PRAISE FOR *SERPENT RIVER RESURGENCE*

"Lianne C. Leddy's book *Serpent River Resurgence* is a welcome addition to the conversation on mining and development in and around the Elliot Lake area. This is a must-read for any person wanting to engage in reconciliation and to understand that First Nations people have been on the frontlines of resource development and have suffered the consequences. This is a timely message for all in the era of reconciliation, and a reminder that First Nations communities have not always been properly consulted or made aware of the consequences, and have been at the whim of the federal government. We must be reminded of our past relationships, and how we got to this point, and we need to hear the truth. This book brings to light some of the truths; it is a welcome addition to the conversation on reconciliation."

Chief Brent (Nodini'inini) Bissaillion,
Chief of the Serpent River First Nation

"For anyone seeking to understand twentieth-century colonialism in Canada, this book offers a compelling on-the-ground story of resource extraction in Anishinaabek homelands. Lianne C. Leddy has done a superb job of tying together uranium demands for American weapons of war, mining boomtown development, and the rich history and culture of the Serpent River people. It is an antidote to settler narratives of progress and a vision of resilient people, land, and future."

Kim Anderson, Canada Research Chair in
Indigenous Relationships and Associate Professor of
Family Relations and Applied Nutrition, University of Guelph

"*Serpent River Resurgence* is a powerful community-based history of resilience and reclamation. Filling a critical gap in Indigenous history, Lianne C. Leddy demonstrates the impact of the global dynamics of settler colonialism during the Cold War while centring an impressive story of Indigenous resurgence."

Allan Downey, Nak'azdli Whut'en First Nation and
Associate Professor of History and Indigenous Studies,
McMaster University

T0341537

"Of bicultural parentage, Leddy situates herself within this story as a member of both sides – Anishinaabe and Canadian. As an Indigenous environmental historian, Leddy explicates the enduring structures of settler colonialism, demonstrating that they are still in force today. To identify those structures, she adroitly deploys the words of her elders, countering their historic exclusion by inserting storytelling into her analysis, while critically approaching and analyzing bureaucratic reports and newspaper articles. A welcome and timely piece of scholarship."

Alan Ojiig Corbiere,
Bne Doodem, Canada Research Chair,
Indigenous History of North America, York University

"A brilliant analysis of uranium mining in Ontario which centres the lived experiences of Indigenous communities, particularly the Serpent River First Nation. Leddy explores deep-rooted Anishinaabe connections to a particular place, situating these conflicts within global processes of Cold War colonialism. Leddy argues that stories have been the foundation of Indigenous resurgence, and the stories she tells are compelling indeed."

Nancy Langston,
Distinguished Professor of Environmental History,
Michigan Technological University

Serpent River Resurgence

*Confronting Uranium Mining
at Elliot Lake*

LIANNE C. LEDDY

UNIVERSITY OF TORONTO PRESS
Toronto Buffalo London

© University of Toronto Press 2022
Toronto Buffalo London
utorontopress.com
Printed and bound by CPI Group (UK) Ltd, Croydon, CR0 4YY

ISBN 978-1-4426-4634-6 (cloth)   ISBN 978-1-4426-6548-4 (EPUB)
ISBN 978-1-4426-1437-6 (paper)   ISBN 978-1-4426-6547-7 (PDF)

Library and Archives Canada Cataloguing in Publication

Title: Serpent River resurgence : confronting uranium mining at Elliot Lake /
    Lianne C. Leddy.
Names: Leddy, Lianne C., author.
Description: Includes bibliographical references and index.
Identifiers: Canadiana (print) 20210334746 | Canadiana (ebook) 20210334878 |
    ISBN 9781442614376 (cloth) | ISBN 9781442646346 (paper) |
    ISBN 9781442665484 (EPUB) | ISBN 9781442665477 (PDF)
Subjects: LCSH: Uranium industry – Environmental aspects – Ontario –
    Elliot Lake. | LCSH: Ojibwa Indians – Ontario – Elliot Lake. |
    LCSH: Environmentalism – Ontario – Elliot Lake. | LCSH: Elliot
    Lake (Ont.) – Environmental conditions – 20th century.
Classification: LCC HD9539.U72 C3 2021 | DDC 338.2/7493209713132 – dc23

We wish to acknowledge the land on which the University of Toronto Press
operates. This land is the traditional territory of the Wendat, the Anishnaabeg,
the Haudenosaunee, the Métis, and the Mississaugas of the Credit First
Nation.

This book has been published with the help of a grant from the Federation
for the Humanities and Social Sciences, through the Awards to Scholarly
Publications Program, using funds provided by the Social Sciences and
Humanities Research Council of Canada.

University of Toronto Press acknowledges the financial assistance to its
publishing program of the Canada Council for the Arts and the Ontario Arts
Council, an agency of the Government of Ontario.

 Canada Council **Conseil des Arts**
for the Arts **du Canada**

 ONTARIO ARTS COUNCIL
CONSEIL DES ARTS DE L'ONTARIO
an Ontario government agency
un organisme du gouvernement de l'Ontario

Funded by the   Financé par le
Government   gouvernement
of Canada   du Canada  Canadä

Contents

Acknowledgments

This book owes a great debt to a great number of people, and I want to start by thanking members of Serpent River First Nation. Chi miigwetch to the Elders who shared their knowledge with me and supported the dissertation upon which this book is based: Valerie Commanda, Arnelda Jacobs, Elizabeth (Betty) Jacobs, Terrance (Terry) Jacobs, Peter Johnston, Frank Lewis, and my grandmother, Gertrude Lewis. Some have passed on in the intervening years, and I will be forever grateful for their generosity and teachings. Chi miigwetch to their families for allowing their words to appear here: Gail Jacobs; Mildred Johnston and her family, especially Buffy Johnston; and Lisa Reid. Miigwetch to Isadore Day, Chief at the time, and Council for their initial support years ago when I began my dissertation research. Miigwetch to Marella Schofield for allowing me to cite from *Connected to the Land*. I am also grateful to Janice Gamble, who ran Elder Tea for many years and was very helpful in pointing me towards important sources.

In the years since I left northern Ontario, my journey has taken me to Waterloo, London, Calgary, St. John's and back again to Waterloo. I've had the privilege to learn from friends and colleagues from home and across these lands known as Canada, including Joe Anderson, Kim Anderson, Kandice Baptiste, Jean Becker, Chantal Bourret, Tarah Brookfield, Sean Cadigan, Marica Cassis, Allan Downey, Rebecca Godderis, Amy Gullage, Karl Hele, Gus Hill, Robert Hughes, Melissa Ireland, Kawennakon Bonnie Whitlow, Arn Keeling, Percy Lezard, Brittany Luby, John and Tammy Maker, Vanessa McMackin, Cheryl Nahwegahbow, Amy Milne-Smith, David Monod, Vanessa Oliver, Jennifer Pettit, Lyndsay Rosenthal, John Sandlos, Irene Tencinger, Darren Thomas, Jocelyn Thorpe, Gary Warrick, Jeff Webb, Dana Weiner, and Jane Whalen.

During my time as a PhD student in the Tri-University Program in History at Laurier, I was lucky to have Susan Neylan as a mentor and advisor. This work also benefited from the guidance of committee members Adam Crerar, Whitney Lackenbauer, Christopher Alcantara, and Paige Raibmon, who all provided helpful comments to move this work from dissertation to monograph, as did three anonymous reviewers. The research at the dissertation stage was made possible by a SSHRC Canada Graduate Scholarship and the assistance of Gloria MacKenzie at Library and Archives Canada, Marthe Brown and Janie Theoret at Laurentian University Archives, and the staff at both the Archives of Ontario and the Elliot Lake Public Library. Thank you to Trevor Stace for his research assistance and to SSHRC for supporting the revisions that brought this work from dissertation to monograph. I am also grateful to the team at University of Toronto Press for their support and assistance. Thanks in particular to Len Husband, for helping me to navigate the publication process and for making me laugh when I needed it.

This book would not have been possible without the support of my family. My paternal grandparents, William and Leona Leddy, raised their family in Elliot Lake, while my maternal grandparents, Lawrence and Gertrude Lewis, did the same on Serpent River First Nation. Thank you to my parents, Peter and Andrea, my sister Patricia, and my nephew Braeden, for your love and encouragement. I am lucky to have in-laws like Hal, Judy, Gillian, Matthew, and "Baby Ben." I am grateful for the support, guidance, and love of many aunties, uncles, and cousins, especially Auntie Diane Meawasige and Steven Baranyai, who were helpful at different stages of this project.

To my husband, Mark Humphries, miigwetch for your constant encouragement throughout this long research journey, as well as your map-making skills. Much more than that, thank you for ensuring that equity starts at home and for giving me the space to do the work I do – and for knowing when to leave tea outside my office door. Paige Leddy, this project started long before you were born and ended as you started kindergarten. Chi miigwetch for choosing me. You are the joy of my life, and my only regret is that you didn't get to meet Gertie.

Waterloo, Haldimand Tract, 2021

Maps

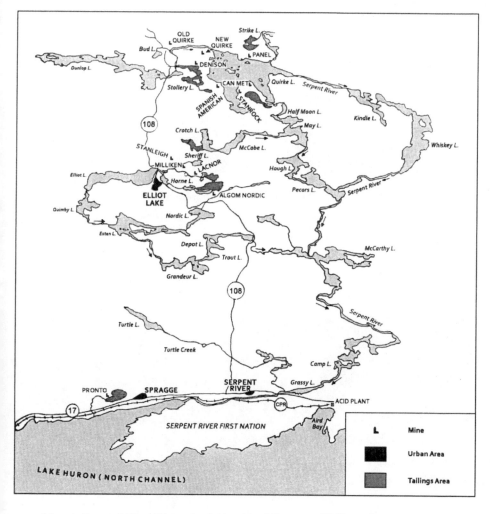

Map 1 Serpent River Watershed, Uranium Mines, and Tailings Area

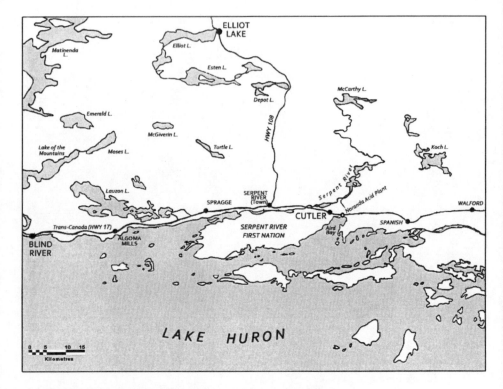

Map 2 Serpent River First Nation and Elliot Lake Region

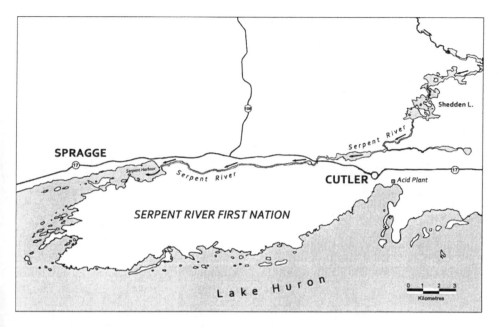

Map 3 Serpent River First Nation

SERPENT RIVER RESURGENCE

Chapter One

Introduction

Long ago, when the world was coming to life, a great serpent came down from the north. As she passed, she carved a wild river through the earth and laid her eggs. Millions of radiant eggs deep in the bedrock. The rains came. The river took on a life of its own. The land grew abundant. As long as the serpent's eggs lay undisturbed, they would do no harm.[1]

– Uranium

The Serpent that shares Anishinaabe territory is said to have a den where the mouth of the Serpent River meets Lake Huron.[2] According to the Elders of the Serpent River First Nation (SRFN), "the reason the river is so twisted is that it was formed by the Serpent as it moved, wiggling its body as it travelled."[3] The importance of the Serpent continues, with Elders and community members sharing sightings from time to time, and, as Arnelda Jacobs shared with me in 2009, "he's there to help us."[4] Uranium mining in the North Shore area of northern Ontario challenged this relationship.[5] The community's traditional role of taking care of the Serpent River, that all-important role of steward, was changed by the effects of mining and the influx of settlers that came to take its eggs.

From the early nineteenth century, Indigenous peoples have had to negotiate a complex system of governance and socio-economic coercion that both Beverley McLachlin, Chief Justice of the Supreme Court of Canada, and the Truth and Reconciliation Commission have termed cultural genocide.[6] More recently, the discourse has rightly started to shift, shedding the "cultural" qualifier. In 2019, the National Inquiry into Missing and Murdered Indigenous Women and Girls referred to the "race-based genocide of Indigenous Peoples, including First Nations, Inuit and Métis, which especially targets women, girls, and

2SLGBTQQIA people" in their final report. It goes on to argue that "genocide has been empowered by colonial structures evidenced notably by the Indian Act, the Sixties Scoop, residential schools and breaches of human and Indigenous rights."[7] Most recently, in the wake of horrific and heartbreaking discoveries of hundreds of unmarked graves at residential schools, public discourse in Canada has featured calls to cancel Canada Day as well as a more widespread acknowledgment of genocide against Indigenous peoples.

In examining the development of the settler-colonial relationship in Canada, most historians have focused on the nineteenth and early twentieth centuries when assimilationist policies were most overt, and as James Daschuk has shown, Indigenous peoples were actively starved, displaced, and dispossessed by the Canadian government.[8] Historians such as J.R. Miller and Sarah Carter, to name but a few, argue that Indian Affairs officials adopted a "bible and plough" policy which used education and agriculture to eliminate cultural and economic traits that the dominant English-speaking society found undesirable in its citizens.[9] On this basis, other historians have analysed the methods, ideas, and procedures of the Indian agents charged with carrying out those policies on the ground, arguing that First Nations were administered in a paternalistic fashion.[10] As Jarvis Brownlie argues, "these officials acted in ways that reinforced the subordination, marginalization, and disempowerment of First Nations people."[11] Paulette Regan extends this argument, presenting a strong critique of the paternalistic colonial relationship that eventually led to the establishment of the residential schools system:

> To those who say that we cannot change the past, I say that we can learn from it. We can better understand how a problematic mentality of benevolent paternalism became a rationale and justification for acquiring Indigenous lands and resources and drove the creation of prescriptive education policies that ran counter to the treaty relationship. Equally importantly, we can explore how this mentality continues to influence Indigenous-settler relations today.[12]

Regan locates the residential school system within a larger and interconnected colonial attitude, one that also gave birth to settler narratives of history that devalue or exclude Indigenous presence and paradigms. Furthermore, she calls on Canadians to take responsibility for the "historical myths and colonial mindsets"[13] that still prevail within the settler-First Nations relationship as they are often present in public discourse. As Adam J. Barker argues most forcefully, the structures of settler colonialism are not just historical in nature but continue to justify and enable seizures of and resource extractions from Indigenous territories and violence against Indigenous peoples whose presence undermines "the legitimacy of Canadian authority and hegemony."[14]

Understanding the dynamics of settler colonialism is especially important in a country where economic development has historically been dependent on resource exploitation.[15] Traditionally, historians have focused on pre-twentieth century encroachments into Indigenous territories and ensuing conflicts.[16] Studies of treaty-making and the growth of mining and timber industries in the Canadian north and west have tended to emphasize policies that furthered the nation-building project and Indigenous responses to them.[17] Historians have thus tended to emphasize the power of Department of Indian Affairs (DIA) actors in shaping the function and outcomes of the colonial relationship. In this analysis, it was difficult to counteract the will of the Indian agent.[18] While some historians have evaluated Indigenous agency within the colonial system, others have cautioned against downplaying the real consequences DIA policies had on Indigenous communities.[19]

Although much of the early literature focused on the late nineteenth and early twentieth centuries, Indigenous agency is also an important aspect of colonial power relations in the post-war period. As the findings of the Truth and Reconciliation Commission make clear, colonial relationships and official and informal aspects of settler colonialism continued to dominate and characterize interactions between the state and Indigenous people throughout the twentieth century, right up to the present.[20] How those relationships were formed, played out, and characterized, as well as how the power of the state was organized and directed to influence or control the lives of Indigenous peoples, was, in turn, shaped by larger national and international phenomena. In examining employment and waged work, social programs, and medicine and healthcare in this period, historians have not only shown the importance of Indigenous agency but also the complexities of official policy.[21]

While the emergence of the nation-state in the late nineteenth century formed the political background to earlier studies of settler colonialism, the Cold War and Canada's economic and military relationship with the United States was central to policymaking in the post-war era. The shifting dynamics of the Cold War, as missiles were amassed and later reduced, which grew and then shrank demand for uranium, had a profound impact on the river, the region, and its peoples. At one time, Cold War historians focused mainly on the political and diplomatic history of that conflict, but in recent years they have begun to focus more on its social and cultural effects on ordinary Canadians.[22] Their research has shown that men and women had different experiences during the Cold War as gender roles became more confining and were later challenged.[23] The rise of consumer capitalism changed how ordinary people organized their lives, made ends meet, and spent their leisure time as well as where and how they lived.[24] But as society and culture were transformed, resistance was possible and ordinary people organized themselves to support environmentalism, advance the peace movement, and fight against the confines of patriarchy.[25] The apparatus of the state, in turn, mobilized to control dissent and non-conformity, targeting immigrants and other groups that were deemed to be less than desirable citizens.[26] As part of this larger project, social programs, education, healthcare, and other interventions were deployed to encourage conformity with dominant norms while deviance was stigmatized.[27] Indigenous communities too continued to fall under the official gaze and they experienced these changes and challenges in unique ways. All the while, new international conflicts and globalization led to further territorial encroachments by the military and industry, both in the name of economic development and national security.

Mining at Elliot Lake was one local part of this global project and it left a long legacy for the Serpent River First Nation, as it did in other communities throughout the country.[28] Researchers have recently begun to look at Indigenous experiences with natural resource use in the post-war period – hydroelectricity, mining, and military presence in particular – especially in Canada's north.[29] Arn Keeling has studied the development of Canadian "yellowcake towns," particularly Uranium City, Saskatchewan, while placing its growth within a larger context of Cold War North America, drawing connections with Michael A. Amundson's 2002 comparison of four uranium townsites in the United States.[30] He argues that the development of uranium mining in Saskatchewan followed a boom-bust cycle and that the community which took shape to extract that resource was shaped by the cultural forces of the Cold War and consumer capitalism. In effect, we can see the post-war period as a new colonial age when communities were planned from the bottom up and settlers flocked to places where non-Indigenous settlement had previously been more limited.

Yet as Keeling and John Sandlos note, until recently little had been written about the experience of Indigenous communities and mining in Canada from an historical perspective, with the bulk of the literature coming from NGOs or government assessment processes.[31] As I argue elsewhere, much of the literature both scholarly and popular on Indigenous peoples and the environment has been connected to the idea of the "ecological Indian," in which Indigenous peoples have a "primitive" connection to the land – a trope that has been widely used by environmentalists and counterculture groups to critique industrialization and development.[32] These ideas have been ably critiqued by scholars and the field of Indigenous environmental history has exploded since the late 1990s.[33] Indigenous or decolonizing methodologies have played an important role in bringing the voices of Indigenous peoples into conversations about land use, water, forestry, and mining in Canada.[34] Indigenous voices complicate narratives of progress and privilege the position of Indigenous peoples in traditional environmental critiques.[35] What this emerging body of scholarship demonstrates is that "even in the postwar period, when status Indians could vote in federal elections and the power of Indian agents slowly eroded, colonial processes were still powerful and facilitated land encroachments and environmental devastation."[36]

A similar pattern is evident in the development of Elliot Lake and its effects on the Indigenous people already living there. Settlers who founded Elliot Lake have generated their own local histories and these authors tend to relate a narrative which emphasizes the "struggle against the wilderness," economic cycles of boom and bust, and urban development as progress – all foundational colonial narratives.[37] Through the use of oral history and interviews from SRFN, Anna Stanley argued that in order for the aims of the Nuclear Waste Management Organization (NWMO) to remain unchallenged, it had to actively silence SRFN. Stanley's study demonstrates that the exclusion of Indigenous voices from debate – which this study examines in a historical context – extends to the present-day.[38] Members of the Serpent River First Nation have also explored the colonial process, taking a more personal and localized approach rooted in deep Anishinaabe connections to the land. The community published its own collection of recorded oral histories entitled, *This Is My Homeland: Stories of the Effects of Nuclear Industries by People of the Serpent River First Nation and the North Shore of Lake Huron.*[39] This community-based collection highlights oral testimony on the negative effects of the uranium industry on the health and environmental well-being of the reserve's residents. Taking an approach that includes both personal narrative and oral history, the editors interviewed community Elders who vividly remember the impacts of the waste on the Serpent River, as well as the environmental degradation that came as a result of the Noranda Acid Plant. A more recent community-based work, *Connected to the Land: Stories from the Serpent's Band*, tells a longer history of the area and people, but also includes sections on the acid plant and cultural renewal.[40]

This book examines the experiences of the Serpent River First Nation as an aspect of the new Cold War colonialism and Indigenous environmental history.[41] In popular culture, this region is known for its mining history and retirement-friendly lifestyle,[42] but the settler town of Elliot Lake did not exist until the Cold War. For the century prior to that, settlers and First Nations had long been engaged in resource development on the traditional territory[43] of the Anishinaabek.[44] The Robinson-Huron Treaty of 1850 established the reserve for the Serpent's Band on the peninsula formed by the mouth of the Serpent River at Lake Huron to the west and Aird Bay to the east, toward Spanish, Ontario[45] (see map 1). In the nineteenth century, mining became important in the Upper Great Lakes area and precipitated the treaty-making process. In the early twentieth century, resource-related encroachment continued on Anishinaabe territory with lumber, agriculture, and the construction of the Canadian Pacific Railway (CPR). These extractive practices, and the patterns of dispossession they established, intensified during the Cold War when the discovery of uranium north of the Serpent River First Nation brought an influx of settlers and industry to the area. Environmental damage related to uranium mining and its secondary industries had a profound effect on the Serpent River First Nation, who had to negotiate the rapid changes and damage caused by uranium mining. As with other aspects of the Cold War in Canada, the international rivalry between East and West brought social and cultural changes as the Cold War left its mark on local communities.

Extractive activities brought new dangers despite promises of modern economic development and employment: the combination of acid production and river pollution resulting from uranium extraction, on or near the reserve, changed how members of the Serpent River First Nation interacted with the land. Mining and industrial development poisoned drinking water for families that drew their supply directly from the Serpent River and many outdoor leisure activities became dangerous. The biggest change brought about by the river's pollution, however, was the impact it had on the First Nation's traditional pursuits of hunting and fishing. The development of Elliot Lake and its mining and refining industries occurred at a time when many local families still relied on a traditional relationship with the land, specifically harvesting fish and wildlife for food. Fur trapping activities that had been ongoing in the area also underwent profound changes, especially for families that earned significant income from those traditional pursuits. While change had been a constant, colonialism in the new Cold War context forced the people of SRFN to confront rapid change on an unprecedented scale in a political environment where their agency and voices were still limited by the constraints of official settler-colonial policies which prioritized development, employment, and assimilation.

This is a book, in short, about Indigenous resurgence in the face of environmental injustice, and a story about defending the land in the face of environmental degradation. Although historical in scope, it examines a later period in the continuous colonial relationship between Indigenous peoples and the Crown. The experience of the Serpent River First Nation suggests that both overt colonialist policies and the broader legacies of Indigenous-settler relations continued to define that relationship throughout the Cold War. Anishinaabek in the area were no strangers to development by the time uranium claims were staked in 1953. What is clear, however, is that this was a time of transition for the community when difficult choices had to be made. These choices were complicated and constrained by the colonial relationship which continued to place limitations on decision-making. As resource development led to river pollution and SRFN experienced the effects of an acid plant built on reserve land, it became painfully clear that the traditional role community members claimed as stewards of the land had been fundamentally disrupted. That is not to say that the community would have rejected economic development and job opportunities, as the people living there may well have accepted jobs as part of the cultural need to adapt and survive. But their inability to *control* the resource development and damage in Anishinaabe traditional territory compromised their role as stewards.[46] This was the key aspect of their relationship to the development of uranium as a resource. It is apparent, however, that as the relationship with the Department of Indian Affairs changed, Indian agents no longer possessed the same authority as they had in earlier periods of development, and so the community was able to overtly voice demands for increased control and monitoring of pollution levels. In the process, the stewardship role was renewed as SRFN leaders had a greater voice in reclamation. Yet even still the community is very much dealing with the legacy of the paternalistic decisions made by federal officials in the 1960s, what I call Cold War colonialism: community leaders had the appearance of control, but their choices were limited by economics, and both policy and practice.

My own background has shaped my approach to this subject in important ways, and in keeping with Anishinaabe protocols, I need to locate myself in the story.[47] I first remember listening to the stories I am about to tell at my grandmother's kitchen table, and my own family history is intertwined with them. I am *Anishinaabekwe* (woman) from the Serpent River First Nation and I grew up in Elliot Lake, Ontario. My father, Peter Leddy, moved to Elliot Lake as a child in the late 1950s when his father, William Leddy, sought employment along with thousands of other men as a uranium miner. As I write in chapter three, this particular boom town was designed as a post-war family-friendly community rather than one that relied solely on camps to house single miners. Like many other wives of miners, my paternal grandmother, Leona (Mickey) Leddy, a nurse in her own right, brought my father and his siblings to the town once their house had been built. My mother, Andrea Leddy (née Lewis) is an *Anishinaabekwe* and she grew up in SRFN, attending school in nearby Blind River and Elliot Lake once the day school closed on the reserve. She and my father met and married in the late 1970s. Gertrude Lewis, my late *Nokomis* (grandmother), ran the post office in SRFN, and was also an outspoken critic of the damage uranium mining did to our territory. She served as an elected Councillor in Serpent River First Nation and was also a school board trustee. My maternal grandfather, Lawrence Lewis, was a hunter and trapper along with his family before he became a labourer for the CPR and later, an employee of the Noranda Acid Plant located on the reserve. Juggling the roles of academic researcher and member of both communities has been both challenging and rewarding, and it also provides me with a unique perspective. This position is reflected in how I have tried to bridge the ways of knowing that come from our traditional stories (*aadizookaanag*) and daily life, or news stories (*dibaajimowinan*) that were the basis for most of the interviews, and archival sources created in a colonial context and held by the Canadian government.[48] This book is a personal story, and I am not merely an objective outside researcher. This is a story of my homeland, of my family, my ancestors, and my daughter.

The role of storytelling in the retention of Anishinaabe community history and culture cannot be overstated. Not only is storytelling our traditional method of sharing information, but it is also an important way for Indigenous peoples to be active participants and recognized experts in academic research. Stories are the foundation of our resurgence, and it is how we have been so resilient in the face of continued colonial encroachment. Indigenous scholars have been at the forefront of connecting storytelling to scholarly methodology. As Maori scholar Linda Tuhiwai Smith wrote in 1999, the political nature of stories is an essential aspect of the struggle for decolonization:

> Telling our stories from the past, reclaiming the past, giving testimony to the injustices of the past are all strategies which are commonly employed by indigenous peoples struggling for justice. On the international scene it is extremely rare and unusual when indigenous accounts are accepted and

acknowledged as valid interpretations of what has taken place. And yet, the need to tell our stories remains the powerful imperative of a powerful form of resistance.[49]

More recently, Indigenous scholars and writers on Turtle Island such as Winona LaDuke, Melissa K. Nelson, Leanne Betasamosake Simpson, and Deborah McGregor are actively calling attention to environmental injustice and the destruction of our territories from Indigenous perspectives.[50] They call on deeper understandings of land and our traditions so that the resurgence of our traditions can be our path out of colonial realities. As Simpson has written, "While theoretically, we have debated whether Audre Lord's 'the master's tools can dismantle the master's house,' I am interested in a different question. I am not so concerned with how we dismantle the master's house, that is, which sets of theories we use to critique colonialism; but I am very concerned with how we (re)build our own house, or our own houses." She goes on with her vision for resurgence: "I have spent enough time taking down the master's house, and now I want most of my energy to go into visioning and building our new house."[51] Her use of Creation Stories and Indigenous knowledge in her work speaks to the importance of storytelling for resurgence.

It is therefore not surprising that storytelling was, for me, the most powerful methodological aspect of this work. Indigenous scholars who have come before me have emphasized storytelling as a methodological tool that is necessary for the research journey, and I have reflected on the importance of oral history and its value in this study.[52] The interviews used in writing this book have been invaluable as they give a clear sense of rapid changes in the community, as well as the significance of the loss of resources and traditional roles. The history conveyed through these conversations – these relationships – is that of lived experience formed by the community's relationship with the land, mining companies, and the government. These themes are central to the community's history and reflect our own Anishinaabe ways of knowing. The interviews I conducted with Elders reflect Indigenous knowledge (IK), which has become increasingly important for the responsible development of resources with Indigenous worldviews playing a growing role in policy development.[53] Although there has been scholarly debate about whether IK perpetuates the image of the "ecological Indian,"[54] there are many examples of how it has been used successfully in environmental planning.[55] Here I integrate IK into the historical analysis of how an Indigenous community experienced and interpreted environmental degradation and economic change. While the uranium industry and other economic development projects on the North Shore were facilitated by a Western understanding of both progress and treaties, the SRFN worldview is more holistic, with an emphasis on the connections between the land, wellness, and social relations.[56]

This story relies on both oral history from community Elders of the Serpent River First Nation, many of whom were politically involved at some point during the post-war period, as well as documentary evidence held in federal, provincial, and local archives. Because this study acknowledges my community's sense of loss, the most rewarding aspect of the research process has been the oral interviews I was able to participate in with my own Elders. I conducted interviews in 2008–9 with Valerie Commanda, Arnelda Jacobs, Betty Jacobs, Terry Jacobs, Peter Johnston, and Gertrude Lewis, followed by a later 2014 interview with Frank Lewis. All were living in the community during this book's timeframe and were affected by industrial development as workers, people who relied on fish and wildlife, and community members with young families. Some of them also became politically active in the 1970s, 1980s, and beyond.

In addition to these oral histories, the book draws upon extensive archival research conducted at Library and Archives Canada, the Archives of Ontario, the Laurentian University Archives, the Elliot Lake Public Library, and the Serpent River First Nation Library. The archival materials, especially records held at Library and Archives Canada in Ottawa, were necessary to tell this story, but I had to always keep in mind that these were records kept by a colonial government to try to control Indigenous peoples in this country. Record Group 10, which contains Indian Affairs records, is comprised of maps, memoranda, letters, and other written sources that tell us a great deal about the colonial perspective in this period. As I have written elsewhere, these records are "distressing evidence of a colonial past and present whereby (mostly) male colonial agents sought to convert, control, and assimilate First Nations people in Canada." Furthermore, the direct words of Indigenous peoples are often hard to find until mid-century, and before then are often "generally relegated to x-signatures, the odd letter from a chief often written by someone else, or an agent's recollection of a conversation."[57] Decolonizing archival research requires reading these records carefully, and trying to find those voices, however difficult it may be.

A further complication was the time period in question, which was, when I started, relatively recent history. At the national and provincial archives, many of the documents that I had anticipated using were closed by law. I pursued Access to Information agreements at both institutions with the support of the Serpent River First Nation Chief and Council and was able to access records that remain closed to other historians although my researcher's agreement requires me to omit the names of some individuals. Newspapers from the community and region as well as other published primary sources have also been important sources for this study.

Melding these two different types of sources equally throughout the narrative was not possible. Readers will find that some chapters rely more on Elders' words and others rely more on archival evidence. This reflects the fact that some of the events, such as the establishment of Elliot Lake, were described in written documents and newspaper articles, while chapters on pollution and politicization were driven by Elders' recollections of those particular times. On the whole, however, these two different source bases reinforce each other. The correspondence between public servants, for instance, tells of the scope of the problems brought by industrial pollution. But these written communications tell one side of the story frozen in time, while Elders have lived experiences and knowledge that memoranda alone cannot encapsulate. I have brought both types of evidence together to tell a holistic historical narrative.

The chapters that follow examine the Serpent River First Nation's experience with mining and industrialization in the context of the new Cold War colonialism. Central to these discussions are questions surrounding environmental and political power relationships, which have affected SRFN throughout the past half-century. Questions about the environmental and health consequences of the uranium industry, Indigenous-settler relations, the importance of traditional uses of land, and what happens when they are compromised by irresponsible environmental business practices have all been central to my research process. The book is organized chronologically, although the chapters that detail the acid plant and the river pollution are contemporaneous.

We begin by outlining the social, cultural, and economic changes occurring in the community during the nineteenth century through to the end of the 1940s. In emphasizing the long history of Anishinaabek presence and worldviews, as well as Indigenous-settler relations and resource use in the area, I demonstrate that while uranium was an important extractive industry in the community's history, it was not the first interaction community members had with the forces of colonialism and development. Fur traders, missionaries, treaty commissioners, and lumber barons had already made their mark and established patterns of interaction, cooperation, and conflict. It was these historical experiences that shaped SRFN expectations and understandings when uranium prospectors arrived in the early Cold War.

Because this is a story of the consequences of colonialism, it is important to provide an overview of the larger Cold War context, one that necessitated exploiting uranium discoveries to make American weapons of war. The town of Elliot Lake was established in the mid-1950s after the discovery of uranium in the area, and while settlers prided themselves on having carved the town from a rock surrounded by wilderness,[58] this narrative excludes the Anishinaabek who were already living and working in the area. The memory is one of "man's" victory over nature, but in reality, Elliot Lake was a planned community, similar to Uranium City in Saskatchewan, that arose from the tripartite relationship between the federal government, the province of Ontario, and mining companies. This exclusion of Indigenous voices facilitated dispossession and the loss of traditional stewardship roles, while also ignoring the environmental legacy of uranium development. Although the focus of this study is the people of the Serpent River First Nation, the development of Elliot Lake provides essential context. As a planned community created to further Canada's commitments to international alliances, it was very much a "top down" story of development and the rapid influx of thousands of settlers without any input from the Anishinaabek. Indigenous perspectives on the events that occurred as boom turned to bust and then boom again are picked up in subsequent chapters.

The story moves from developments at Elliot Lake to explore the impacts of the Noranda Acid Plant on SRFN land. Sulphuric acid was used in the leaching process to obtain uranium oxide to sell to the United States government and was thus a secondary industry to operations at Elliot Lake. Through the involvement of DIA, which saw employment opportunities on the horizon, Noranda leased land from the community for the purposes of building an acid plant. Community members faced the dilemma of choosing between jobs and the traditional role of defending territory, which bore the legacy of continued injustice. While they contended with the presence of the acid plant, they also had to confront the degradation of the river system. The promise of a steady wage economy, and especially the pollution it brought, threatened the traditional pursuits that had been central to community identity, as some had feared. Uranium and acid development hampered peoples' ability to interact with the land as they once had, and it altered the community's social relations. Although the Ontario Resources Commission had monitored the area since the start of mining operations, results of water quality studies were not reported in a timely fashion. For its part, the federal government saw no conflict of interest between protecting the well-being of Serpent River First Nation and its facilitation of the uranium industry: uranium mining was important for the purposes of international relations and economic development, and the acid plant would provide a significant economic opportunity for the community. This dual purpose defined the colonial relationship in the context of the Cold War.

As the environmental, health, and social legacies of uranium became more apparent, Serpent River First Nation leaders sought new ways to assert traditional responsibilities to and relationships with territory. The community's tactics changed as members made public presentations, engaged the media in their struggle, and also resorted to more radical means to press their concerns. Ultimately, it was the community members of the Serpent River First Nation who forced a reluctant government and public to acknowledge and address the environmental losses that formed the legacy of Cold War colonialism.

The history of Cold War colonialism and uranium extraction was devastating for the Serpent River First Nation. The Serpent's radiant eggs, which had lain undisturbed since time immemorial, were harvested while settler resource exploitation threatened the Serpent's home. But the lasting legacy of the new colonialism was not only environmental injustice, but also resurgence.

Chapter Two

The Serpent River Anishinaabek before 1950

First the white men came and trapped all the mink and otter and beaver, then they came back for the trees and all we had left were the rocks. Then the SOBs came back for the rocks.[1]

– Gilbert Oskaboose, *Uranium*

In an interview for the 1990 National Film Board film, *Uranium*, SRFN Elder and journalist Gilbert Oskaboose succinctly outlined more than four hundred years of resource exploitation in northern Ontario. Sustained contact with settlers was not a new phenomenon on the North Shore in the 1950s. Indeed, traders and missionaries had been present for centuries, the Robinson-Huron Treaty had been negotiated in 1850, and timber had been a major economic catalyst in the area at the end of the nineteenth century. These processes brought new technologies, modes of transportation, and demands for different resources. Resource exploitation, then, was not a new process, nor had it excluded the Anishinaabek as active participants. In fact, the early nineteenth century marked a time of negotiation between Indigenous peoples and Europeans that was characterized by trade and cultural exchange. It is after this period, however, when the federal government introduced such legislation as the Indian Act in 1876 and established the Department of Indian Affairs, that the relationship changed significantly; afterwards settlers invaded Anishinaabe territory in more substantial numbers. The land transactions and development projects that affected reserve lands between 1850 and 1945 reflected larger resource patterns as northern Ontario moved from a pre-industrial economy to an industrial economy. Settler lumber and farming initiatives in the later decades of the nineteenth century increased non-Indigenous settlement, exacerbated DIA interference, and began to threaten traditional relationships to the land. Indigenous peoples on the North Shore had been living in a reciprocal relationship with their territories since time immemorial and had participated in traditional, post-contact forms of hunting and trapping since the early days of the fur trade while continuing to manage those resources effectively. From the 1830s onward, the colonial and federal governments enacted several laws and policies to administer First Nations and the lands they occupied, with a particular focus on Christianizing and civilizing. As historian John L. Tobias has argued, "protection, civilization, and assimilation" had formed the foundation of Indigenous policies both before and after Confederation, enshrined in successive pieces of legislation including the Gradual Civilization Act (1857), the Enfranchisement Act (1869) and the Indian Act (1876).[2]

The forms of land and resource use that settlers considered useful reflected their Euro-Canadian values that land should be productive. First Nations resisted the growing importance of mining in the mid-nineteenth century and the displacement it brought with it, as it infringed on their rights and excluded them from the process. This resistance in what would become northern Ontario resulted in the negotiation of the Robinson-Huron Treaty in 1850. As industrialization intensified in late nineteenth-century northern Ontario, DIA policies worked to undermine Indigenous attempts to negotiate their relationships with settlers as they had done in the past. Attempts to force First Nations' adaptation to Euro-Canadian values and goods also sought to displace past practices of cultural exchange, extending into processes of resource exploitation. It was still possible for Indigenous peoples to exert agency and assert traditional relationships with the land, but DIA legislation, surveillance, and the interference of Indian agents often constrained these efforts.

This chapter examines the history of the Serpent River First Nation before the discovery of uranium in northern Ontario and the subsequent establishment of Elliot Lake. It demonstrates that the community's experience with uranium is not the only encounter of historical significance. To that end, it includes an ethnographic review of Anishinaabe worldviews and the socio-political aspects of Anishinaabe life. It also examines the encounters of the Anishinaabek with other Indigenous groups, settlers, and resources. As infrastructure improved, so too did the intensity of resource extraction activities. At the same time, Indigenous sovereignty and agency were under attack by a supposedly benevolent government. While resource development was not new in the area in the 1950s, uranium extraction and increased settler populations marked a departure from previous colonial processes while still relying on entrenched patterns of encroachment and dispossession.

Up to that point, many Indigenous people lived traditional and semi-traditional lifestyles, relying on hunting and fishing to fulfill at least some of their dietary needs and trapping as part of an emerging mixed economy.

As Anishinaabek, we place great importance on oral traditions passed down through generations. Such stories emphasize place, space, and the connectivity of animate beings. In Anishinaabemowin, the Ojibway language, the key (and most difficult) linguistic differentiation is whether an object is animate or inanimate. As Ojibwe language teacher Patricia M. Ningewance states, "the obviously alive objects are included in the animate class, such as people, animals, and plants. But there are such nouns as rocks, pants, spoons, socks, pens, the sun and stars, clocks, pipes, etc. in the animate class."[3] She goes on to recall the memory of hanging a broken household object on a tree, which she interpreted as "giving it a dignified burial at the end of its life as a useful object. Or, maybe its life could be extended by being planted in the arms of a living tree. The fact that it was 'just a thing' made no difference."[4] She emphasizes the tie between the way the language works and the cultural importance of respect: "We all have importance – human, animal, plant or inanimate object. One is not worth more than the other ... I guess that's an illustration of one of the *Anishinaabe* teachings: respect for everything."[5]

Indeed, the common Indigenous phrase "all my relations" gets to the heart of this idea of respect and mutual responsibility and challenges the idea of an environment as separate from us. As Deborah McGregor reminds us, environmental justice is about "justice for all beings of Creation, not only because threats to their existence threaten ours but because from an Aboriginal perspective justice among beings of Creation is life-affirming."[6] She uses traditional teachings to demonstrate this point more clearly, pointing to the need to explore these connections more overtly in the context of environmental justice. Our instructions for how to live are in our stories, McGregor reminds us, underlining the importance of storytelling as a didactic method.

Our re-creation story describes how the world was re-created on the back of the turtle after a great flood. It is said that several animals attempted to dive below the water in order to secure earth for the turtle's back, but only the muskrat was successful.[7] Sky-woman breathed life into the soil, and it expanded. She went on to have two children, a boy and a girl. The new people were called the Anishinaabek, the "spontaneous beings."[8] As Basil Johnston reveals, "the island formed in this way was called Mishee Mackinakong, the place of the Great Turtle's back, now known as Michilimackinac."[9] The story emphasizes the connection between place and Indigeneity for the Anishinaabek, as it is the reason why some Indigenous nations refer to North America as "Turtle Island."

Our other traditions feature Nanabush, the trickster figure born of a human mother and spirit father, and sent by the Creator, or *Gitche Manitou*, to teach the Anishinaabek. He exemplifies the difficulty in maintaining binary differences between human and spiritual creation because he is often said to have adopted certain physical characteristics of animals through his behaviour. Despite having been sent by the Creator, Nanabush is nevertheless imperfect. As Basil Johnston explains, this imperfection is what makes him important in Anishinaabe traditions: "From Nanabush, although he was a paradox, physical and spirit being, doing good and unable to attain it, the *Anishinaabeg* learned. For his teachings, they honoured Nanabush."[10] As can be seen in the cultural importance of the Anishinaabe re-creation story and the traditions involving Nanabush, the connectivity among humans, spirits, traditions, and the environment is made clear. The turtle's generosity, as well as that of the animals that risk their lives to dive for earth, do so to assist Sky-woman. They continued to come to her aid to get through their first winter.[11] These connections rely on relationship and renewal, and when they are broken, there are consequences that affect not only the land, but our ability as human beings to thrive. As John Borrows reminds us, there are relationships, or treaties, that must be maintained if we are to respect our own Indigenous laws.[12]

Anishinaabe territory is in the Great Lakes area, and extends out to the north, west, and south.[13] People moved throughout the area at different times in the year. Politically and socially, the Anishinaabek – comprised of the Ojibway, Odawa, and Potawatomi peoples and their allies – were brought together in the Council of the Three Fires.[14] These nations emerged separately from one group near Michilimackinac,[15] a place of great importance in our traditions because it is the site our re-creation story, and each had important roles within the Council: the Ojibway were faith keepers, and were responsible for maintaining the sacred birch scrolls; the Odawa were traders; and the Potawatomi were the fire-keepers.[16] The Three Fires alliance, which predates contact with Europeans, was important for trade, military, and social purposes; the latter included intermarriage and the continued maintenance of important kinship ties.[17] Our ancestors gathered together at specific times to make decisions as allied nations. Although Olive P. Dickason and David T. McNab describe them as being "a not particularly effective counterbalance to the Five Nations,"[18] the Anishinaabek have oral traditions describing military victories over the Haudenosaunee that historians have, in recent years, revived for the scholarly community.[19] However, it is also our treaty relationships with the Haudenosaunee that help form our understandings of shared territory and what international relationships looked like before the Robinson-Huron Treaty of 1850. When the Haudenosaunee extended the Dish with One Spoon principle of their Great Law to the Anishinaabek, the *Gdoo-naaganinaa* or "our dish" agreement affirmed that overlapping territories had to be shared between both confederacies, and each were responsible for maintaining them without impinging on the other's sovereignty.[20]

The area now known as a former uranium boom town, Elliot Lake, has significant cultural and historical importance for the Serpent River Anishinaabek. Rooster Rock, where Anishinaabe ancestors drew pictographs, is one of our sacred sites. Elders interviewed by Perry Shawana in 1984 recalled that Rooster Rock (*Pakakwanakenda* or *Bakakwehngenda*) was so named because the Anishinaabek sometimes heard crowing in the area.[21] It is now part of a tailings management area accessible by an old mining road and by boat. *Mosgetmasowamis* was the name of the area upon which the townsite of Elliot Lake was built.[22] Memories of a village camp near the present-day hospital at Elliot Lake are still alive in the community, and clash with recently proposed developments near the site.[23] The cultural importance of the community's sense of place and history can be further seen in the significance of the Serpent, a being that is said to have made its home in the river after which it was named.

The Anishinaabek celebrate a long relationship with the territory along the North Shore of Lake Huron and important ties to places there; this history is far older than settler narratives suggest. It began long before the arrival of people searching for uranium to fuel nuclear weapons and generate electricity. Health, wellness, history, and community are inextricably linked in a culture that has connectivity at its core. Balance and respect for Creation are paramount, and this was reflected in the ways Anishinaabe ancestors interacted with the land and with the settlers who came first for furs and non-Christian souls, then for trees, and then finally and most destructively, for uranium.

The settler historical narrative, on the other hand, usually tells the story of the expansion from the St. Lawrence into the Great Lakes region from the perspective of the French explorers, ranging from Cartier and his unsuccessful attempts to find the riches of the Saguenay, to Champlain and later explorers. Narratives about "The Heroic Age" – the time from French contact to 1663 – are often told in terms of explorers' contributions to the establishment of Canada, and in particular, the roles these contact relationships had in establishing a nation based first on mercantilist extraction and later on a capitalistic relationship with resources.[24]

W.L. Morton wrote about Champlain's efforts to explore New France's hinterland in the early 1600s, and how he joined Algonkian forces against the Haudenosaunee in both 1608 and 1609 in order to facilitate the St. Lawrence fur trade.[25] Champlain first arrived in the Georgian Bay area in 1615 via the French River[26] and initiated a pattern in which the French inserted themselves into existing tensions between Indigenous groups, working to establish missionary and trade relations with the Indigenous peoples they encountered. During the seventeenth and early eighteenth centuries, New France sought to expand its influence in the Great Lakes region, resulting in both a system of trading and military posts along the shores of the Great Lakes and south on the Mississippi as well as alliances with Indigenous groups such as the Anishinaabek, Huron-Petun, and others.[27] Jesuit missionaries established mission communities among the Wendat in their homeland, *Wendake*, around what is now Georgian Bay and Lake Simcoe beginning in 1634,[28] then expanded their missionary work north and westwards over the next three decades.[29] Reaching to the North Shore of Lake Huron and the eastern boundary of Lake Superior in 1668, missionaries founded a church at Sault Ste. Marie, followed by the St. Ignace mission at Michilimackinac three years later.[30] Economic and spiritual endeavours were intertwined in these Jesuit activities, provided they were consistent with their faith.[31]

Yet throughout the period, Europeans were never free to define trade or engagement on their own terms. Indigenous expectations and protocols framed the exchange of European goods for furs and featured systems of alliances, ceremony, and negotiation that integrated these exchanges with Indigenous worldviews and approaches to diplomacy.[32] In the western Great Lakes region, Indigenous peoples traded with French agents while Wendat brokers operated near Georgian Bay, facilitating trade further to the south and east.[33] Military forts first appeared in the central Great Lakes region in the 1670s and 1680s between Michilimackinac and Grand Portage.[34] These followed the formal claim of Simon François Daumont, Sieur de Saint Lusson, in 1671 that the interior belonged to France.[35] As Michael Witgen has argued, this extension of the French empire into the Great Lakes region "represented the rhetoric of empire rather than a genuine expansion of political sovereignty,"[36] but it nevertheless signified an attempt on the part of the French to assert sovereignty and protect trade routes as well as access to brokers and resources. Anishinaabek would have had hardly seen themselves as subjects of the French Crown, despite efforts to claim them as such.

European competition over the fur trade, chiefly between Great Britain and France, led to further territorial invasions. When this rivalry resulted in the defeat of New France at the close of the Seven Years' War in 1763, England issued the Royal Proclamation and its terms were ratified by 2,000 Indigenous chiefs and dignitaries at the Treaty at Niagara the following year.[37] While the document is often cited as establishing British supremacy in North America, for Indigenous peoples its importance lies in the recognition of "Indian Territory" and the need to enter into treaties before European settlement could take place. This treaty – following the protocols of Indigenous diplomacy that featured gift-giving, wampum, and symbolism – signified a new relationship between the Anishinaabek and the British Crown from an Indigenous point of view that is still remembered in our communities today. This relationship was defined by mutual respect and recognition of Indigenous rights and has underpinned the expectations of Indigenous Nations since that time.

As the French before them, the British Government at Niagara was chiefly concerned with securing military alliances with Indigenous peoples in the interior of North America to secure what the British saw as the "frontier" against incursions by rivals. Even so, the relationship remained multidimensional, characterized by self-interest on both sides, although the British were in no position to press their demands. During the American Revolution, the Anishinaabek often partnered with the British, supplying approximately 6,150 Anishinaabek warriors from the Upper Great Lakes to assist the Crown against American patriots.[38] Yet other groups also chose to remain neutral.[39] When war broke out again in 1812, Indigenous leaders chose sides based on their own interests, the most important being to defend their lands from further American encroachment. On the North Shore of Lake Huron, the British success at Michilimackinac on 17 July 1812 encouraged the Anishinaabek to support British forces.[40] Anishinaabek from the Sault Ste. Marie area, led by Shingwaukonse, fought with Isaac Brock in southern Ontario while Assiginack led others from Manitoulin Island at both Michilimackinac and Prairie du Chien.[41]

Both Shingwaukonse and Assiginack retained considerable political influence well into the mid-nineteenth century which gave the relationships forged at the end of the eighteenth and beginning of the nineteenth centuries enduring significance. Cory Silverstein, in his analysis of Indigenous stories about the War of 1812, highlights the Anishinaabe connections made between identity, land, and history in its aftermath.[42]

In *Connected to the Land*, Elders recount the roles of Anishinaabe leaders and warriors in the conflict, after which some at Michilimackinac – that sacred place from oral tradition – moved north to Manitoulin Island and the North Shore of Lake Huron when it was turned over to the Americans.[43] The change of fortunes in the Indigenous-settler relationship would be marked by a continuation of invasion, the dispossession of Indigenous peoples of their lands, and increased assimilationist policies in the nineteenth century as the British Crown gradually lost the need to partner with Indigenous groups to maintain security and the fur trade declined, eventually giving way to settlement.

As settlement gradually pushed north during the early part of the nineteenth century, the government of Upper Canada and the British Crown sought to exert control not only over territory, but also the people who lived there. As part of this process, Protestant and Roman Catholic proselytizers renewed missionary efforts beginning in the 1830s, including attempts to establish a series of mission communities in Upper Canada.[44] Peter Jones (Kahkewaquonaby), an Anishinaabe Methodist minister, helped to create a community at Credit River in 1825, while two years later, William Case, a Methodist missionary from the United States, established the Grape Island community, which was later relocated to Rice Lake in 1836. Indian Affairs agent Thomas G. Anderson was responsible for two Anishinaabe settlement communities, both of which were largely unsuccessful as settlement projects: Coldwater on the Narrows in 1829, followed by Manitowaning on Manitoulin Island in 1835.[45] All of these settlement schemes would have served to root people in one place who had previously moved across a vast territory with the seasons, opening the road to settlement.

These failed schemes foreshadowed Sir Francis Bond Head's plan to solve what settlers saw as the "Indian problem" by relocating many groups along the coast of the Great Lakes to Manitoulin Island. Bond Head, the lieutenant governor of Upper Canada, had little hope for assimilation and integration of the Anishinaabek and settlers, and instead, argued "that the greatest kindness we can perform towards these intelligent, simple-minded people, is to remove and fortify them as much as possible from all communication with the whites."[46] His plan to move Indigenous peoples to Manitoulin Island to enable them to live out their remaining days without settler interference was certainly part of the nineteenth century stereotype that romanticized "primitive" Indigenous peoples, but more than that, it offered an opportunity to open Indigenous lands for settlement.[47] To that end, in the summer of 1836, Bond Head arrived at Manitoulin Island for a meeting that included gift-giving and the exchange of wampum, as well as a speech that recalled the Treaty of Niagara. His speeches to the Indigenous peoples gathered there consisted of a treaty that would have the Anishinaabek "relinquish [their] respective Claims to these Islands, and make them the property (under the Great Father's Control) of all Indians who he shall allow to reside on them."[48] The Roman Catholic community at Wiikwemikoong rivalled Manitowaning, and twelve other permanent villages had been established across the island, but the mass migration Bond Head had hoped for never materialized.[49]

At the same time, there was no pressing need to extinguish title in a rocky region where farming was difficult, if not impossible, and the fur trade had declined in importance. Until the 1840s, settler interest in the area was limited to that of members of religious orders, traders, and government and military officials.[50] But tensions increased as the importance of mineral development grew in the mid-nineteenth century, and settlers saw the Upper Great Lakes region as a potentially lucrative resource hinterland for both the newly renamed Canada East and Canada West to exploit. Historians cite the Mica Bay incident, one of the more notorious conflicts surrounding settler incursions into Anishinaabe territory, as one of the catalysts for the treaty process in the Lakes Huron and Superior region.[51] As licenses and permits were given to mining development companies beginning in 1846, Indigenous leaders became vocal about asserting their rights and concerns over their exclusion from the tendering process. Shingwaukonse, the Anishinaabe chief from the Sault Ste. Marie area who fought in the War of 1812, pressed his grievances against invasion by visiting Montreal twice, in addition to petitioning for compensation for lost timber and minerals.[52] In one such petition, Shingwaukonse acknowledged the wealth present in Anishinaabe territory: "Great things have been found in these places. I see Men with hammers coming to break open my treasury to make themselves rich and I want to stay and watch and get my share."[53] When repeated efforts to assert Anishinaabek sovereignty had yielded no result, Shingwaukonse, another Chief named Nabenagoching, and a large group of Métis and Anishinaabe men defended the land by taking over the Quebec Mining Company at Mica Bay and closing its operations.[54] Allan Macdonell, a settler with mining interests and fluency in Anishinaabemowin, accompanied them. The colony of Canada West's response was to deploy one hundred men to end the confrontation, arrest the chiefs, and bring them to Toronto. Throughout their subsequent incarceration, Anishinaabe leaders continued to press their demands for compensation, and it was decided that a formal treaty should be signed in accordance with the Royal Proclamation.[55]

The treaty-making process began in 1849 when Alexander Vidal and Thomas Gummersal Anderson were appointed commissioners and sent to discuss land cessions.[56] This was followed a few months later with the appointment of Willian B. Robinson by Order in Council on 11 January 1850 to go to the region to negotiate and sign a formal treaty.[57] Robinson, a fur-trading businessman with strong connections to the Family Compact, had instructions to treat with chiefs representing approximately 3,600 First Nations people around Lakes Huron and Superior in an effort to obtain land. He was provided with £7,500 to accomplish this task and was specifically instructed against gift-giving, meaning that his negotiations would be in breach of Indigenous diplomatic expectations.[58] Representatives from Indigenous groups from across the North Shore of Lake Huron and the eastern coast of Lake Superior took part in the treaty-making process, including the people then living on the banks of the Serpent River and the peninsula that stretches out into Lake Huron where the river meets the lake.

The Anishinaabek see the treaty-making process as the beginning of a sacred relationship. We see the agreements that were eventually signed as more than simple written contracts: they are a comprehensive living agreement based on a nation-to-nation relationship. The fact that the relationship is sacred has linguistic and cultural importance, as an important distinction in Anishinaabemowin is whether or not something is animate. In this case, the paper and the relationship it represents are alive in our language. There were verbal aspects to the treaty, in addition to the written portion, but the latter is privileged by the western viewpoint of the federal government. Nevertheless, the notion that this was and still is a sacred agreement is very much alive in Anishinaabe communities. From the Anishinaabe point of view, the treaty-making process did not represent a one-time transaction whereby land was surrendered permanently. Elders have said there is no word for "title" in Anishinaabemowin, emphasizing the worldview that land and resources cannot be bought or sold, and a responsibility for humans to fulfil our duties in relationship with creation, not as owners.[59] Furthermore, this relationship with the land needs to be protected for future generations, a teaching that ensures that any decision-making process today needs to look at possible impacts beyond the present day. Although the Serpent River Anishinaabek had been living around the peninsula for some parts of the year long before the treaty was agreed to, the concept of a reserve – a small piece of land to which present and future generations were bound – would have been foreign and divergent from Anishinaabe understandings of territory and responsibility.

The Indigenous perspective of the treaty-making process was very different from the settler perspective which emphasizes the specific language of the final agreement. Among its clauses, the following terms were emphasized:

> That for, and in consideration of the sum of two thousand pounds of good and lawful money of Upper Canada, to them in hand paid, and for the further perpetual annuity of six hundred pounds of like money, the same to be paid and delivered to the said Chiefs and their Tribes at a convenient season of each year, of which due notice will be given, at such places as may be appointed for that purpose, they the said Chiefs and Principal men, on behalf of their respective Tribes or Bands, do hereby fully, freely, and voluntarily surrender, cede, grant, and convey unto Her Majesty, her heirs and successors for ever, all their right, title, and interest to, and in the whole of, the territory above described, save and except the reservations set forth in the schedule hereunto annexed; which reservations shall be held and occupied by the said Chiefs and their Tribes in common, for their own use and benefit.[60]

From a settler perspective, this was the most important part of the agreement known as the Robinson-Superior Treaty, signed at Sault Ste. Marie on 7 September 1850, followed two days later by the Huron Treaty.[61] Between the two treaties, from the settler perspective, title to 52,400 square miles had been sold and Canada West had secured the rights to those resources.[62] The Vidal-Anderson commissioners wrote that the Serpent Band requested "a small reserve at the mouth of the Serpent River, where they have ground cultivated."[63] They were the seventh group listed in the Robinson Treaty, led by Windawtegawinini, and negotiated to keep "the Peninsula east of Serpent River, and formed by it, now occupied by them."[64] The name chosen by the band reflected the importance of their stories about the Serpent and the treaty makers clearly understood that the land and the river itself were of great importance. As the people of the Serpent River came into more sustained contact with the apparatus of the emerging state in Canada West, their lives – or rather the aspects of their lives deemed important to settler societies – were documented in growing detail. Using settler documents describing assimilation in order to write Indigenous history can be problematic, but these documents can also reveal resistance and resilience.

Not long after the treaty negotiations, the Province of Canada developed an interest in keeping a closer eye on Indigenous peoples and the lands they occupied, in part to ensure that they adhered to the restrictions and terms of those agreements. In 1856, Governor General Edmund Walker Head appointed a panel of special commissioners, including Richard T. Pennefather, the superintendent-general of Indian Affairs, as well as Froome Talfourd and Thomas Worthington, to investigate "the best means of securing the future progress and civilization of the Indian Tribes in Canada" as well as "the best mode of so managing the Indian Property as to secure its full benefit to the Indians, without impeding the settlement of the country."[65] The commissioners found that the population of Windawtegawinini's Band at Serpent River had decreased from seventy-nine at the time of the treaty in 1850 to seventy-one when they next reported in 1858.[66] Linking Christianization to a larger process of civilization (and thus pacification), they remarked on the conversion rates of the North Shore, which were not, in their eyes, sufficiently high: "With the exception of the Indians at Garden River," they wrote, "there are not many inhabiting the North Shore of Lake Huron who have renounced heathenism."[67] Clearly, the Anishinaabek were still practicing ceremonies and traditions on the land as they had before the treaty. Fathers Hannipeaux and Ferard, the Catholic missionaries at Wiikwemikoong on Manitoulin Island, estimated that of the approximate 578 people "yet inhabiting the forests between Penetanguishene and Bruce Mines," about 261 Anishinaabek chose to remain "heathen."[68] In fact, a tally of converts indicated 294 Catholics and 23 Protestants, but none of them are listed in the Serpent River area.[69]

It is clear that in the 1850s, the people of Serpent River continued to live a traditional lifestyle. Although reports described the habitual lifestyle of North Shore Anishinaabek in dismissive terms, they also affirm their continued traditional land use practices:

> These tribes live for the most part by hunting, and on the produce of their fisheries, although they do raise a few potatoes, and a little Indian corn; and they find a market for disposing of their peltries and supplying themselves with the necessaries at the posts of the Hudson's Bay Company. They are quite nomadic in their habits, seldom living, or remaining long in one spot, and contented with the shelter afforded by a bark wigwam or a hut of reeds. It is only during the spring and autumn, when they come down from the high grounds to the border of the Lake, that they are accessible to those who would urge on them the necessity of Christianity and civilization. There is no difficulty therefore in accounting for the small apparent results of the labours of the missionaries.[70]

Throughout the latter part of the century, state officials would continue to document, however disparagingly, the "nomadic" nature of the

Anishinaabek on the North Shore and their traditional connections to their territory. Yet given the remoteness of the place from settler population centres, the community was largely left alone. As was the case in decades past, the Serpent's Band participated in a seasonal round focused on the river, along which they typically lived in the summer months. Hunting, fishing, gathering, limited farming, and trapping remained the most important economic activities.

While many people continued to engage in traditional seasonal movement throughout Anishinaabek territory, those who settled in the area were subjected to growing surveillance by officials from the new Department of Indian Affairs. As scholars have documented, the policies of the new Dominion of Canada directed at Indigenous people aimed to assimilate them into settler society and various benchmarks were used to measure progress toward that goal including religion, mode of subsistence, and health.[71] No longer were Indigenous peoples regarded as equal partners by state officials, but as wards of the state to be transformed gradually over generations into ideal citizens. In his 1874 annual report, J.C. Phipps, visiting superintendent, echoed the concerns from 1858 about the daily lives of the Serpent's Band: "The Indians raise only a small quantity of corn and potatoes," he wrote. "They maintain themselves by hunting and fishing. As is the case with most of the mainland Bands, Paganism prevails to a great extent amongst them." Their homes were said to take the form of log houses, and even the state of their physical bodies was subjected to scrutiny: they were said to be "comfortably clad" and "possess a fine physique; but from hardships and exposure appear old at forty years. They suffer from scurvy, and diseases of the eye are common amongst them."[72] The description of the Serpent River Anishinaabek was consistent with what Mary-Ellen Kelm has called "diagnosing the discursive Indian."[73] DIA categorized them as hunters with fine physiques on the one hand, but described their bodies as being riddled with preventable diseases, simultaneously emphasizing an undesirable lack of material and hygienic progress.

As late as 1884, Phipps reported that there were still several families who chose to remain on the land, at least for part of the year, rather than settle on their reserves along the North Shore. Those who were still "for the most part nomadic in their habits" did not raise crops but came to the reserve area in the summer. The day schools were kept open to accommodate these children and those belonging to families who did settle.[74] DIA attempted to mitigate the Anishinaabek's rejection of large-scale settled agriculture and their insistence on continuing to practice a seasonal round by extending the school year, hoping to work toward assimilating their children.

While the Anishinaabek continued to live their lives as they had, incorporating change that served their needs, more settlers moved to northern Ontario to participate in timber extraction. These repeated encroachments complicated Anishinaabek views of territory, as leaders had to navigate increasing government intervention through Indian agents and the Indian Affairs bureaucracy which sought to implement a series of centralized policies that supported development and saw adherence to the capitalist economy as an important aspect of assimilation.

Facilitating development required efficient access to the region though. To that end, Indian Affairs obtained a surrender for a CPR right of way through reserve land on 30 January 1882, which was ratified by eleven Chiefs and principal men, who, according to the terms of surrender, constituted a majority in the community.[75] Six years later, an extra 9.3 acres of land were purchased for a railway station at Kenabutch,[76] translated as "maybe" or "it is uncertain," one of the first official names given to the community in settler documents.[77] Elders tell stories about the first to settle in the area of the station, which was on their reserve as defined by the 1850 Treaty. Babamosh was a late nineteenth century Chief and worked for the CPR. He is said to be the reason the community was called Kenabutch: when the railway was being built through the reserve, CPR representatives asked what the name of the place was. Babamosh's response was "kenabutch," or in English, "maybe."[78]

While the arrival of the railway was an important milestone in the eyes of Indian Affairs officials as it provided access to Western goods and new economic opportunities, the people of Serpent River were not passive actors. As passing trains posed threats to livestock, they asserted demands for protection. The ledger for the 1896 DIA Annual Report, for example, lists compensation amounts for two community members. The CPR provided $30 to David Panasie for his cow and $75 to Jacob Oshkaboose to replace a horse, both of which were killed by passing trains.[79] In 1904, the Indian agent Samuel Hagan reported to the Secretary of Indian Affairs that he had been approached by the Chief and Councillors about their losses and the fact that there was still no fencing in the community to protect their animals.[80] In a follow-up letter, Hagan was more specific about the community's past and present concerns, indicating both the long-standing nature of the problem, and the inconsistent compensation measures: "The Chief said he lost a good horse in the summer of 1902 and he wrote to the Railway authorities, but got no answer ... I think the Indians are very moderate in what they ask so there is nothing to prevent their stock going on the railway."[81] It appears that the Chief and others who lost valuable animals to the unfenced railway were unsuccessful in dealing with the CPR directly,[82] and turned to DIA to assist them in securing compensation. After correspondence that spanned more than a year and a half, a fence was built in accordance with the community's wishes.[83]

While the Department and community members could collaborate in some situations, this was not always the case in questions related to development and land surrenders. Nevertheless, the people of Serpent River resisted encroachments on their territory and rights and fought to receive compensation when development appeared inevitable. One of the most serious disagreements occurred in 1912 as the CPR sought to extend its lands in the reserve to build a branch line to Sault Ste. Marie. Chief William Nahmiwan succinctly outlined his community's grievances in a letter dated 7 August 1912: "I beg leave to inform you that the CPR Company are building another branch into the Serpent River Reserve, about two miles west of Cutler and we have not been consulted, in this matter, nor have we had a meeting, or any information in connection with same." He went on to describe their memory of the previous transactions a generation before; the CPR "never settled with the Serpent River Reserve band of Indians, for the building of the Soo Branch." Chief Nahmiwan was eager to have DIA address the issue before construction continued: "What we would like, and request you to look into, is a settlement of this latter work, before they do anything further with the siding they have now started as noted above."[84] According to the records of Indian Affairs, the CPR was seeking to build over an additional thirty-two acres across the heart of the community.[85] Rather than address the community's concerns, the Department of Indian Affairs allowed the CPR to secure a surrender by producing a signed contract with the Chief, which went against the requirements of the Indian Act and the Royal Proclamation. The contract produced by the CPR and sent to Ottawa was written on company stationery, dated 17 October 1912. Attributed to Chief William Nahmiwan but written in different handwriting than the letter he sent to DIA in August, the document reads: "I Wm Namawan Chief of the Serpent River band of Indians consent to the Canadian Pacific railway Co taking possession of their railroad as shown to me on plans. [I'm] to do their work and grading and I am satisfied to let the Indian land department settle the price of said right of way and borrow pit."[86] The Department accepted this dubious contract, rather than going through the legal process of preparing a surrender document or receiving the support of Chief and Council as was the case in 1882, and went on to work out the financial details in secret.[87] Yet when the terms of the deal became known at Serpent River, Nahmiwan again wrote to the Department to protest the sale, this time with the support of Council. He countered that because the band "never got one cent for" the original CPR agreement, they would only cede the width of the railway track and no more.[88]

J.D. McLean, secretary of the Department of Indian Affairs, did not hesitate to inform the chief of the powers residing in his department as a result of the Indian Act: "A railway company may take the necessary land in an Indian Reserve with the consent of His Excellency in Council," he succinctly replied. McLean was referring, most likely, to the power of 1884 and 1894 amendments to the Indian Act which allowed for land appropriation in order to raise revenue,[89] or the 1911 amendment to expropriate reserve land for public purposes.[90] Undeterred, J. Simpson, the Chief Councillor at Serpent River, wrote back to McLean with the support of the entire Council, demanding that the CPR pay 50 per cent more than had originally been negotiated, a request that was eventually met.[91]

The right of way for the CPR running through the reserve had both real and symbolic importance for a larger process of dispossession that was being perpetrated "from sea to shining sea." The railway facilitated mineral and timber extraction as well as agriculture, and it opened the door to increased settler incursions into northern Ontario. The establishment of a sawmill on leased reserve territory, and the notions of economic progress and development that it signified, was an example of an earlier Indigenous-settler relationship framed by resource extraction in Ontario's northern "hinterland." While mining development in the Lake Superior region had been a catalyst for treaty-making a generation before – and would be a significant site of renegotiation two generations later – it was the increase in non-Indigenous settlement related to timber in the second half of the nineteenth century that defined resource extraction. As more American logging companies sought timber rights and established mills on the North Shore, DIA facilitated their occupation of reserve lands and it is clear from Indian Affairs reports that as the various mills in operation in the area provided important employment opportunities for the Anishinaabek, development would be an important priority in the department's program of assimilation.

Timber played an important role in the local settler economy starting in the mid-nineteenth century when mills were established in several settlements throughout the North Shore area. One of those was at a white settlement on leased reserve land near Aird Bay, called Cutler. The settlement was known to the Anishinaabek as "Frenchtown," a reference to the fact that many of the settlers who lived and worked near the timber plant were of French-Canadian descent.[92] In the 1980s, Elders linked the timber industry to families coming to settle more permanently on reserve territory in the mid to late nineteenth century and said that there were also many Anishinaabek then living nearby in what is now Spragge, or *Mooshmazaagiing*, a mill town situated on the other side of the river from the peninsula that formed the reserve.[93] There had also been a village at *Giteoodinang*, the "old town" right across the water from Spragge and west of the present-day village, which families left to move closer to the village at Cutler.[94] Timber harvesting and mill jobs on the reserve were used to entice community members to settle on a more permanent basis nearer to Cutler village, as they would have access to wage jobs, a school, and other amenities.[95]

The development of the mill coincided with the Department's pursuit of measurable benchmarks of assimilation including material prosperity and hard work. The first lease was agreed to in March 1894, when George S. Chitty, Timber Inspector, obtained a surrender from Chief Antoin Ojowashkogijig (Bluesky) and eleven other men in the community.[96] Herman F. Harbeck, a lumberman from Spring Lake, Michigan, originally leased 424 acres of reserve land for $300 annually for twenty-one years. By October of that year, however, the lease was assigned to the Cutler and Savidge Lumber Company.[97] Harbeck himself was from the same town where Cutler and Savidge was operating, and he was listed as their Secretary in 1887, suggesting that he had secured the lease on behalf of the company, which was lauded as one of the most prominent in the industry.[98]

The settler village that developed on leased reserve land as a result of the mill was named after Dwight Cutler, one of the owners of the company. Within a year of the assignment to Cutler and Savidge, B.W. Ross, Indian Superintendent, summarized the movement of many of the 122 band members to Cutler during the previous summer in order to take advantage of employment opportunities at the mill, and noted that they were "doing well."[99] While the sale or lease of reserve resources for the benefit of Indian administration was not a new concept, it appears that, from the perspective of DIA, this land transaction had the added bonus of curtailing Anishinaabe movement and encouraged them to settle in one place to take advantage of wage labour opportunities.

In 1901, Cutler and Savidge assigned their lease to N.N. Wright and Co.,[100] comprised of partners Ralf Loveland, Edwin P. Stone, and Nathaniel N. Wright from Saginaw, Michigan.[101] A 1903 fire insurance plan prepared by Charles E. Goad estimated the population of the mill town to be 500 people.[102] That same year, a new assignment was drafted to transfer the lease to Loveland and Stone, which appeared to be a new partnership that excluded Wright.[103] Within a year, Loveland and Stone were interested in buying the property outright in order to establish a factory on site. Indian agent Samuel Hagan supported the sale in a 1904 letter to Frank Pedley, deputy superintendent-general of Indian Affairs: "These factories would be of inestimable value to the Indians of Serpent River Band by giving many of them, young & old, steady employment in the factories, and in the woods."[104] The local MP at Thessalon, A.E. Dyment, was also interested in the surrender and asked Pedley for an update on the land sale to Loveland and Stone: "I believe it would be greatly to the Indians' advantage to have this sold as it will mean considerable more work for them there for a long time to come."[105] Again, this sale of land and resources for the "benefit" of the First Nation continued DIA's plans for perpetual employment and efficient land use. Dyment's true motives, however, are less clear: he was the son of Nathaniel Dyment, who established the mill at Thessalon in 1877, and was himself a lumber merchant and stockbroker.[106]

Hagan expected that the surrender process would proceed quickly. It did not. He had asked for the surrender forms in his December 1904 letter, citing money distribution to band members on 1 January as a reason for quick action.[107] The original lease had listed 424 acres of reserve land, but Pedley indicated that much of that was under water, and therefore DIA could not sell it. The surrender papers, which had yet to be signed, covered only 198 acres of the reserve which were not covered by water. Hagan soon learned that it would be difficult to hold a meeting, or at least one that would result in his desired outcome. He maintained the community was interested in voting on the potential surrender, but they were "scattered about," making it difficult to call a meeting for that purpose. His letter betrayed another reason for the delay in that he was "informed that the chief has turned against the others and wants more than the company will give" and proposed a solution that would undermine the chief's authority: "[t]he act says the surrender shall be assented to by a majority of the Band. Can this be done by a majority of the Band, without the sanction of the chief." Hagan was hopeful in his new estimated date for the surrender vote: "I think the Indians will be all out of the woods about the first of March when I hope to have this affair closed up."[108] The reply was in the affirmative: a majority was required, but it did not require the Chief's agreement,[109] again marking a significant departure from the leadership requirements affirmed in treaty-making fifty-five years before.

It is unclear what changed over the course of the year, but on 6 February 1906, Chief Robert Bluesky sent a telegram asking for the surrender papers because they were "in from Hunting grounds" but were "anxious to get back."[110] Hagan sent a letter to Ottawa the same day with similar urgency, but wrote that they "wanted to get away to the Lumber woods."[111] While the former suggested a desire to return to the land,

Hagan's letter emphasized the male community members' eagerness to return to wage work in the very lumber industry the land surrender was meant to facilitate. The surrender was obtained by the Crown on 10 February 1906. Chief Robert Oshowskukhezhik (Bluesky) and eight other men from the community made their mark on the agreement, which encompassed 198 acres of reserve land. There was even a note referring to Chief Bluesky's signature: "this man Indian Chief being unable to write his name made his mark to same after having it read over to him and by him fully understood."[112] As we shall see, the oral record in the community indicated that this was not in fact the case.

The surrender was negotiated between the Crown and the Chiefs, but department correspondence sheds light on DIA's dealings with the company over the price they ought to pay for the land. Hagan originally suggested $500 as a fair price,[113] but Pedley recognized the potential loss in revenue, as the original lease stipulated a cost of $300 per year for nine additional years. He made adjustments based on the fact that DIA could not sell land covered by water, and thus recommended "that the sale be made for a sum based upon the capitalization of 3% of half the rental, which would be $5000.00."[114] On 9 June 1906, J.D. McLean wrote to Hagan, notifying him that the $135 in annual interest would be distributed "in the usual way" while $5,000, less 10 per cent, would be credited to their capital account.[115]

This practice, while typical of land and resource surrenders, would lead to community frustration. In August 1909, community members still did not see the benefits of the sale and boycotted the company store because they had not been compensated.[116] McLean instructed Hagan to make the interest and capital policy clear to the community. Hagan's reply was that "the Indians know all about the money that was paid by the company" but apparently, for reasons unknown to Hagan, they did not receive their interest payment that year. He assessed the reasons for damage done to the company store's business and indicated that the Anishinaabek were "always looking for money." He promised to "have a pow wow about it" when he visited the community.[117] Since traditional dancing was illegal at this time, Hagan's choice of words was unfortunate.[118]

In his response, McLean indicated that the interest on SRFN's capital account was used to pay for a doctor, a constable, and for schools, leaving nothing to distribute to individuals.[119] SRFN members thus had to pay for the administration of their own colonized community rather than actually control how the money was spent. In 1912, Chief William Nahmiwan wrote to the Department asking for the deed for the Loveland & Stone property and listed all of the amenities that were present in the community, including the mill, wharf, store, pool room, and housing structures. While he did not state his purpose in writing, he appeared to be attempting to call attention to the settler development that had taken place on the land and to ensure that the sale was in fact legal. DIA sent a copy of the surrender and informed the chief that the land was sold after the surrender was obtained in accordance with policy.[120] No mention was made about including a copy of the deed, thereby highlighting the two-step process of reserve land surrenders, the second of which often excluded the input of community leadership. By the end of the decade, the deed for the parcel of land had been taken over by Spanish Mills Company.[121]

By 1920, DIA attempted to encourage yet another sale to a lumber company – this time to Spanish Mills Company – for an extension of the lumber yard. Hagan brought the request directly to DIA in August 1918 before consulting with the community. McLean had directed him to do so before the surrender would be considered, but Chief John Kijadjiwan's[122] letter to DIA in January 1920 suggested that Hagan took a more coercive approach: "Our Indian Agent of Tesslon [Thessalon] has asked the Indians of this Reserve to sell or Grant some number of acres of land to the Spanish Lumber Co. The said Agent claims if we should not agree to this, the land will be taken and the Indians will get nothing for it." He went on to ask for clarification about the power of DIA, writing, "[s]hould this be possible we would like to know."[123] McLean clarified that a land surrender was in fact required under the Indian Act and stated that the Department would pursue "the best prices obtainable in the interest of the Band."[124] The chief immediately requested a new copy of the Indian Act and relayed the community's requested price for the land, especially given the significant amount of birch on the parcel in question.[125] In early March, the Chief Kijadjiwan reiterated the community's openness to the idea of surrender, provided a fair price was offered, but that any surveying should wait until the end of the month because of the deep snow.[126] A meeting was held on 8 September to vote on the issue. Hagan recorded that sixteen of the twenty-five eligible voters were present and all were in favour.[127] It is unclear how the other nine men felt about the potential surrender as they were not present for reasons Hagan did not discuss. On 5 October 1920, Chief John Kijadjiwan and six other male community members surrendered an additional 179.4 acres of land.[128] It was not until after the surrender was agreed to, however, that the land was valued at $4 per acre.[129] The Spanish Mills Company paid $717.60 to extend their lumber yard, although it did not last long. The mill burned in 1924,[130] and the Spanish Mills Co. Ltd. sold both parcels of land (179.4 acres and 198 acres) to the Spanish

River Lumber Co. Ltd. in March 1925.[131] Not long after this time, the town of Spanish Mills, located on Aird Island across from the reserve, was abandoned, indicating the company's financial problems.[132]

Men from the community remembered these land transactions much differently in their correspondence. On 16 May 1925, perhaps because the Spanish River Lumber Company had taken over from Spanish Mills Company two months earlier, William Nahmiwan wrote on the behalf of the community to ask for information about Spanish Mills Company leaving Cutler: "there was to be work all the time in order that our son's [sic] could work at their plant but since the mill burned down there is no sign of putting up another plant." The transition from traditional pursuits to wage labour – one that DIA had so doggedly pursued in the late nineteenth century – was now threatened by the boom-and-bust cycles that typify resource economies. Chief Nahmiwan further stated that they had not sold the land, but rather only rented it to the company, and wanted to know what the company's plans were for the land.[133] Charles Rothers, the new Indian agent for the Thessalon Agency, wrote to the Spanish River Lumber Company about the question of whether or not the company owned the land outright, as he did not have a record of it on file. The company representative wrote back and stated that they had in fact taken over the land that had been originally purchased by Loveland & Stone, but that they had no immediate plans for it.[134]

In 1930, Chief John Lewis (Kijadjiwan) wrote again about the land and asked "what form is the Spanish Lumber Company holding a portion of our reserve which was Leased to Cutler and Savage about 45 years ago," further stating that the community "would like to know how that portion of land is held by the Spanish Lumber Co." DIA did not file a response to the letter, if any was given.[135] Three years later, Chief Alex Meawasige asked for clarification about the nature of the transactions, as the community leadership had no paperwork on file. He asked DIA if the Spanish River Lumber Company had a deed for the land, as the community Elders remembered the situation differently: "From what I hear from the oldest members of the band is that the plant was only leased, and it was understood that after the company was through operating the mill and not doing any more work and were leaving the place, all the houses were to be left there for the Indians, and the lease was to end." He went on describe the actual outcome once the company left: "But instead the company has sold nearly all the houses with the Exception of 5 or 6 houses and if they have the deed please tell me the year and month that the deed was made."[136]

Chief Meawasige, in another letter, called attention to the fact that the company, once they decided not to rebuild the mill, sold the remaining wood, docks, and houses that they did not destroy. In response, the community posted notices against trespassing or removing property from the site but were dismayed to see those notices removed by the company. Chief Meawasige continued a pattern set by his predecessors in pointing to the fact that the community had not been compensated for the presence of the company on their land: "The Indians of our Band are not satisfied with this as we have no knowledge of getting rent or remuneration of any description since before the Spanish River Lumber Co. came here."[137]

Serpent River community members – especially the former leaders who were by this time Elders – remembered the lease but were consistent in their rejection of any notion that a sale had taken place. The community memory indicated a profound misunderstanding of the meaning of the paperwork that was being presented to them at the time. It is not that the negotiations were forgotten, as the promises that had been made verbally (and then promptly broken) were still remembered. Such promises included the houses being left for the use of community members and that their sons would have work long into the future. This suggests that the differences between leasing land and surrendering it for a sale were not made clear, and the paperwork itself actually looks quite similar. The community Chiefs and Councillors made their marks rather than writing their names in full on the forms in question, suggesting that they were not literate in English. Finally, the fact that they surrendered the land to the Crown before it was then sold to the companies in question (and the leases and deeds could be assigned to other companies afterwards) highlights the ways in which DIA's colonial power excluded community leaders from any negotiations with those companies after they obtained the surrenders. Community leaders, however, continued their resistance to such practices.

In the 1940s, when the mill and settler residents at Cutler were long gone, the community wanted their land back. A resolution dated 6 August 1943 stated "that we ask the Indian Affairs Branch to try and buy back the land which now is held by the Spanish River Lumber Co for the interest of the Band as the land is lying idle there now."[138] Once again, DIA brokered the deal and gave permission for the community to use their capital account to buy back a portion of their reserve. DIA negotiated with the company in April 1944, and as a result, they agreed to pay $2209.60 for both parcels of land, including $700 worth of buildings still standing on the properties.[139] The land was transferred to the Crown on 23 February 1945, after two years of negotiations. More than half a century of lumber extraction on reserve territory officially came to an end with the community's purchase of its land back.

By the 1940s, timber extraction remained an important part of the local economy but many families continued to live a more or less traditional lifestyle, at least for part of the year. As several of the Elders interviewed by Perry Shawana recalled, families were, at that time, still involved in trapping, keeping community gardens, and producing maple syrup.[140] Participation in the waged economy was clearly important, but it was only one aspect of how many people lived their lives. Although resource extraction and development brought significant changes to the community, the importance of the cultural relationship continued, and community members voiced their concerns when promises were broken.

The arrival of the railways, growth of the lumber trade, and disputes over land use all dominate the relationships between the community as a whole and increasingly large settler populations. While the people of Serpent River First Nation worked at local mills, on the railway, and in the lumber trade, community leaders continued to assert their rights and to resist developments that threatened the interests of the community. In this respect, there was ongoing, significant, and effective resistance to the actions of the Department of Indian Affairs and settler-owned industries. This resistance and adherence to traditional community-based values emphasized their relationships to territory and allowed community members to negotiate their own interactions with the state, industry, and settler society. Some benefitted from the waged economy, others continued to live a traditional lifestyle, while most probably engaged in a mixture of the two. Yet at no point were traditional relationships fundamentally changed: the river remained the focus of the lives of the people of the Serpent River First Nation.

Chapter Three

Carving a "Jewel in the Wilderness": The Establishment of Elliot Lake

Elliot Lake Mining Camp – Evidence of radioactive ore prompted Aimé Breton and Karl Gunterman to stake claims south of here near Lauzon Lake in Long Township in 1948. Geologist Franc R. Joubin became interested and persuaded mining financier Joseph H. Hirshhorn to fund drilling operations. In 1953 they located the ore body that became the Pronto Uranium Mine. The discovery of further uranium deposits near Quirke and Elliot lakes led to a mining boom. The town of Elliot Lake flourished until the US stopped buying Canadian uranium in 1959. By the late 1960s, non-military uses for uranium were being developed, and mining activity revived. By 1970, the Elliot Lake camp had produced uranium oxide worth 1.3 billion.

– Ontario Heritage plaque at Elliot Lake

I'm concerned about the fact that the mines have closed. The owners are moving away and leaving the mess that we have to live with. My Grandpa is a trapper. He tells me stories about the way the land was a long time ago. He trapped in the Elliot Lake area. He tells us about how things have changed in the land and the animals and doesn't trust those things anymore. That makes me worried about the water, animals, and the land. This is very important to me and my community. Please make sure they clean it up right. Meegwetch.[1]

– Angela Lewis (Kijadjiwan), 1993

The provincial historical plaque, when juxtaposed with the words of a SRFN youth, point to very different understandings of the region's heritage. While the plaque commemorates man's victory over nature in the name of economic development, the speech of a young girl to a decommissioning board emphasizes the true cost of uranium operations from an Anishinaabe perspective. One narrative privileges the story of a municipality's determination to overcome a boom-bust cycle, and the other demonstrates the social, cultural, and environmental consequences the development of settler society has had on the First Nations in the area.[2] This chapter continues the story of land incursions on Anishinaabek territory and demonstrates how mining companies and different levels of government joined forces to establish and protect a settler mining town in the context of the Cold War. This chapter traces the local settler history of the area and examines the establishment of the mines that had such a profound impact on the territory that the Anishinaabek had been using for centuries. We have seen how the Anishinaabek at Serpent River had resisted settler encroachment in dynamic ways. However, in the context of Cold War uranium development, the community had to contend with profound change brought on by further settlement and industrialization. In other words, SRFN had to face an expensive, modern townsite that had been built to house miners and their families and the mining operations that threatened the river system after which the community was named.

French explorer Jacques Cartier was first told of the riches of the Kingdom of the Saguenay in the early 1500s.[3] From the mid-nineteenth century onward, prospectors and miners were travelling north to explore mineral development in the area. Indeed, as has been discussed in the previous chapter, the Robinson Treaties of 1850 were commissioned largely in order to extinguish Aboriginal title along Lakes Huron and Superior for the purposes of resource extraction. Indigenous resistance to settler mining development at Mica Bay necessitated treaties in the area, and the colonial government undertook such processes to support European expansion and settlement.[4] This pattern of government intervention in the planning of the so-called frontier would continue with mineral developments more than a century later, particularly at Elliot Lake.[5]

The 1850 treaties paved the way for the development of "new" Ontario, supported by a resource extraction economy,[6] and as the incident at Mica Bay indicates, mining has been an important pursuit in the region since the mid-nineteenth century. Sudbury, for example, which started out as a CPR stop in 1883, soon gained economic importance as copper and nickel deposits were found,[7] and the railway town became a settler mining boom town very quickly.[8] Prospectors found gold near Red Lake in the northwestern region in the 1890s[9] and the Porcupine Gold Rush to the east started the mineral development of towns such as Timmins and Kirkland Lake after 1909.[10]

Overall, the mining industry in Canada was credited with being a major factor in the country's economic growth, and between 1925 and 1950 the industry's output rose from $214 million to $806 million.[11]

New sources of mineral wealth were discovered with a regularity that created an air of speculative possibility in the minds of private prospectors and governments alike. By the late 1940s, the North Shore of Lake Huron thus had a long settler history of fur trading, mining, and forestry boom towns, and the countryside was dotted with settler farmsteads and mining headframes on the Precambrian Shield.[12] This settler economy was reliant on resource extraction for its prosperity, and the Cold War would both intensify the need for mining and bring a new and significant influx of settlers.

Atomic weapons were developed in the United States during the Second World War and used against Japan in the summer of 1945. The sheer power of first atomic weapons and later the hydrogen bomb was meant to deter the Soviets from starting a conventional war, which would be unwinnable for the NATO alliance. When the Soviets tested their first nuclear weapon in August 1949, however, this sparked an arms race in which the United States sought to build and maintain an arsenal of nuclear weapons large enough to deter a Soviet conventional or nuclear attack. Thus, finding large quantities of uranium for use in building nuclear weapons was a key requirement for developing a successful American nuclear weapons program. While Canada was not interested in cultivating its own home-grown offensive nuclear weapons – although it did obtain American-built and controlled Bomarc defensive missiles – from the early years of the Manhattan Project Canadian governments had a vested interest in supporting the American weapons program and maintaining cooperation between their British and American allies. To this end, Canada could provide the uranium required for the job.

In 1930 Gilbert LaBine discovered pitchblende, a uranium-rich mineral, at Great Bear Lake in the Northwest Territories and founded the Eldorado Gold Mining Corporation to extract trace radium from the uranium.[13] During the Second World War, American demand for uranium to develop and build atomic weapons led the Canadian government to nationalize Eldorado and take over its mining operations.[14] In the post-war years, demand for the mineral continued to climb, thus renewing private interest in prospecting and extraction: private companies could mine uranium legally again starting in 1948.[15] Companies preferred deposits that were both accessible and closer to American markets and refining operations. This eventually led to the discovery of uranium near the North Shore of Lake Huron and the establishment of the town of Elliot Lake.[16]

In Ontario's mining belt, anxious citizens followed the prospecting rush as it unfolded across the country. In 1950, they learned that in

Quebec, seasoned prospector Captain John R. Beauchemin, backed by more than twenty years of experience and a trusty Geiger counter, made a new uranium discovery near Saint-Siméon in Charlevoix County.[17] The prospectors' staking of 15,000 acres of land following the discovery was met with great excitement, but this was not for economic reasons alone. It was also a reason to ask the Duplessis regime to extend the Quebec-Chicoutimi highway to Saint-Siméon.[18] From this, newspaper readers could infer that uranium would bring important infrastructure and development money wherever it might be found.

For a region of Ontario dependent on the discovery of new resources for sustained economic growth, uranium strikes elsewhere in Canada captured the imaginations of the settler readers of the *Sault Daily Star*. In 1949, sixty groups prospected in Northern Saskatchewan, while the following year it was predicted that their number would double thanks to fifty claims staked in the Lake Athabasca area.[19] Readers learned of another high-grade deposit in March 1950 when Adolph Studer announced his discovery in the La Ronge area in Saskatchewan.[20] The next month, three claims near Lac La Ronge were made "commercially feasible" to mine deposits by the increase in the value of uranium.[21] The *Star* delighted in reporting that the regional prospecting supervisor, Malcolm Norris, explained that "the new price basis will mean a boost of $7 a ton on top-assay ore" and "the other two known deposits would get a 'reasonable' price increase."[22]

As the *Rotarian* told its interested American readers, the Canadian uranium prospector's "bible is the Government issued *Prospectors' Guide for Uranium and Thorium Minerals in Canada*."[23] The *Prospectors' Handbook*, as it was colloquially known, was in its third edition by the spring of 1950 and northern Ontario prospectors picked up copies to learn how to join this new mineral rush.[24] It provided a description of radioactive minerals, a geological and geographical overview, and provided tips about how to use and care for one's Geiger counter.[25] The Provincial Department of Mines encouraged development of this new industry through free evening prospecting classes which it organized and funded in Toronto.[26] As the Sault Ste. Marie newspaper reported, uranium fever in the area reached frenzied levels when the government guaranteed prices for the ore in April 1950, effectively doubling the price.[27] Excited editors suggested that prospecting and exploration of the radioactive ore would soon rival the area's already solid tourism industry.[28] In 1955, the *Bruce Mines Spectator*, a local paper for the small North Shore town, even suggested that readers interested in outdoor tourism also do some prospecting on the side.[29] "Bring a Geiger counter to Ontario!" it suggested. "You may not strike it rich but you will have a lot of fun with the ever-growing group of holidayers who use their vacation time to look for radioactive minerals while enjoying the great Ontario outdoors."[30] Anyone could become a prospector, thanks to direct government intervention, a nationalized pricing scheme, and a seemingly unlimited market south of the border.[31]

Despite settler enthusiasm for uranium discoveries, the initial search for large deposits in the Upper Great Lakes region bore little fruit. Interest was sustained at a fevered pitch by smaller but tantalizing discoveries made by 1950 on the eastern shore of Lake Superior north of Sault Ste. Marie as well as in northern Michigan.[32] Local newspaper articles reminded readers that even these finds had economic value and that even greater ones were just around the corner.[33] For three years, prospectors and mining company representatives kept busy buying and renewing mining licenses throughout the region, gambling on what they hoped would be a big strike. Meanwhile, the newspapers assured readers that, despite apparent setbacks, a brighter future lay ahead.[34] Three long years later, settler luck finally changed, with grave consequences for Anishinaabek in the area.

The largest uranium find in Ontario took place under mysterious circumstances, known colloquially in local lore as the "Backdoor Staking Bee." Catharine Dixon, a long-time resident of Elliot Lake and a former journalist, details the search for uranium in the area east of Blind River from the late 1940s onward. She attributes the discovery of uranium to independent prospectors, likely encouraged in their endeavours by local news reporting which promised that a successful claim would pave the way to personal economic fortune. By the 1950s, more and more independent prospectors were staking claims, and a Sault Ste. Marie hotel owner by the name of Aimé Breton and his employee, Karl Gunterman, purchased several lapsed claims from Long Township in the District of Algoma. In 1952, Gunterman also allowed the claims to lapse, even though Breton had instructed him to maintain them. Franc R. Joubin and Joseph H. Hirshhorn purchased the twice-lapsed claims. Gunterman had met Joubin on the land when they were both prospecting in the area, and Joubin had subsequently become very interested in the potential of the Breton-Gunterman claims.[35]

Joubin, an independent geologist backed by financier Joseph Hirshhorn, hypothesized that the oxidization process had rendered surface uranium nearly undetectable, but that the elusive element was lurking just below the surface. This supposition spurred the "Backdoor Staking Bee" during the spring and summer of 1953, in which a group of independent prospectors as well as some employed by Joubin and Hirshhorn chartered flights from the Porcupine region (near Timmins,

Ontario) and flew into the area in secret. Over the next six weeks, more than seventy prospectors, geologists, cooks, and pilots worked to stake 8,000 claims in the area, but their activities did not become public until 12 July 1953, two days after their claims were filed. When their secret was leaked, excitement swept the region as prospectors jumped on the bandwagon, hoping to cash in on a potentially large find. Popular and official hopes abounded for a boom in what was regarded as the latest mineral frontier in northern Ontario.[36]

The local popularity of the story of Breton's and Gunterman's lost opportunity and a lucrative secret summer staking bee underpins a romanticized view of a wild uranium-packed frontier waiting to be exploited by those gifted with courage and vision. Indeed, in one account of these events, the history of Elliot Lake is recounted as a pioneer narrative. "The first discoveries in the area occurred during 1953," writes a local historian, "and with the faith of financier Joseph Hirshhorn in Franc Joubin and in uranium, plus the rugged pioneer-spirit of thousands of individuals, a part of Canada's great north began its transformation."[37] While the people who came to the area in search of wealth, employment, or a stepping-stone to a new life certainly took an economic chance, the reality did not reflect local rhetoric about individualistic enterprise in a rugged, untouched wilderness area. Instead, from the very beginning uranium prospecting was but another chapter in a long history of regional resource exploitation, this time backed by government price guarantees and a Cold War market driven by an American demand for nuclear weapons.

While the physical act of prospecting is, at one level, an individual undertaking, from the very beginning the exploitation of the claims staked in 1953 became a private-public partnership involving mining companies and both federal and provincial governments. This partnership created the town of Elliot Lake, which is evident in the geographical names of the town today. One of the community's unique features is the street names which reflect the links between environment, industry, and government. In one area the streets are named after tree species, while in the centre of town they are named after the leading private individuals responsible for the establishment of the mining industry. In a third neighbourhood, the names of prime ministers are used, with Pearson Drive situated as its backbone. It is not surprising that the urban geography should reflect this reality in a town built and sustained by a partnership between industry and government. Indeed, as we will see, there would be several points in the town's history when the industry at Elliot Lake would only be sustained by government stockpiling initiatives in the absence of international buyers for uranium. The uranium economy at Elliot Lake – which was subject to a boom-bust economic cycle like any other single-industry town – was thus shaped by larger socio-political changes and private-public partnerships from its very beginning.

But it was the "Backdoor Staking Bee" described earlier that began the rush of mining companies to the area. The stakes claimed in a Z formation belonged to the Algom Mining Company, and it investigated the best 630 stakes it had claimed and quickly put a diamond drilling program into place.[38] Consolidated Denison was not far behind during the summer of 1953. A.W. Stollery and F.H. Jowsey staked the company's claims, while R.I. Benner began the geological mapping of the staked area the following spring.[39] The drilling done at these mine sites and the others that soon followed demonstrated the staggering amount of uranium that had been discovered. "Before the end of 1953," writes Dixon, "it became evident that ore bodies at both Quirke and Nordic [two mines that were established] might be larger than those at either Gunmar, or Beaverlodge in Saskatchewan. They would yield more uranium oxide than Great Bear Lake in the Northwest Territories and probably twice as much as Pronto."[40] The quantity and concentration of uranium underground was unprecedented at the time, and twelve mines quickly came into operation in order to extract it: Algom Quirke, Algom Nordic, Consolidated Denison, Panel, Can-Met, Stanrock, Stanleigh, Spanish-American, Buckles Mine, Milliken, Lacnor, and Pronto.[41] The federal government entered into a $1.6 billion contract with the Atomic Energy Commission in the United States in 1957, underlining the extent to which the state was involved in uranium production and its export.[42]

Between 1955 and 1961, uranium extraction was extremely profitable; by the end of the 1950s, Canada had become completely embedded in the American uranium economy, and that relationship was a lucrative one, with the annual uranium trade bringing in approximately $300 million every year throughout the late 1950s. The United States imported about half its uranium and most of that came from Canada, further cementing the economic and military relationship between the two countries.[43]

On a Monday night in October 1956 at the Blind River Legion hall, Lester B. Pearson, then Secretary of State for External Affairs and Member of Parliament for Algoma East, explained the direct relationship between uranium extraction in his riding and Canada's international relations: "Ninety-six percent, perhaps more, of the product of this area, is going to the production of weapons of war – weapons almost too much in horror for the human mind to grasp."[44] Pearson was well aware of the importance of making peace and not war; he won the Nobel Peace Prize the following year for his efforts during the Suez Crisis.[45] While nuclear war horrified him, Pearson conceded that deterrence was necessary: "We must look for other means to peace, but it looks to me as if it will require this deterrent to aggression for some time to come."[46]

The purpose of the Blind River meeting was to brief the public about an international conference in New York. The topic of the conference was the peaceful use of atomic energy, and Pearson had hoped to enlighten his constituents about the importance of their area and the new industry. "If we in New York can make a success of this conference," he said, "we will do two things. We will prevent any countries, other than those who already atomic weapons have – United States, United Kingdom, and the USSR – from using atomic energy for purposes of war. And we will try to increase knowledge of atomic power in other countries, so that we can find new uses for uranium and atomic energy. If we can do this, it will have a direct bearing on this area."[47] In his address, Pearson pointed out the importance of Algoma's uranium to winning the Cold War, both as an essential component of the West's deterrence policy, but also in hopes that it would provide important energy alternatives or other peaceful uses.[48] He was keenly aware that both were good for the Algoma economy, and that the latter alternative would fuel the uranium economy after nuclear weapons were no longer needed.

Pearson's rousing speech was in keeping with the Canadian government's excitement over uranium prospects, which had led to Eldorado's nationalization in stages from 1942 to 1944.[49] At this time, Eldorado had a monopoly on mining and milling uranium ore after its interests turned from radium to uranium in the post-war period. Once the ore had been milled, it was then processed into uranium concentrates at Port Hope, Ontario, and then shipped to the United States for refining into pure uranium metal. Although Eldorado had a monopoly on uranium contracts, in 1948, the government announced that privately owned mines would be encouraged to replace government-owned mines in uranium development.[50] Previous to this, two of the three other mines that were in operation were located at Port Radium in the Northwest Territories and in the Beaverlodge area in northern Saskatchewan. Crown-owned Eldorado Mining and Refining Corporation ran both of them, while Rix-Athabasca ran the sole privately owned mine in production in Canada in the Beaverlodge area as well. Two other companies, Gunnar Mines and Consolidated Nicholson, were set to begin production in the Beaverlodge area, while Pronto Uranium was in development in the

Blind River region of Ontario.[51] Thus, the North Shore area of northern Ontario, whose economy had always been defined by resource extraction, added uranium as one of its key economic drivers – a mineral that was to shape both economic and public perception of the region in the years to come. However, unlike previous economic developments, cooperation between private business and federal and provincial levels of government would define this new phase.[52]

A cooperative public-private partnership was imperative to create a townsite closer to the ore body so as to facilitate its extraction. Blind River, where Pearson's meeting took place, is located seventy kilometres from the present-day site of Elliot Lake. The main ore body was also thirty kilometres from the Trans-Canada Highway, the North Shore of Lake Huron, and the local branch line of the CPR. Given the remoteness of the mine sites to existing towns and transportation infrastructure, it was clear that a townsite would have to be "carved from the rock," to borrow the title of a recent historical documentary on the history of Elliot Lake.[53] In the beginning there were makeshift camps to house male employees, but mining officials thought that there should also be more permanent sites for housing.[54] The campsites bred their fair share of criticism:[55] in 1957 the United Steelworkers of America union supervisor, Terry Mancini, drew media attention to the inadequate living conditions faced by his members at their work camps. Stating that some of the buildings were nothing more than "broken down barns" and making reference to the forty reported instances of food poisoning, Mancini publicized his demands for a clean-up of conditions.[56] "We saw men retching and throwing up outside between huts," he reported. "Inside we saw men lying sick in bed while somebody was trying to spoon hot tea into them."[57] Mancini insisted that his members deserved better.[58]

In 1957, a thousand men walked off the job at the Algom Nordic Mine in protest of the crowded and poor conditions to which they were subjected. Campsite conditions were controlled by the mining companies themselves, which made living conditions an aspect of collective bargaining. Indeed, it was a recurring issue for the workers and their union and a journalist's description of camp housing underscores their grievances:

> Some of the men's attempts at adding the homey touch are indeed pathetic. Small shelves erected around double decker bunks hold personal gear, pictures pasted to the walls, and even a jam pail used as a bed lamp. This spells home for these men. Lines strung across the rooms add to the general atmosphere ... and drying socks and underwear to the smell. In these

latter huts toilet facilities are very poor. Long line-ups are the order of the day for the use of porcelain wash basins ... a man objects to washing in another man's dirt.[59]

While authorities from Ontario Public Health inspected the site and found no evidence of overcrowding, the miners who lived sixteen people to a twenty-by-sixteen-foot room disagreed.[60] The overcrowding was a by-product of the rushed construction of the temporary work camp, which had been established to quicken workers' access to the sites. As the mines developed and the population increased, it is hardly surprising that employees who planned to stay in the area for the long-term wanted to bring their families. But this was impossible so long as they did not have access to proper single-family housing.

Since the mines and government had been initially reluctant to support a permanent building program as had been established at other single-resource sites elsewhere, alternative housing had developed in close proximity to the individual sources of employment – the actual headframe of the mine, for example. This often created a hodgepodge of loosely connected and sometimes isolated clusters of housing sites which, given the boom-bust nature of the economy, were unsustainable in the long-term.[61] At the uranium camp at Elliot Lake, it was decided early on that there should be a single community established for mine employees regardless of where they worked. Representatives from Algom Uranium Mines Ltd. had advocated for this plan since 1954, and a brief presented to the Ontario Municipal Board on 20 July 1955 echoed that sentiment:

> A prime objective of Algom Uranium Mines Ltd. and indeed of all mining companies is to ensure their labour force favourable living conditions in pleasant surroundings. As I understand it, this objective can be readily attained through the incorporation of an Improvement District. It can be met by building town-sites at the individual mines or by fostering a central community. This Company and its employees favour a central community and have in the past and will continue in the future to work with government agencies to encourage this movement.[62]

The brief, an example of the lobbying efforts undertaken by the mining companies, underlines many of their goals for business and community development in the area and their concern in particular that the latter support the former. The establishment of the townsite was not to be a haphazard settlement in northern Ontario. Instead, the provincial government and the mining companies joined forces in the planning for this modern town, a relationship that stemmed back to the previous year. As Robert Robson argues in his study of government intervention in resource townsite planning in northern Ontario during the 1950s, "the provincial government, through its efforts to rationalize northern growth and expansion, committed itself to the notion of comprehensive planning."[63]

A meeting between representatives from the Departments of Lands and Forests, Highways, Health, Municipal Affairs, Mines, the Hydro-Electric Power Commission of Ontario, the CPR, Algom Uranium Mines Ltd., Technical Mine Consultants, and the Roddis Lumber and Veneer Company on 19–21 September 1954 was surprisingly productive given the number of people present, each with his or her own interests. The purpose of the meeting was to discuss planning options for the townsite.[64] In a statement made on 26 January 1955 to the provincial Cabinet Subcommittee set up to deal with the Elliot Lake question, the Administrative Committee on Townsites expressed the need for the establishment of a townsite and detailed the skeletal provisions that were already in place in the area.[65] Perhaps most importantly, these recommendations noted the bright future of the industry in order to emphasize the area as one of growth and prosperity. In other words, although the statement was no doubt an accurate assessment of the conditions on the ground, the recommendations highlighted not only the need for a townsite, but that its establishment would also make economic sense in the long-term.[66]

Over the next year, cost-sharing schemes were ironed out through meetings of the Administrative Committee on Townsites and the provincial Cabinet Subcommittee chaired by the minister of municipal affairs; Franc Joubin provided written assurances of Algom's willingness to contribute. Shortly thereafter, the Improvement District of Elliot Lake, an area that now spanned 396 square miles, was born of an amalgamation of nearly a dozen townships.[67] Once the Improvement District was designated, the townsite was divided into three subdivisions to be built consecutively all under the supervision of the committees comprised of mining and government interests.[68]

While the urban planning for Elliot Lake reflected post-war utopian ideals and a government desire to promote order and rationality in development, one peculiar aspect was the structure of the town's governing body.[69] Due in part to the initial transient population (labourers and miners came and went) as well as the rapid transition from work camp to townsite, the province appointed a board of trustees, comprised of three men who answered to the Department of Municipal Affairs, to act as the governing structure in the community.[70] In fact,

the minister of planning and development at the time, W.K. Warren-
der, issued an order under the Planning Act to protect government
and business interests by establishing standards of development for
the area. Government interests and legislation would control development until "such time as local municipalities are established to assume
responsibility for the permanent administration of the area."[71] The
chaotic free-for-all that characterized some boom towns was not to be
repeated on the North Shore. Instead, a joint task force between business representatives and government ministries would closely control
the area. Joubin, who was now the President of Algom Uranium Mines
Ltd., E.B. Gillanders, Algom's Managing Director, and B. Willoughby,
the director of Can-Met Explorations Ltd., were chosen to sit on the
Board of Trustees effective 1 September 1955,[72] the same day that the
area was designated a township municipality.[73]

As Robert Robson argues, the province of Ontario was heavily
involved in municipal planning of northern Ontario "resource town"
development in the post-war period, and Elliot Lake was no exception.[74] The fact that the community was planned by a partnership
between business and government interests did not mean that development would be wholly orderly. In his government report entitled,
"Improvement District of Elliot Lake," J.W.P. Carter indicated that the
timely transfer of surface land rights from the Crown did not impede
development in the townsite, but the clearing process delayed the availability of lots. At the very end of his report, he also mentioned that the
companies, "with their attitude of urgency, improperly sited the school,
a water tower and some of the water services – to rectify these matters
all take [sic] time."[75] This embedded statement underscores the rapidity
that characterized the development of the townsite and demonstrates
that even carefully controlled planning can be unduly influenced by
time constraints. While Carter believed that "the preparation of the
town-site at Elliot Lake [had] proceeded with acceleration and that
community development [had], as much as possible kept pace with the
mining development of the area,"[76] it appears that one of the three board
directors disagreed. Joubin, in a letter to W.M. Nickle, the minister of
planning and development, outlined his concerns about the townsite's
pace of development: "the development of the town-site must also be
accelerated to keep step with the development of the mines. The provin-
cially directed townsite field-planning crew has varied from three men
to twelve and back to a present four in number; a ridiculously small
force for the scope and urgency of the project in hand."[77] Joubin's letter,
written on Algom Uranium Mines Ltd. stationary, presents a scathing
criticism of the pace of this organized planning. As both president of

Algom and a member of the Board of Trustees for the Improvement District, he was in the position to compare the development of both the economic and social aspects of the region.

The problem of organized planning was not lost on other board members. E.B. Gillanders, the Vice-President at Rio Tinto Company and a member of the Board of Trustees, called attention to the delays associated with townsite construction and the impact they could have on uranium extraction: "We realize we can't operate these mines without homes for the workers ... We want to get away from two or three contractors stumbling over themselves when they get on the job." He also emphasized that government interference caused delays in planning and construction: a lack of coordination on the part of provincial departments, as well as the federal government's "tight money policy," had a negative impact on much-need financing. "From the company's viewpoint," he wrote, "if we could handle our homes [sic] construction in the same way as we handle construction for our mines then all these bottlenecks that have caused housing delays would have been eliminated long ago."[78] The complicated ties between government and business, although necessary for the establishment of the townsite, were also to blame for delays.

Financier Joseph Hirshhorn downplayed this partnership and instead told the local newspaper that the town was his own idea: "I'm building this entirely on my own."[79] Egotism aside, Hirshhorn's comments reveal that the mining and town development process was understood to be a permanent and lasting process of directed evolution. It was, he said, something that was important not only locally but to the nation as a whole. "This is a big thing ... Not a boom, but a planned expansion," he told the paper. "The next 20 years belong to Canada – and during this period this district from Sudbury to the Sault is going to expand."[80] Clearly for Hirshhorn and others in the community, Elliot Lake symbolized the post-war optimistic spirit that framed economic development in the 1950s.[81]

Newspaper reports of the time highlight the rapid and sometimes unnerving pace of development but always emphasized that the local settler population was engaged in an act of civilization building, literally carving a new and "useful" town from what was formally "underused" wilderness, in stark contrast to Anishinaabek views of land. One newly arrived woman, whose husband was having difficulty finding their assigned lot, told the newspaper: "They said it was on high ground. It better be on high ground. I don't want to live down below. The contractors said it was high. It better be. But you can't tell about contractors." While the reality of moving to a new townsite may have been unnerving, the newspaper used romantic language to describe the creation of the town. "The square of concrete foundations yawned vacantly in the afternoon sun," read the story in the *Bruce Mines Spectator*, which doubled as the local Elliot Lake paper at the time; "in the distance were the colourful row of trailer homes; the barracks-like parade square of bunkhouses; men swarming over half-completed homes – some roofless, some windowless – against the sky's blueness." Then the story quoted the same woman as saying, "you know, it's going to be wonderful here."[82] Clearly the building of the town was construed as a positive and creative act, making beauty and wonder from what was perceived as an empty and unused space.

While people moved to the area in droves, many new settlers were concerned about the bunkhouses and shacks that were built to accommodate the transient members of the population. For many new arrivals, however, there were few other options. A front-page story in the new Elliot Lake local, the *Standard*, told of the shacks that were "mushrooming overnight" and the health and fire hazards they presented.[83] Twenty to thirty shacks had been constructed outside the townsite as a response to the need for housing. The absence of power and water facilities, as well as the crowded living conditions (two adults and twelve children in one ten-foot square room in one instance), worried the Department of Lands and Forests and the local fire department to the point that they outlawed further construction of such shelters. Community officials were pressed to act due to their proximity to the bush as well as the lack of sanitary measures.[84] The following week it was reported that the Board of Trustees, backed by mining representatives, had passed a new by-law against shack-building and unauthorized trailer parking. Fire and health officials were the first to voice concern over this grassroots response to controlled town planning; then the Board of Trustees chairperson, Joubin, presented his new plan for the "registration of trailers, the assessing of trailers outside authorized sites, and for the policing of mine properties by mine managers."[85] Although the construction of new homes was proving to be a long process, it was clear that the Board of Trustees would not allow housing to go "beyond the limits of control," as Joubin referred to the issue in the meeting.[86] The act of building an ordered and rational town reflected post-war idealistic values and not just growth itself. The former provided evidence of progress while uncontrolled growth seemed to recall an older, unenlightened age.

Local officials thus continuously struggled to maintain control over the development process. The townsite construction problems outlined by Joubin himself at the beginning of 1956 in his letter to Minister

Nickle were still being addressed the following year.[87] By the summer of 1957, 1,050 housing units were scheduled for construction.[88] It is perhaps no coincidence that the announcement came one month after the conflict over ramshackle housing made news. The units would be divided among the three neighbourhoods built in the 1950s, unimaginatively but rationally referred to as Neighbourhoods One, Two, and Three. While some lots had been cleared for individual purchase, Stanrock, Stanleigh, Consolidated Denison (through Con-Ell, its housing subsidiary), and Rio Tinto Mines (through its housing subsidiary, Elliot Lake Building Corporation) held control over many of them in order to address the housing needs of their employees.[89] In this way, growth was planned by government but then became the responsibility of the mining companies themselves.

While the clearing of lots had begun in the spring of 1955,[90] the building plans for Neighbourhood One were not fully registered until January of the following year. Although trailer park sites remained available, it was still some time before miners, construction workers, and their families could occupy these new single-family homes. Housing construction was completed in some areas of town by the spring of 1956, and it was not long before residents commented on the fact that all the houses looked the same. As in many company towns, citizens could only choose from one of three types of home: bungalow, story-and-a-half, and two-story houses with little variation in the floor plans in each category. The uniformity of the houses reduced costs through economies of scale while also reflecting the principles of order and rationality that underlay the town's planning.[91] While company towns tended to offer less variety than independently planned communities, the move toward standardized housing models was common in Canadian corporate suburban communities.[92]

In a new town populated by young miners and their families, it was not long before they identified the need for educational provisions. But schools were only planned once the construction of permanent housing began. At the end of October 1956, construction began on an eight-room elementary school, which was meant to provide some relief to the 350 students studying in the three-room school that had only recently been built. As for the education of adolescents, the town theatre doubled as the high school.[93] A year later, the *Standard* reported that work on the elementary school was being rushed because the three-room school was overwhelmed by the more than 375 students who had to cope with the "stagger system," whereby children attended school in shifts in order to access the limited supply of classroom space and teachers.[94] Nevertheless, demands for schools appeared to be as much a symbol of the community's success as it was understood to be a symptom of the problems of overcrowding and rapid growth.

As with schools, the churches initially made do with a shortage of meeting space through haphazard, temporary arrangements. Parishioners started building Our Lady of Fatima Catholic Church in early 1957 while Father Farrell said mass at the townsite's recreation hall, as well as at Denison and Can-Met Mines.[95] Unitarians were still in the process of building their church thanks to volunteer labour and several work bees.[96] That said, these temporary arrangements did not hamper the growth of church communities on the townsite. By May 1957, Catholic women had formed the Ladies' Auxiliary of Our Lady of Fatima parish and the Anglican Ladies' Guild had started meeting at the same time.[97] The Catholic Auxiliary discussed the need for a tea and the Anglican Guild planned a dance and attended to the matter of arranging a room for the newly arrived rector. Female parishioners were already successfully building their respective church communities while the church buildings themselves were either still under construction or masses were being held in temporary locations owned by the mines.[98]

Local and provincial governments had the responsibility to invest in state-of-the-art infrastructure, which would showcase the town's efficiency and functionality. It was an expensive proposition: it was estimated that roads, sewers, and water would cost $1.4 million. As mining waste was routinely discarded into the local environment, including the water systems, finding a clean, safe supply of drinking water was of the utmost importance. Carter's report on the development of the townsite, mentioned earlier, outlined these concerns and the measures that would need to be taken to address them. "An exhaustive survey is under way [sic] to ensure an adequate supply of water for domestic purposes of the town-site and for mining purposes," he wrote. "Simultaneously a careful study is being made to ensure that tailings dumps of the Mining Companies are so arranged that there will be no contamination of water supply for domestic use."[99] The notion that rapid development, no matter how controlled and planned by governments and private business concerns, may have compromised the safety of residents was glossed over and dismissed as an issue simply related to the growth of the site itself. In some ways, infrastructure – like the schools and churches – was understood to be a victim of the town's success. Nevertheless, rationalized growth was seen as the solution and it was the state's job to ensure that any such shortcomings were rectified. While the safety of the water system in the settler town was of the utmost concern for residents, government, and the companies, we shall see in the following chapters that the same needs of the First

Nations community that had lived in the area since time immemorial were neglected in the process.

Safe drinking water was not the only infrastructural concern that needed to be addressed quickly in order for Elliot Lake to grow on schedule. The provincial government was also concerned about the construction of the main road from the Trans-Canada Highway to the townsite and then on to the mine sites. Local oral histories continue to emphasize the broken-down cars that littered the old road due to the inadequacy of the road surface. In the spring of 1955, the management of Algom Uranium Mines Ltd., in a letter addressed to P.T. Kelly, the minister of mines, outlined the urgency of an adequate road and fore-saw disastrous transportation issues if a fix was not soon forthcoming:

> the fact that the four mines have already announced production plans on a large scale and the possibility that at least two more producers may be added to the list in the near future should substantiate our view that nothing short of a two-lane gravel highway will suffice to meet requirements. Furthermore, if development in this area is to continue without serious delay, the construction of this highway should be undertaken immediately.[100]

The letter not only served as a follow-up report to a meeting that had taken place the previous week, but it also appealed to the minister's business sense: a region so valuable in resources required adequate roads not only for the construction phases of mining operations but also for the establishment of the townsite itself.[101]

The slow development of roads threatened the centralized townsite that both government and mine representatives so desired: "the matter of town-site planning depends entirely on road conditions, as it is planned to accommodate approximately 1,000 men in the new townsite. Present plans are that these men would commute by car and bus from the town-site to their respective places of employment. However, if commuting is not soon practical, the companies will be forced to accommodate their entire working crews at each of the mines."[102] A press release issued by the Ontario government a few months later echoed this sentiment and the desire to create a planned municipality:

> Past experience in Ontario has indicated very clearly that population expansion, such as that which is presently in prospect for the Blind River area [soon to be the Elliot Lake area] into areas which are not organized municipally can, and usually does, lead to the creation of many serious problems of sanitation, education, transportation, protection and

administration. All of these problems, if permitted to develop and expand unimpeded, would seriously detract from the potential economic benefits which would otherwise accrue to the local region and to the province as a whole.[103]

In other words, the province understood its duty to be ensuring that the townsite was planned in an orderly manner and that growth was properly managed to so as to avoid the problems of the past.

Private interests in the area saw the government's main role as being the facilitation of expansion, rather than its management. To them, the economic importance of Elliot Lake was justification enough for timely government expenditures on important infrastructure projects. These sentiments were echoed by Algom Uranium Mines Ltd. President Franc R. Joubin in a letter to P.T. Kelly dated 6 April 1955. He did not mince words about the economic importance of the area to the province, and this formed the basis for his request for a highway. "Five mines to-date have developed proven and semi-proven ore with a gross value of approximately $800,000,000 at current uranium prices. Widely spaced exploratory diamond drilling indicates that this reserve can be tripled."[104] Joubin went on to specify the contracts that were expected and those that were already in place, as well as their potential outputs and employment figures. As for the expected $1.5 million price tag for the highway, he explained that it was "a sum that will probably be returned to the provincial treasury at least three times over prior to 1961."[105] The main road into town was yet another infrastructural challenge for the mines and government committees in charge of developing the area. Joubin, no doubt a fiscally minded man, pointed out in no uncertain terms that the road was imperative to the development of this resource-rich area and that the project would pay for itself within a few years. Elliot Lake was to be an investment rather than an expenditure.

The slow progress made on the only road into town did not deter some visitors who wanted to see Canada's newest nuclear boom town. The 45th Annual Meeting of the Ontario Chamber of Commerce, held in Sudbury in May of 1957, included a bus tour to the Elliot Lake area and a visit to one of the mines.[106] Governor General Vincent Massey's visit to area in May 1957 brought national attention to the city. He visited the Consolidated Denison and Algom Quirke mine sites and was accompanied by representatives from both companies. After meeting school children and attending a reception, he went on a tour of the Noranda Acid Plant at Cutler on SRFN reserve land, underlining the links between the communities through economic development and capitalistic views of progress.[107] The hosts held up Elliot Lake as a model city in urban planning, emphasizing the way in which its economic activity had practical uses for the Canadian nation and the NATO alliance in the context Cold War security.[108]

It was a municipal concept and a private-public partnership which local and provincial officials were eager to promote. A tour organized in August 1957 by Lands and Forest Minister Clare Mapledoram provided an opportunity for several Members of the Legislative Assembly (MLAs) to visit northern Ontario and its newest mining town.[109] After the MLAs toured the townsite, the mill at Algom Quirke Mine, the site at Consolidated Denison, and then stopped for a luncheon at Milliken Mines, members of the local Chamber of Commerce presented a brief that outlined their concerns about development in the area, including roads, schools, housing and trailers, fire service, and jail facilities.[110] The Elliot Lake project was also highlighted in such public venues as the Ontario Exhibit at the 1957 Canadian National Exhibition, where a model of the commercial area was displayed.[111] This was yet another opportunity for the Department of Planning and Development to showcase its newest project and it not only underlined the planned nature of the town, but also the stake the province had in it. Although the exhibit showcased the area as the future of natural resource development in the province, local residents took such opportunities to emphasize the interconnectedness of economic and social successes, which meant finding a way to address the problems of rapid growth and expansion.

Almost as soon as the town was built in the late 1950s, the problem for the public-private partnership project became one of managing a declining population and economic base rather than addressing the problems of unbridled growth. In 1959 it became public knowledge that the United States government would no longer buy uranium after its contract expired in 1962. In response, the mining companies looked to the government to maintain demand through nationalized stockpiling programs. Uranium, which had fuelled the boom, was now a commodity without a market. As a result, just as quickly as the town began, people had to leave in search of employment elsewhere. Some mines closed around Elliot Lake as the federal government decided which companies would get contracts and which ones would not. Again, the relationship between government and the uranium industry set the pace of the town's decline.

The Diefenbaker government was acutely aware of the situation arising at Elliot Lake. Interested parties had lobbied the prime minister, who "wondered what could be done about the matter."[112] In a telephone conversation with Ms. O'Brien, chair of the Elliot Lake Women's Delegation to Ottawa,[113] Diefenbaker reportedly assured her that "votre problème me touche très profondément et j'ai travaillé à le résoudre toute la semaine et la fin de semaine."[114] Despite the prime minister's assurance that the plight of Elliot Lake was at the forefront of his agenda for the week, there was little his government could – or would– do to appease the town's concerns. Gordon Churchill, minister of trade and commerce, reminded him that the United States' decision regarding uranium contracts had not been a surprise. "Elliot Lake had over-expanded," he explained. "Its population of 24,000 was expected to shrink to around 10,000 but the lay-offs would be spread out over a period."[115] Churchill also wondered why the Central Mortgage and Housing Corporation (CMHC) had authorized 25-year mortgages in a single-industry town in the first place.[116] The government worried that the failure of state supported resource towns would cause it a significant degree of embarrassment.[117]

Elliot Lake was one of several resource towns built nationally in the mid-1950s to exploit uranium deposits, and while the main burden in each case was provincial, Ottawa was the common link. Uranium City in Saskatchewan, for example, would also be severely impacted by the end of the American contracts. Unlike in Elliot Lake where mining was a private venture, in Uranium City, the Crown corporation was responsible for mining in the area, and this provided the government with an opportunity to subsidize operations so as to keep the town alive. Uranium City, unlike Elliot Lake (Pearson's riding), was also represented by Conservative MP Stanley Korchinski, a member of the Standing Committee on Mines, Forests, and Resources in 1958.[118] When it came to choosing which mines would get a limited number of continuing federal uranium contracts, Uranium City ultimately became the clear winner.[119]

Elliot Lake stood to lose out as the federal cabinet debated how to deal with the end of American uranium contracts. Whereas Uranium City was supported through new contracts awarded to Eldorado, it was understood that most of the private mines at Elliot Lake would likely close as there were simply not enough contracts to go around.[120] Mr. Churchill reported that:

> after several discussions, the Committee had decided to recommend that the contracts held by Stanleigh and Stanrock Mines be transferred to Rio Algom. While some people in the district had voiced disapproval of the proposal, others had endorsed it. The former was saying 'do not sell Rio Tinto,' while the latter approved the transaction because would mean other mines in the immediate vicinity would remain open longer thus assuring the employment for a larger number of miners.[121]

David James Walker, the minister of public works, elaborated that "under the Rio Algom offer to Stanrock, the former would assume all Stanrock's obligations except the mortgage amounting to $770,000 owing to Central Mortgage and Housing Corporation in respect of a primary industry loan for the construction of 104 houses at Elliot Lake."[122] Housing in Elliot Lake, and specifically the fact that the CMHC had guaranteed mortgages for 24,000 residents, was a concern, but it was not enough to force the government to artificially support a declining market. In concluding months of investigation and deliberation about the situation at Elliot Lake, Diefenbaker's cabinet decided that, in the end, "the government simply could not be responsible for every community which declined because of economic and technological changes."[123] Nevertheless, if anyone from the government were asked for comment they were to remind reporters that the "position of the province as having a major share of the responsibility for this matter should be emphasized ... [and] that the community's case would not be improved by anyone making abusive statements."[124]

The decline of Elliot Lake – and federal support for its mines – remained a political issue after Diefenbaker was defeated by Lester B. Pearson's Liberals in 1963. Pearson's seat was, after all, located in the Algoma East riding, which included Elliot Lake. Suddenly artificial support for the private mines became politically viable.[125] Stockpiling – the accumulation of vast quantities of uranium by the government for resale at a later date when prices improved and new markets opened up – became the preferred solution to the Elliot Lake problem. In effect, it amounted to the nearly wholesale subsidization of the industry and town by the federal government, albeit wrapped in rhetoric that equated a healthy uranium supply with national security. "If [stockpiling] was required to maintain existing mines at their current level of operations until the market strengthened" then, concluded Pearson's cabinet, "so be it."[126] A federal stockpiling scheme was one solution to an absence of an export market, and it is what allowed the remaining mines to operate after the American contract came to an end. It did not solve the problem, but it was one way to mitigate it and thus keep the model public-private partnership alive.[127]

The clandestine strike that characterized the Backdoor Staking Bee in 1953 set in motion a unique sequence of events that resulted in the rapid development in the area that complemented large-scale uranium extraction. The local lore maintains that a "city was born" out of the bush, an image that constructs a dichotomy between humans and the land, when in fact it originated out of a closely planned partnership between the mining companies and the provincial and federal levels of government. Unlike the stereotype of a single-industry town born of a frenzied prospecting spree, this was no haphazard town. Although there were certainly individuals who led the mining companies to success, the development of the town and the industry itself was not left to chance and individualist enterprise. The provincial government, particularly its municipal branch, was involved almost from the very beginning, while the federal government was keenly interested in the development of a resource that would help solidify its new relationship with the superpower neighbour to the south. The mining companies were eager to have the support of these levels of government. The industry collapsed in 1959 with an announcement that the US would no longer rely on Canadian uranium, a decision that would devastate the town.

Elliot Lake was a community that, in many ways, continued the long tradition of the Saguenay mythology. Just as Cartier had been lured beyond the St. Lawrence by tales of the area's richness centuries before, so too had mining prospectors and companies arrived in search of mineral wealth. The town of Elliot Lake symbolized the settler search for economic development in the wild, and it would shape Indigenous-settler relations in the area. But while earlier use of the area's resources had, at some points, been conducted in partnership with local Anishinaabek, the extraction of uranium marked a new era in the region's history. The partnership that allowed mines to be established, to flourish, and then to be saved from decline existed between the various levels of settler governments – but they excluded the First Nations from the decision-making process.

This settler narrative of progress and economic boom and bust silences Anishinaabek voices, on whose homeland these mines were built, while ushering in a new stage in the colonial relationship. The area thirty kilometres north of Lake Huron had long been the traditional trapping, hunting, fishing, and spiritual centre for the people of the Serpent River First Nation. While the Robinson-Huron Treaty signed in 1850 relegated them to a reserve on the North Shore of the lake, community members still fostered their strong ties to traditional land. One hundred years later, prospecting, luck, and a peculiar pact between big uranium business and government had a profound change on the entire ecosystem, having disastrous impacts on the First Nations community that found itself downstream from the self-proclaimed "uranium capital of the world."[128]

Chapter Four

"It took all the trees": The Cutler Acid Plant and Its Toxic Legacy

When we lived right across from the plant, we couldn't even leave the windows open in the summertime because of the fumes.[1]

– Gertrude Lewis

Just as in Elliot Lake, the street names on the Serpent River First Nation also point to the history of the area. Wiigwaas Road refers to the birch trees that are abundant in the region. Walkhouse Bay Road leads to a wharf at the end of the peninsula at the edge of the reserve. Perhaps one of the most telling names in the community is Sulphur Circle, the cul-de-sac that once housed non-Indigenous employees of the Noranda Acid Plant, near the old plant site. The street was on a parcel of land leased by Noranda Mines Ltd. and later Canadian Industries Ltd. (CIL) and is a testament to the relationship that continues to bind the Anishinaabek to the legacy of the uranium industry that boomed thirty kilometres north in Elliot Lake starting in the 1950s.

This chapter discusses that relationship in detail and examines its genesis in the 1950s. The roles of mining companies, Serpent River First Nation leadership, and community members as well as the intrusion of the Department of Indian Affairs are central to this story. Through the paternalistic arm of DIA, the federal government sought to control the affairs of the First Nation while at the same time maintaining a vested interest in the private-public partnership in uranium development at Elliot Lake. This chapter argues that this conflict of interest proved disastrous for the people of the Serpent River First Nation, who were experiencing the contradictory nature of mining as an agent of modernization: while the acid plant provided both leasing revenues and job opportunities, these were as short-lived as they were environmentally disastrous.[2] DIA continued the process of leasing reserve land for resource exploitation – a pattern that began at the turn of the twentieth century when logging companies and the CPR became interested in the area – but this time did so within the Cold War context. Community members, on the other hand, negotiated their roles as workers and stewards as best they could.

As uranium replaced timber as the top local resource in the 1950s, Noranda Mines Ltd., a major player in the resource extraction business, was eager to gain access to the profits from this booming industry.[3] The Serpent River First Nation's proximity to key transportation infrastructure (the CPR, Trans-Canada Highway, and the North Shore of Lake Huron) and the Serpent River watershed – not to mention its colonial relationship with DIA – offered this chance.[4] Noranda did not seek to operate mines in the Elliot Lake area, but instead looked for land where it could build a sulphuric acid plant.[5] Sulphuric acid was essential to the leaching process whereby the local low-grade uranium was extracted from the rock, and thus an acid plant capable of producing the chemical locally would benefit from a lucrative secondary industry.[6] At the same time, however, its production was dangerous: sulphuric acid is a highly corrosive substance and inhaling its fumes can lead to irritation and damage to the mucous membranes of the lungs, throat, and nose. The Centers for Disease Control and Prevention lists the following symptoms of exposure: "irritation of eyes, skin, nose, throat; pulmonary edema, bronchitis, emphysema; conjunctivitis; stomatitis; dental erosion; eye, skin burns; dermatitis."[7] The acid itself was to be produced by burning elemental sulphur in a roaster.[8] Despite the known risks of sulphuric acid exposure, SRFN members were not told about the severity and extent of possible environmental damage arising from this process.

Noranda leased the land from the reserve, and DIA employed similar mechanisms that had been used in the context of lumber in the decades before, all in the name of Cold War economic development, but at the expense of the local Anishinaabek. DIA had a history of attempting to make First Nations communities pay for their own "upkeep," in effect forcing them to contribute to the colonial relationship that had already been imposed upon them. Although community members initially welcomed the prospect of employment, especially when they saw the prosperity of the other boom towns springing up in the area, they could not have foreseen the extent of the damage it would bring, and they were also denied an active voice in controlling the process. While community members had wanted their own legal representation in negotiations with the company, DIA denied this request in order to further larger federal commitments to the settler community in Elliot

Lake as well as Canada's allies. The establishment of the acid plant would leave a lasting legacy of toxicity in the community that continues to be felt today.

The summer of 1955 brought news of a new acid plant that was planned for the Blind River area. The local production of sulphuric acid to extract uranium was essential to building the industrial basis for the planned town of Elliot Lake, and the local newspapers focused solely on the economic and industrial benefits of such a plant. "To produce the large daily tonnages of sulphuric acid required in the chemical leaching process to be used on the Blind River [Elliot Lake] uranium ores, Noranda Mines will construct a multimillion dollar acid plant in the area," reported the *Leader-Spectator* in 1955. "The all-important raw material will be pyrites from its own Rouyn holdings. A unique Noranda-developed process will turn-out daily: some 350 tons of high grade iron sinter; around 70 tons of elemental sulphur; an estimated 500 tons of sulphuric acid."[9] The plant, which was to be built and run by Noranda Mines Ltd., provided an important means for that mining company to be involved in the booming uranium industry without actually running a mine.[10] The newspapers also lauded it as another example of industrial consolidation and efficiency that would contribute to the area's positive economic and social development: the plant would make use of Noranda's own pyrite production while providing an important secondary industry to the North Shore area.

The papers extolled the virtues of secondary industrialization, equating it with the modernization and progression of an "empty" wilderness area, as the plant would contribute to the viability of other resource extraction industries in the region.[11] The plant could also provide refined iron to American or Canadian steel mills, if constructed in an area suitable for a deep-water wharf, while its main output, sulphur, might also be used in processing at pulp and paper mills.[12] The newspaper article was meant to laud the area's recent coverage in the national paper, the *Financial Post*, and it was hence hopeful and celebratory in tone, particularly in the way the development of the region was tied to achieving national and international economic and strategic security goals. Concerns that the plant would not be open in time to effectively service the new mines were offset by faith in technological ingenuity and more temporary expediencies: "If not, Noranda is confident it can operate a temporary process producing only acid, and switch to the bigger and more economically desirable process when the special equipment is available."[13] As it happened, the plant was indeed built in two phases, the first of which was undertaken by the Cleveland-based Arthur G. McKee Company in 1956, after which initial operations began, and the second by the Leonard Construction Company, which allowed full production to start in 1957.[14]

The decision to construct the acid plant on the Serpent River reserve was made for several reasons. In his book, *Noranda*, Leslie Roberts describes the company's desire to choose a location that was close to existing transportation and nearby locations for housing employees.[15] Government economic development policy also stipulated that a new townsite should not be constructed if at all avoidable, and thus an existing local community would have to house the plant.[16] But the North Shore was also a tourist and recreational sportfishing destination and heavy, dirty industry might actually be opposed in some settler communities that relied on vacation lodges for employment.

That said, there were plenty of settler communities along the North Shore that would have met those criteria, including several which already had operating mine sites.[17] But the Cutler site provided a perfect opportunity to meet the company's needs. The site that once housed an old abandoned pulp and paper mill, as described in chapter two, would provide the physical space needed for the plant, which could be situated between the CPR branch line from Sault Ste. Marie to Sudbury and the main channel along the North Shore.[18] The bay at Cutler was also deep enough to support a wharf to facilitate Great Lakes shipping if the plant proved viable.[19] At the same time, the Cutler site would situate the plant near the existing settler community at the town of Spanish, Ontario, some ten kilometres east of the reserve. As Robert Robson argues, this made the Cutler site ideal as Spanish could still become "the home community for its anticipated workforce of from 100 to 150 men."[20]

This "ideal site" was located on the Serpent River Indian Reserve (as it was then called) and was thus on land controlled by the Department of Indian Affairs which could be influenced by federal interests in promoting development at Elliot Lake as well as the strategic considerations to find uranium. The Department was also already anxious to promote industrial employment for the local Indigenous population, which it saw as clinging to a backward way of life.[21] "Trapping is still a very important factor in the Indian economy and will be for many years yet," lamented a 1959 departmental report on the economic development of Indigenous peoples in northern Ontario. "This type of work, arduous though it may be, is accepted by those Indians who have not been in close touch with industrial development. But where they have been so exposed more and more are realizing the benefit of steadier work and a regular income."[22] It is clear that DIA saw steady wage work as the way to encourage the community to "progress."

The building of the acid plant at Cutler was thus seen as an important step in the colonization of local Anishinaabek. The Department of Indian Affairs attributed the community's dismal economic situation to their tendency to cling to such "outmoded" economic means as trapping and subsistence hunting and fishing and the Department saw industrialization as a way to move reserves and their occupants into the twentieth century. "The general economy of the Indian population in the northern Ontario region improved during the past year," read the 1957 departmental report on the situation of Indigenous peoples in northern Ontario. "Though hunting, trapping, fishing and lumbering are still basic to their economic welfare, many Indians were employed in construction work on such projects as the Mid-Canada radar line and electric power and industrial projects. Indians were also employed in mining at Kirkland Lake, Red Lake and other areas."[23] Moreover, the Department saw employment at the acid plant as a way to make reserve residents less dependent on government funds. "With the excellent opportunities for employment now available on the reserve, relief should be at a minimum," reported the local Indian agent to his district supervisor.[24]

Full-scale participation in the wage economy and resource extraction in the area was seen as a positive development as it would "advance the situation of the Indian." This sentiment dominated the interactions of DIA with Indigenous peoples at the time, as modernization and integration were important general tenants of Indian Policy.[25] In this case, government policy reflected popular opinions, and locally, the press lauded the idea of modernization through industrialization. "In Cutler, Noranda Mines provides a regular source of employment here and the Serpent River Reserve is *luckier than others*," read an article in the Elliot Lake *Standard*. "Previously the Indians living there depended upon fishing, trapping, and the lumber industry.[26] In days gone by local Indians functioned largely as family units, hunting and moving from place to place, practicing conservation as they went."[27] The equation of industrialization with economic progression and the success of the colonial relationship is obviously ethnocentric. But official and popular ethnocentrism, and the Whiggish acceptance of Western capitalist concepts of labour and wages that it entailed, actually justified the paternalistic need to control and encourage Anishinaabek economic life.[28]

It was a view of progress shared by the local settler population. "The Indian Affairs Dept., and the Dept. of Education, Community Programs Branch have all played an invaluable part together with the spiritual work of the missionaries, in helping adjust the past with the present," read another article in the *Standard*. "Unfortunately however the Indian still does not trust the non-Indian."[29] The notion that the Anishinaabek were "lucky" to have the interference of DIA and missionaries, and as an extension of those colonial relationships, the opportunity to work in the acid plant (or indeed, have it located prominently on the reserve) privileges the notion of Western capitalistic ideas of "progress" and "development."[30] In fact, the challenging situation faced by the community members of the Serpent River First Nation in the late 1950s was actually the result of a rapidly changing way of life and colonial processes – not any inherent backwardness or inability to adapt. SRFN had to adapt once economics, geography, and colonial policy goals converged. The reserve's existence as a racially segregated space legislated and overseen by the federal government, but located close to a white settler community, was thus a determining factor in the establishment of the plant.[31]

In early 1955, Noranda approached the community and DIA about the possibility of establishing an acid plant on the reserve. DIA officials were thrilled with the prospect as they had been encouraging economic development and secure employment in the community since the nineteenth century. At this point, SRFN was not a "self-sustaining" reserve economically and roads, houses, and facilities had all fallen into disrepair.[32] When Noranda offered to pay $7,162.50 to lease land for the acid plant, J.T. O'Neill, the Superintendent for the Sault Ste. Marie Agency, reported to Ottawa that the reserve's problems would be solved. "With the industrial development in that area, I expect a general increase in all matter pertaining to this Band."[33] Indeed, O'Neill used the expected prosperity to justify the First Nation's budget, which included repairs to roads and buildings, as well as recreation equipment.

The methods through which the acid plant came to be located on the Serpent River First Nation reveal the continuation of the colonial relationship between the federal government (particularly DIA) and the reserve. It also emphasizes the complexity of the colonial experience as many in the community welcomed the jobs that the plant seemed to offer as a means to escape the poverty imposed by the reserve system.[34] Even so, the leadership and some members of the community attempted to ask questions so as fulfil their traditional relationship with land and water.[35] DIA had a history of using land and resource transactions for the upkeep of the community.[36] This often meant that their land and or resources were sold or leased, when possible, for the upkeep of the community in order to curtail government relief obligations, and as was discussed in chapter two, SRFN Councils had taken decisions to lease land very seriously. The only major surrenders to that point had been to the CPR and then to the Spanish River Lumber Company.

The community had, for the previous two decades, shown a growing interest in not only retaining its lands but reacquiring lost lands. Land had become politicized on the reserve and the community's assertion of land rights had even contributed to an attempt to remove a sitting Chief from office.[37]

But by 1955, there was a new resource boom and community leadership had shown an interest in surrendering land and the mineral rights on a portion of the reserve to Noranda.[38] A copy of the Band Council Resolution (BCR) granting approval was found in the Indian Lands Registry, but it bears only two signatures. Dated 22 June 1955, it reads that the Council resolved:

> That the offer of Noranda Mines Ltd to lease not more than 125 acres of our reserve land for a period of 99 years, at an annual rental of $25 per acre be accepted.
>
> First payment, due on signing of the lease will be for two years rent. This being payment of the first and last years charges.
>
> That the agreement will contain the usual clause giving Indians preference in employment, further that when any Indian employee falls down on the job that the Chief and Council be notified.[39]

The BCR indicates that the community leadership was primarily interested in economic development opportunities provided by the uranium industry, through both leasing and employment prospects.

But not everyone in the community agreed that industry and jobs should be accepted so easily. Community members' oral history suggests that DIA – anxious to bring industry to the reserve – controlled the negotiations and pushed through the lease of the land.[40] Several public meetings were held, which many Elders remember attending. Gertrude Lewis recalled the ways in which DIA officials at those meetings downplayed the fears of community members. "The community was invited to all these meetings," she says. "[Although] most of the people thought it was a good thing ... some of our young people would want to ask questions and the Department of Indian Affairs people would tell them ... We'd try to ask for a lawyer to look into it. And they said we didn't need a lawyer because the band didn't need a lawyer 'cause they had all the lawyers they needed in Ottawa – Indian Affairs."[41] Indeed a report entitled "Background Information: Highlights of the History of the Cutler Acid Site," commissioned in the mid-1980s by SRFN's leadership, supports these community members' recollections. "The Band was concerned about the lease with Noranda for the construction of the sulphuric acid making factories and requested the presence of their own lawyer," it reads. "The Department of Indian Affairs officials told the Band that the government lawyers would protect the Band's interests."[42]

The complexity of this land transaction is amplified when one understands that there were also legal reasons why the surrender was accepted when the community had only repurchased the land the decade before. The minutes from a meeting of the Privy Council in February 1956 refer to the land transactions from the early part of the century, stating, crucially, that "these lands formerly were part of Serpent River Indian Reserve Number Seven but were surrendered and sold then later repurchased *but never again added to the Reserve under the provisions of the Indian Act.*"[43] While Chief and Council had bought the land back in 1944, several documents from the 1950s indicate that the transaction had not been completed in compliance with the Indian Act. It is unclear why this was so: the Order in Council PC 53/5770 is dated 26 July 1944 and was stamped by the Department of Mines and Resources (responsible for Indian Affairs at the time) as received on 31 July and registered on 3 August of that year.[44] Nevertheless, this was one of the reasons given for the Privy Council's approval. Since Noranda had "applied for the lease of the said lands for the site of a sulphuric acid manufacturing plant and related purposes for a term of 99 years," continued the clerk, the committee, on recommendation of the minister of citizenship and immigration (which held the Indian Affairs portfolio), approved the application.[45]

The BCR, when read without the context provided by oral history, seems straightforward. Community history suggests that Chief and Council were told that the land on which the plant was being built could be leased to Noranda Mines Ltd. without band approval because it had been previously leased to the Spanish River Lumber Company: according to former Chief Earl Commanda, "We had a pulp/timber mill here in the community back at the turn of the century. Land was leased to that lumber company. It was called the Cutler Salvage Lumber Company.[46] Indian Affairs took advantage of that surrendered land – the leased land, the surrendered land – to negotiate with Noranda Mines to build a sulphuric acid plant right in the middle of our community in the early 1950s to service the uranium mines."[47] Chief Commanda's description of the way in which reserve land was passed from one company to another illustrates the long history of colonial attempts to encourage reserve members to participate in the local industry, be it timber or uranium.

Former Chief and Band Manager Peter Johnston pointed out that this was part of a larger continuing process of reusing land set aside for one purpose earlier in the reserve's history in order to fulfill another but different role at a later point in time. It also served to minimize the need for discussion or debate, allowing DIA officials to continue an interventionist role in reserve life. Because of this, "a referendum wasn't necessary, which would have been the case in any other situation," Johnston says.

> If, for instance, [a company] came in and wanted to set up their operation, they had to go through the federal government again, in that situation and the federal government had to have a referendum. The majority of the electors of the band had to approve it. In the case of Noranda, though, the land had already been approved. This land had been given up for sale and leased to ... Cutler Savidge and Sawmill way back in the 1800s. And when the sawmill ceased operations, the land should have returned back to the federal government, but it never did. It had [to be] returned back to the band as band property, but it never did. And so what somebody realized, and the negotiations went on with Noranda was that they didn't require a referendum because the land had already been given up.[48]

As Johnston suggests, control over the leased land should have been returned back to the reserve after the company left and the community bought it back, but this never happened.

Ultimately, the lease was signed between the Crown and Noranda on 10 April 1956. Again, the lease made mention of the fact that the band's repurchase of lost land in 1944 was "never again added to the Reserve under the provisions of the Indian Act." The lease of 95.5 acres, "more or less," was for 99 years, to last from 1 July 1955 to 30 June 2054.[49] Soon after, the plant was built on the reserve to support its industrialization (furthering departmental goals), supposedly for the benefit of its inhabitants. This particular lease was a continuation of the pattern of repurposing reserve land that was labelled as under-used or "wasteful" for capitalistic pursuits. Whether through the 1884 and 1894 changes that allowed the Superintendent-General of Indian Affairs to "lease undeveloped reserve lands without surrender or band consent" or a 1911 Indian Act amendment to expropriate reserve lands for public purposes, DIA had a history of using its power to entrench setter-colonial views of productive land use, often to the detriment of First Nations reserve boundaries.[50] In the case of SRFN and its rapid changes, DIA officials used their ultimate authority over the land and desire for economic development and presented the plant as an easy and quick fix that would solve most of the reserve's problems. Throughout, the process was overseen and controlled by DIA and shaped by the economic legacy of colonialism, which served to minimize debate and opportunities for dissent.

The complexity of the colonial relationship – and the ways in which community members had to choose between preserving traditional worldviews or survival – is apparent in their recollections. The Elders who shared their knowledge with me recalled the reasons why many in the community welcomed the plant and they suggested that the promise of economic development was one of the primary factors that led many to support the lease. For instance, Peter Johnston recalled that community members wanted to ensure that reserve members were given the opportunity to work at the plant and be given priority in hiring.[51] DIA agreed to this as it was one of the reasons its representatives were so enthusiastic about the scheme, and it was outlined in the lease that the company "give preference to members of the Serpent River Band of Indians ... and that if an employee from the Band is not efficient on the job he will be warned and the Chief and/or Council of the Band so notified."[52] Employment began during the construction phase in 1955 and the plant was completed in 1956.[53]

It was not long after the plant began operating that community leaders realized that not all problems were solved. William Meawasige, who had overseen the reacquisition of band lands a decade before, was quickly re-elected as Chief. One of his main initiatives after his re-election was to try and rescind the band's surrender of its mineral rights and to begin pressing for compensation to personal property that was damaged by the fumes from the plant.[54] When the plant's lease was renegotiated in 1964, Chief and Council hired their own lawyer and fought off the sale of the plant to protect its interests.[55]

In only a few short years, there would be no talk of renegotiations or sales. As those who had been skeptical of the plant had feared, any economic prosperity was fleeting and left a legacy of environmental destruction that hurt rather than improved the long-term prospects of the reserve.[56] "Of course we thought it would be a good thing for our area because there was no work in this area," recalled Gertrude Lewis. "And we thought there'd be employment and our living would be better. We weren't thinking of the destruction of our wildlife and trees and gardens that followed from the plant. We didn't know about that ... they didn't tell us how it would affect anything."[57] For Lewis, employment was clearly only one part of a larger picture that included responsibility for protecting the environment. Terry Jacobs had similar reflections about the process of consultation and why band members agreed to the plant's establishment. "No, we didn't know what the consequences would have been, you know?" he said. "I suppose we would have known if maybe we had one of our members of the community or council to go out and see … – like, Noranda, it was in operation then – what damage there had been around that area. Maybe we wouldn't have accepted it."[58]

But at the same time, some families were still working in traditional activities like hunting, fishing, and trapping.[59] The plant was thus built at a point in time where many people were still living off the land and participating in moditional economies;[60] the community was in a state of transition. DIA was equally interested in providing jobs to minimize its expenses on the reserve while also keeping community members away from their traditional pursuits.[61] In other words, employment at the plant was a way to further the goal of assimilation. Community members were interested in jobs, but this came as a result of economic necessity and poverty.[62] They were not opposed to the prospect of steady employment, and indeed, many of them welcomed it in the face of prosperity arising elsewhere in nearby settler boom towns. The concept of survival was paramount, and not in and of itself inconsistent with IK. For members of the community, the ability to provide for their families was seen as a continuation of traditional responsibilities, even when the reality of the resource economy meant they could be seen as contradictory.

Industrial development threatened the dominance of a traditional worldview in which economics, community, and place were inseparable. Traditionally, members of SRFN had relied on the land in a relationship founded on reciprocity and respect. Whereas Western conceptions of land and environment evaluate usefulness in purely economic terms, Indigenous peoples traditionally evaluate the environment through a more holistic worldview, as described in chapter two. With an Anishinaabe worldview, the acid plant's effects on the broader ecology of the Serpent River system and the living beings that depended on it – including humans – could not be separated from its economic potential. Indigenous knowledge defined the relationship between community members and their environment at a time when many were still living off the land at least part of the time. It was precisely this type of worldview that DIA officials hoped to destroy in the process of assimilation. The separation of economics from environment and community were essential precursors to an acceptance of Western capitalism. The uncritical acceptance of the need to build the acid plant by DIA thus underlined the differences between Western and Indigenous conceptions of "useful" land and systems of knowledge. From the perspective of DIA officials, resources were a purely economic matter rather than a single aspect of a more holistic worldview.

It would be anachronistic to suggest that environmental concerns would have been on DIA's radar in the 1950s. Settler communities such as nearby Sudbury, Ontario, welcomed industrialization because to those living in the area, the economic wealth generated by mining and refining processes was paramount. The environmental devastation, which was the by-product of that development, was either ignored or downplayed until the benefits of development were outweighed by its negative side-effects. In some communities the balance between the two quickly tipped; in others it never has. But it would be equally anachronistic to suggest that First Nations in the area did not see what many settlers refer to as the "environment" as a key consideration. It was a very real concern for the members of the community who attempted to speak out about the acid plant while attempting to address their traditional relationships with the land by trying to promote discussion and debate about the plant. Jobs were certainly a factor but unlike in settler communities, they were not the only consideration, and this is a key point. Because of the nature of the colonial relationship, however, there was no such opportunity for questions. From the perspective of the First Nation, concern for environmental damage to the land would have been an important consideration but was not consistent with settler resource development elsewhere in the region.[63]

But the jobs that followed were both fleeting and dangerous. While the influx of steady employment was beneficial to some community members in the short-term, many found that working in a sulphur plant had dire health consequences.[64] In the case of Lawrence Lewis, Gertrude's husband, this meant that the purchase of new uniforms and equipment was often necessary due to damage incurred by the hazardous work environment:

And then [his] clothes were always burned. Almost every week he had to buy new clothes for work 'cause they had little holes in them, burned. I guess it depended on where you were working in the plant, too you know, if you were working right where the fumes were and everything … And then he just worked on labour work and that was, that was dirty. Working right in, you know, where all that dirt was and everything. And he got burned on his face with some of the acid. I don't know how that happened. He still has a scar there today on his face. You can see it if you look at him. A little mark there.[65]

The plant provided jobs, but it was dangerous work. Terry Jacobs described some of the hazards that he encountered. "There were times you couldn't wear the gas masks in there," he said in an earlier interview. "The diaphragms would freeze up and you'd choke your-self. You didn't get anything else. About 175 people worked there."[66]

For some, this led to breathing problems, which the workers attrib-uted to the dangerous fumes they often inhaled:

> The guys would be working in there like I say without respirators ... I'm sure everybody must have inhaled a lot of that – like you say – sulphur gas. Sulphur gas itself, it was hard to breathe. And I worked in the roaster plant and the number one, number two acid plant and they had two 500 horsepower motors and they sucked all the gas from our plant but when we got a power failure, all that reversed and we got it back into the roaster plant, and we inhaled that ... I was working on the floors and I had to go check everything else, how everything was running. Put some covers back on and if you got stuck in that gas, there's nothing to breathe. I remember about two o'clock in the morning one time I had to come down a four-inch pipe, about 80 feet down the side just to get into the [control room] – 'cause all the gas was gone up. I went in, I couldn't breathe anything. I couldn't breathe. So I shimmied down the pipe just to get back into the control room, and I took my chances, but if I'd stayed there, I don't know, I could have been suffocated by the gas. When you hear that, it just dries your throat right up.[67]

While community members were benefitting in some ways from their new jobs and were able to purchase things that many could not until that point, it came at a potentially high cost.[68]

Employment in the uranium industry cost at least one man his life.[69] Wilfred Commanda, a non-smoker, submitted his workplace compen-sation claim while dying of lung cancer, to which he succumbed in 1992. A decade later, after a fifteen-minute recess, the Workplace Safety and Insurance Appeals Tribunal found that his lung cancer was in fact due to his employment at the acid plant and at the mines in Elliot Lake and provided a settlement to his widow, Valerie.[70] Frank Lewis, in his recollection of being a young man in the community, remembered wor-rying health impacts on workers who worked inside the plant: "When I worked at the plant the guys that I worked with now they're all gone. Every one of them ... but the boys I'm talking about, they all worked inside the plant. And I used to see them coming out at five o'clock, four o'clock. Gagging away, you know. Coughing, coughing. And I don't know maybe that's the cause of it, I don't know."[71] The lack of safety equipment and health and safety precautions, in conjunction with the dangerous work being carried out, quickly undermined any financial benefits that came with employment.[72]

The introduction of the plant had an impact on the reserve, both positive and negative, and change was rapid: "A lot of big changes, eh? It felt like a big change," recalled Betty Jacobs.[73] Community knowledge holders indicated that these changes and their increased purchasing power were beneficial: "It was nice to see people starting to buy cars, you know ... after a few years they started buying the comforts of life you might say. TVs and all that you know."[74] Arnelda Jacobs remembered the plant changed her life, too: "our men were working there and then my husband worked for a construction company and we got paid every week. So I could go to town to do the shopping, the grocery shopping and it changed our way of life so ... we were able to buy food."[75] The plant itself brought profound social and economic changes to the community. All remember that this new material wealth came at a high cost, but it must also be acknowledged that many community members desired better paying jobs. This is why some supported the acid plant in the first place. Yet the desire for a better life, at least in material and economic terms, was in direct competition with traditional desires and obligations to the community's lands. In fact, the uranium industry and the plant compromised the very ability of the community to balance those two competing demands through the destruction of the land.

The river pollution on one end of the reserve, which severely compromised the community's fish and game resources, was compounded by the pollution in Aird Bay as a result of the acid plant operating on the other side, seriously curtailed the community's ability to continue its traditional practice of subsistence fishing. Elders recalled that the effect of the pollution was to make the fish in the bay soft, and therefore not suitable for consumption.[76] When the fish were eaten, in some cases, the pollution could be tasted. "We got a nice bass," recalled Terry Jacobs. "One of those nice ones. In the evening, eh? I thought when we go home we're going to cook that right away. And we tried, I tried it but, it tasted like it was rotten."[77] According to Peter Johnston, the fish population of the bay area also decreased. "Well, I think that what happened is that it used to be common to fish close by," he said, "and then as the effects of the effluent from the plant over the years got worse and it accumulated in the lake, the fish just couldn't take it anymore and the ones that didn't die just didn't come in. They weren't there anymore. They found other places that were more habitable to live in. And so you didn't have the fish in the lake anymore that you used to have."[78] Fishing was a traditional economic and subsistence activity that connected the residents of the Serpent River Reserve to cultural and ecological traditions of stewardship and reliance on the land. The pollution and effects of the acid plant not only sickened the residents of the area but also threatened to undermine and destroy important cultural traditions.[79]

Even after the acid plant shut down, many people in the community saw it as having caused significant and ongoing environmental degradation in the area. Several research groups such as Rosalie Bertell's International Institute of Concern for Public Health and the Institute for Environmental Studies at the University of Toronto have studied the effects that air and water pollution had on the community.[80] From the very beginning, the acid plant had a noticeable and detrimental effect on the environment and landscape. The damage to trees and vegetation in the area, particularly near the plant, was extensive and one of its earliest and most obvious effects. As Arnelda Jacobs recalled, "it took all the trees, the northern wind used to blow south and it used to affect the trees ... There were no trees up there on the side of the hill."[81] Deforestation represented the physical scarring of the landscape, which members of the Serpent River First Nation had traditionally held in trust.

As early as 1959, the SRFN community leadership expressed concern about the effect the plant was having on the land.[82] Noranda recognized such losses only in economic terms and, as per an agreement signed in 1959, the company paid annual compensation for lost timber potential. Thus, the damage to community land was seen in terms of economic loss rather than from a holistic perspective. Eventually, in 1963, a reforestation project was undertaken by Noranda Mines Ltd., DIA, and the reserve, which was intended to end Noranda's responsibility to the band for its loss of wood and timber, rather than restore an environmental wrong.[83] From the beginning this scheme was compromised by the very fumes that had killed trees in the first place, as G.S. Lapp, regional supervisor of Indian Agencies, wrote: "Those trees that were planted in the bush survived the summer. The trees that were planted in the open, northeast of the acid plant ... showed extensive damage."[84] It was essential from the company's point of view to finish the project as quickly as possible as, according to J.O. Hinds, the Assistant Secretary at Noranda, they hoped that "adequate reforestation has been done so that we can discontinue the compensation that we have been paying for each year to the band."[85] While many of the buildings had been simply abandoned on the site, trees were the one aspect of the reserve landscape that was to be returned to its original state upon penalty of compensation to the community – it was the only thing deemed to be of economic and thus measurable value. This is not surprising as the reforestation project itself was defined by the relationship between DIA and Noranda rather than the company and the community. Letters between Noranda and DIA again describe the reforestation project in purely financial and compensatory terms. On the few occasions in which band leadership was included in the correspondence (usually only to administer payments to the community members who worked as labourers for the project), that correspondence was copied through DIA. In this sense, then, compensation was construed in purely financial terms in the context of the public-private partnership and often excluded community members.[86]

In a memo from Lapp to the Superintendent of the Sault Ste. Marie Agency, there were to be no more payments due after May 1964 "or when reforestation was carried out." It would also appear that DIA waited until March 1965 to ensure the payments for the preceding years were paid. Furthermore, despite the fact that Lapp stated, "it will be August 1965 before the full results of the reforestation can be determined," he went on to definitively state that, in any case, the 1964 payments would be the last.[87]

DIA and Noranda discovered that the replacement of trees was easier said than done. An October 1964 inspection of the reforestation efforts reported that:

1. Ninety percent of plantation trees showed fume damage, but 50% had 1964 growth.
2. There was no appreciable damage to the residual forest as the most susceptible tree white pine had previously been salvaged. Many small white pine, less than 8" d.b.h. [diameter at breast height] were dead, but these were either too small for the 1961 cut, or were dead and contained too large a cull factor.
3. Some of the hardwood species indicated delayed budding in May 1964 which might be caused by 1963 fume damage.
4. The 150 tree seedlings planted in three places away from the plantation and under an overstory of hardwood or brush were quite healthy.

On May 14, 1964, Mr. Dunfield and Mr. A. Meawasige walked over the fume damaged area and determined where the 40,000 trees were to be planted. The trees arrived at noon on May 14.[88]

As this report suggests, the fumes from the plant compromised most of the trees that had been replanted, but some began to recover after the plant's closure in 1964. The repeated visits and tree inspections speak to the concern about the reforestation project as a whole, but, more importantly, they demonstrate that the company and DIA were well aware of the damage caused by the plant's operation. Even using their own Western economic standards to measure damage to the community, it was evident that the plant was destroying the long-term ability of the community to support itself (despite DIA's aim to make them self-sufficient) and it would prove costly and time-consuming to reclaim. The scope of the efforts needed to reforest the area speaks to the degree of environmental damage: the same report concluded that about 10,000 trees would have to "be planted in the gullies on the side hill opposite the acid plant, 10,000 in the former plantation and 20,000 scattered throughout the bush."[89] But hopes of success remained marginal. "Unfortunately, Lands and Forests have said they do not wish to assist in this project as they are afraid of the poor publicity if the trees fail to survive," it read.[90] Thanks to the extent of the pollution, forestry would never again (or at least for a long while) be an important source of wealth for the community, thus making reforestation a SRFN problem. "Reforestation could be a bigger project on this reserve if we had assistance in investigating planting sites," concluded the DIA report. "It could be a Centennial project for the Band, and partly seen from Highway 17."[91]

It is telling that at Serpent River, DIA officials ultimately returned to the theme of protecting the local tourism industry even in discussions about reforestation. Many in the region, especially those with vested interests in the tourism industry, found the now abandoned acid plant site to be an eyesore, untimely and detrimental to the public image of northern Ontario as a haven for outdoor enthusiasts.[92] If new trees would hide the damage to the community, it would remove a potential obstacle to wilderness tourism and recreational land use in the area.[93] DIA's suggestion that the community build a centennial forest was also in keeping with various other projects that were funded in the mid-1960s by all levels of government to celebrate the country's hundredth anniversary.[94]

But it was not only the trees in the area that had been devastated by fume damage from the plant. At least one family launched a claim against Noranda Mines Ltd. for fume damage to their dwelling.[95] The investigator submitted the following to the company upon visiting the house:

> The rust from the nail heads was showing through the paint as claimed. The roof whuch [sic] is of rolled roofing is leaking because the mastic used to seal the joints has died and allowed the laps to separate. The normal life of this type of roofing is about five years and the rate of deterioration is considered to be normal and not due to fume. The nail heads in this type of roof application are exposed and in this case show some rusting but not to the extent that it is causing the roof to leak.[96]

Despite the findings of the investigator – that there was indeed damage but that it was not due to the acid plant fumes – the plant manager of the Sulphuric Acid Division at Noranda Mines Ltd. nevertheless agreed that it was "possible that the rusting of exposed nail heads in this building was accelerated when some fume was discharging from the acid plant stacks prior to March 1960 and Noranda Mines is prepared to allow [X] the sum of five hundred (500) dollars to pay for repairing this damage."[97] In other words, although the company did not agree that there were grounds for the community member's complaint, they were still willing to pay a not insubstantial sum to address the claim.[98]

There was some discussion as to the necessary level of DIA involvement in the case. In a letter to the superintendent of the Sault Ste. Marie Agency, Hinds described the settlement: "we have drawn a general release for the signature of [X] however, before approaching him, Mr. Wearing felt that we should contact your office to make sure that the Department of Indian Affairs is fully advised of the situation and if we require the consent of any other parties, perhaps you would be good enough to advise us."[99] In response, the new superintendent of the Sault Ste. Marie Agency, A.R. Aquin, described DIA's involvement in the matter as being "arm's-length": the company was to negotiate directly with the complainant, but that once the agreement was signed, they were to send a copy to Aquin "in order to protect this office against any future discussions."[100] DIA, although responsible for bringing the acid plant to the reserve in the first place, was not interested in involving itself in securing compensation for damage done by the plant to the reserve. It also accepted a settlement which came with the proviso that the company would be forever released from responsibility for further damage, despite the fact that the plant was still running in June 1961 when compensation was offered to family X. "It was fully explained to them at the time of signing that they could have no further claim against the company for smoke, fume, or acid damage as a result of our plant's operation," Hinds told Aquin. "As far as they are concerned, the matter is settled once and for all time."[101]

But damage to the homes and property of reserve residents was common, as the oral histories of Serpent River Elders confirm. According to Valerie Commanda, "the roofs never used to last that long … and the cars, too, eh, they used to rust. They only lasted a couple years."[102] The Lewis family was forced to move from their home, which was in an area directly across the highway from the acid plant, because of the damage: "our roof was burned … from the plant. The roof in our house. And I believe that's why [DIA] asked us to move from there. We had to move up this way."[103] This damage not only resulted in the relocation of a family, but also the community post office, which Gertrude Lewis ran from her home until the 1990s. It appears that the destructive influence of the plant was pervasive on the reserve. More than one resident recalled the clear signs that all was not right with plant's emissions. Terry shared "that dust was so fine it blew across the community when you got an east wind. And anybody who had nice white clothes or sheets on the line – it would all turn rusty when they brought them in. Of course, this calcine was 65% iron in it."[104] Gertrude Lewis recalled the holes in her clothes: "even when we hung out our clothes out on the clothesline – now this is being laughed about, but it really happened – when I'd hang my clothes out on the line they'd have little weeny, tiny holes in them."[105] Damage to clothing does not appear on any of the records for claims, but it was widespread enough to have become a dark joke on the reserve among the Elders, particularly among the women who were usually the ones doing the laundry.[106] It is thus difficult to determine how frequently individual families launched claims against the company.

Property damage was superseded in the minds of residents by the health effects the acid plant had on reserve members. People who lived in close proximity to the plant found themselves inhaling the fumes that were killing trees, rusting cars, setting fire to roofs, and putting holes in clothing on a daily basis. "Well, the sulphur fumes were really bad," recalled Lewis, "because when we lived right across from the plant, we couldn't even leave the windows open in the summertime because [of] the fumes."[107] Serpent River First Nation residents also complained about the impact that the poisoned water had on their children. Terry Jacobs recalled the effects that swimming in Aird Bay had on his child and others in the community: "all the leaching from the acid plant ... went into the bay, and it contaminated all of the shorelines ... our daughter would go swimming and she'd come out with all – with a rash, and most of the kids did."[108] Valerie Commanda noted that her children suffered from the same condition upon swimming in the same area.[109] In an effort to avoid these rashes for her children, Gertrude Lewis remembered mistakenly thinking the river was a safer place for water leisure activities: "we thought the water was so dirty down here in the bay and they were breaking out, you know, they were getting sores on them. So instead of swimming there, they went up to the Serpent River ... And the Serpent River was nice and clear. And we thought, oh, they're safe up there ... And here we found that there's radium 226 in that river! We weren't supposed to use that water at all!"[110] Other children, particularly those who lived in "Sulphur Circle" suffered from undiagnosed conditions. In a 1985 report on the health effects of the water pollution on those who swam in the river, one child was described as having discolouration on their gum line, which was a possible indication of metal poisoning.[111]

While it was not long before the community had to contend with the negative effects of the plant, any positive developments were fleeting. The jobs soon disappeared. By the time the plant closed in 1963, it had been in operation for less than a decade. The long-term economic consequences of the plant closure were devastating for the community. "Since the closing of the acid plant here on the Serpent River Reserve," wrote the Chief to an official in the Mineral Resources Branch of Indian Affairs, "We are in a very depressed area, there is no work here at present. We feel that something else could be started, for example a rock quarry."[112] For short a time the plant had provided jobs for the community.[113]

In its 1959 annual report, Noranda had been excited about its operation at Cutler, where it was operating close to capacity, and had even explored acquiring federal government support for the building of a wharf to enable the plant to increase its output capacity.[114] Just two years later, the company report sang a very different tune. "The Cutler acid plant was lower at 344 tonnes of acid per day, about 35% of capacity, due to reduced demand for acid from the uranium mines," it read. "Some 85,000 tons of pyrite concentrate was burned to yield 125,500 tons of acid and 57,000 tons of iron calcine."[115] The decrease in output in 1960 – versus the growth which had been anticipated a year earlier – was directly tied to the "bust" period of Elliot Lake in the uranium industry of the early 1960s.[116]

The following year, Noranda transferred its leasehold to Cutler Acid Ltd. (CAL) for $2 after the price of uranium plummeted with the public announcement that the United States would not renew its contract with Canada.[117] CAL, which operated the plant for Canadian Industries Ltd. (CIL), bought the plant most likely because it competed with another plant it owned near Sudbury and closed the Cutler operation.[118] Even as operations slowly resumed at some of the mines toward the end of the decade, it was thought to be more financially sound to truck sulphuric acid from the Sudbury area than to continue running the plant at Cutler.[119] When the plant ceased operations in 1963 and the jobs dried up, environmental pollution and social change meant that it was too late to return to the old ways. The fish in the bay were either gone or inedible, and the fish and game in the Serpent River system were contaminated, compromised by mining operations upstream at Elliot Lake. If DIA had intended that jobs at the plant would decrease the Serpent River First Nation's reliance on moditional economic activities and move its members more permanently into the local resource-based economy, they had succeeded. Members of the Serpent River First Nation were now part of a modernized boom-bust economic cycle and unable to rely on traditional economic pursuits like fishing, hunting, forestry, and trapping as they once had.

The Elliot Lake *Standard*, which had once extolled the virtues of building the plant on the reserve in the hope that it would "advance" the progress of the "Indians," now talked about the abandoned structure as a blight on the landscape and a danger to the tourism industry. Articles in the paper described it as an eyesore visible from the highway, saying it had the "scabrous look of deserted and derelict buildings" and posed a danger to the well-being of the larger community.[120] For his part, Chief William Meawasige wanted to be able to use the land for a practical purpose, but CIL refused to cooperate with plans for demolition. DIA was also unresponsive. In an ironic twist, when the lease expired the plant land was deeded back to the reserve, but CIL did nothing to decommission the site and it was therefore unusable and continued to pose a significant health and safety hazard to the community. SRFN could not finance such a remediation project independently, and in 1967 Chief Meawasige wrote letters to Prime Minister Pearson, who was also the member of Parliament for the area, asking him for assistance.[121]

The government's answer came two years later in the form of "Exercise Powder Serpent," a training exercise held for 110 members of Number One Field Squadron, Royal Canadian Engineers.[122] The exercise was intended to both demolish the plant and provide the army with an opportunity for live fire training. In late August 1969, the unit began a multi-week operation that was witnessed by interested parties of both the Canadian and American armed forces.[123] The squadron camped near the site and had its food and water transported from Elliot Lake. By the end of October, all the buildings had been blown up at a cost of over $100,000.[124] The demolition by explosives levelled the building but scattered contaminated pieces of rubble over a wider area. Larger pieces of debris were piled in the nearby ravines.[125] A new Chief and Council were elected soon after and in February 1970 they raised the issue of the refuse, which was still on nearly 100 acres of reserve land.[126] Although the plant had been demolished, the site remained unusable and a danger to community health and safety.

While the Cutler Acid Plant brought some degree of economic prosperity to the reserve, it came at a high cost. The Cold War brought with it new imperatives that trumped First Nations interests, and it also led to an entrenchment of the colonial relationship that had already existed.

The community had to contend with colonial pressures to modernize and their own desires for wage employment, while at the same time trying to assert their stewardship role by asking questions and writing complaints about acid plant damage. Although the community initially welcomed the prospect of jobs in the face of economic disparity, their attempts to investigate the offer through their own legal representation were squashed. The Elders' recollections of wanting work in the community, especially as mining would lead to the depletion of the very resources upon which they had relied and intimately understood for centuries, highlight the complexity of extraction in a colonial context. As more and more settlers came to the area, the inequality was readily apparent to them, and while the prospect of steady jobs was initially positive, they could not have anticipated the extent of environmental damage. The jobs would be fleeting, but the legacy of toxicity would remain for decades.

Even when it came to working in the plant, employees had to contend with occupational exposure to acids and dangerous chemicals, and reserve residents watched as their trees, homes, cars and even laundry were affected by the constant presence of fumes and red dust. Community and family gardens and traditional pursuits of fish and game were replaced by store-bought groceries. By the time the plant closed and the wages disappeared, there was no possibility of safely returning to those practices as they had been contaminated by the plant and mining operations at Elliot Lake. CIL had little interest in taking with them anything other than what could be moved cheaply and quickly and left the buildings where they were. DIA had not negotiated a clean-up clause in the lease to Noranda despite the suggestions made by reserve residents and the community priest in 1954–5. More than a decade later, Chief Meawasige had found some success in publicizing the eyesore to an increasingly sympathetic Canadian public, but it was left to future leaders to ensure that the decommissioning process was carried out. In the meantime, children played on the site, fires erupted in the sulphur heaps left behind by the Royal Canadian Engineers, and the water still burned the skin of anyone wanting to swim in the area. All these issues would persist over the next half-century, while reserve leadership became increasingly militant in its calls for proper environmental reclamation of the site. In so doing, community members would reassert their relationships with the land more explicitly and renew relationships with the land in accordance with Anishinaabe tradition.

Chapter Five

"We weren't supposed to use that water at all!" Uranium Mining and the Serpent River

All the animals in the area, that was their source of drinking water as well.[1]

– Terry Jacobs

The Anishinaabek have interacted with the land on the North Shore of Lake Huron since time immemorial. Evidence of early occupation in the area of what is now Elliot Lake has long been documented: *Bakak-wehngenda*, or Rooster Rock, is an important cultural site located in the community's traditional territory.[2] Now it is part of a uranium tailings management area. As community members continue to reclaim and use sacred sites such as this, it is apparent that although their ways of interacting with the land have been compromised by uranium extraction, their dedication to tradition has remained strong. This chapter examines the many changes that have occurred in the Serpent River watershed since mining development started, and the effects these changes have had on the people of Serpent River First Nation. Community knowledge holders remember early use of the land and water system, and the changes that took place once mining activity began in the 1950s. The development of industrial and mining operations brought about a dramatic change to the myriad ways in which members of the Serpent River First Nation interacted with their traditional territory.

Community Elders have long memories that recall family ties to the land and river system. Terry Jacobs recalled that his father had made his living hunting and trapping near Black Creek (part of the watershed), but this livelihood was compromised by the river pollution, as more and more Elders of his generation realized that the animal population had diminished and those that remained – the beaver in particular – had been affected to the point where it threatened the community's ability to harvest.[3] Betty recalled that her father-in-law had to stop trapping altogether due to the poor quality of his pelts and the difficulty in obtaining them, saying, "He had to quit … Even the fur – he was trying to do whatever they do to skin the beaver – broke right off … Even the fur was no good."[4] Her husband, Terry, described a generational shift in dependence on the land as a result of pollution, and the loss of rich resources:

> Most of the elders – I'm an elder now, I'm seventy-two – but the elders just before me, they enjoyed all this trapping, hunting and trapping. And they had to get away from that. The meat might be contaminated. [Pause] And I know Betty, she used to like beaver tails, eh? And the beaver that she used to get were all from the Black Creek. She ended up with colon cancer. I don't know, I can't say for sure that was the result of eating that beaver tail because it was really good, really rich. And she, she enjoyed that, eh? She enjoyed beaver as well, all the meat.[5]

This personal history not only contains important information about changes in the community's access to resources over time, but it also underlines one of the main concerns that Serpent River First Nation members have had about uranium: its effects on their well-being. It was more than the disturbing fact that the traditional ways of life were disrupted – they could also make one sick. The connectivity that had always been part of life was now threatening it.

In the minds of the Elders in the community, this was directly tied to the river pollution. As Terry recalled,

> Oh, yeah I guess a lot of leaching came from Elliot Lake. All the water emptied into the Serpent River, eh? Came right down. I remember first of all when I was a young fella I could swim in the Serpent River and it didn't matter if the water was really four or six feet deep. You see right down to the bottom. The stones down below, they looked like jewels. It was very, very clean.

However, once the mines started, he said, "a lot of their leaching emptied into the Serpent River. The bottom of that Serpent River was just like a greyish gunk, eh?[6] And I guess that had to be all from Elliot Lake. And it's still not – after being closed for so many years – it's still not completely cleaned up." According to Jacobs, the water had many uses: "That water used to be good for drinking, swimming, washing, washing your clothes. And I guess all the animals in the area, that was their source of drinking water as well. The animal population went down, eh?"[7] The ways in which Elders understand the effects of the uranium industry on their community is through their well-being, a holistic concept that privileges the connectivity between health, environment, culture, and spirituality. Threats to community well-being form the foundation of this collective understanding. As mentioned in chapter four, economic gain may have been a catalyst for the establishment of such industries, but it was not worth the price paid in the loss of resources and the erosion of community health. As seen in the Jacobses' recollections, health is understood to be directly tied to land, and as one is diminished, so too is the other.

Uranium production was one of the biggest threats to the Serpent River watershed, which covers approximately 1,274 square kilometres[8] and eventually flows into the North Shore of Lake Huron. When companies and various levels of government were cooperating in the establishment of the uranium industry at Elliot Lake, there was little consideration for the safe and responsible disposal of the by-products and waste of extraction. Calls to investigate the water disposal methods of mining companies came as early as 1955 after the Pronto Uranium Mine (south of present-day Elliot Lake) began operations, and, as one newspaper put it at the time, "initial concern was for impoundment of tailings and neutralization of acid wastes. Although waste treatment and disposal methods were not entirely satisfactory in the beginning, improvements which were made in the first year of operation appear to have been adequate."[9] It was the responsibility of the Department of Lands and Forests (which later became the Department of Natural Resources Canada) to study water quality and tailings disposal areas, as well as to "assess the pollutional effects of liquid wastes which must, of necessity, be discharged."[10] The newspaper article described the scientific process of tailings and their disposal, as the uranium itself had to be extracted from the ore using sulphuric acid.[11] This process, called leaching, separates "the insolubles (tailings) and [passes] the clarified solution (with pH adjustment) through ion-exchange resins. The final barren solution and the water-borne tailings are mixed and fed to mixing tanks where lime slurry is added under automatic pH control to give pH 6.5 to 7.5. After adequate agitated retention in the neutralization plant, the mixture is discharged through wood-stove pipe line to a disposal area."[12] The tailings would then be held in a pond where they could settle. The newspaper, even in the boom days, acknowledged that the sheer magnitude of the 35,000 tonnes of uranium mining capacity of the mines in operation near Elliot and Quirke Lakes "indicated a tremendous waste disposal problem."[13]

There are twelve decommissioned mines in the area – Buckles, Can-Met, Denison, Lacnor, Milliken, Nordic, Panel, Pronto, Quirke,

Spanish-American, Stanleigh, and Stanrock – and all are either in the Serpent River watershed or near the North Shore of Lake Huron further south of Elliot Lake. A 2004–5 report of the Serpent River Watershed Monitoring Program, prepared for Rio Algom Ltd. and Denison Mines Inc., described the tailings management areas left by these mines: "Associated with the mine sites are ten decommissioned tailings management areas (TMAs) ... Tailings were also historically deposited in Buckles Creek, so this area is also considered a source of mine-related contaminants within the licensed area of the Lacnor-Nordic TMA."[14] The maintenance and security of these tailings sites thus continues to be an important issue in the area, and are managed by Rio Algom Ltd. and Denison Mines Inc.[15]

The tailings process was explained by a short 1967 report by A.E. Armstrong, entitled "Pollution in Serpent River Water," written to communicate the extent of the effects of the uranium industry, and the consequences for fish and wildlife were clear even then:

The main sources of waste from the milled process are:
   (1) The tailings, or finely divided waste rock that remain after the separation from the uranium-bearing acid solution
   (2) The barren solution that remains following the removal of the uranium oxide concentrate
   (3) Mine water that is pumped from underground
   Approximately twelve lakes in the Elliott [sic] Lake area are receiving tailing decants, and without a doubt this has affected the fish or at least has curbed the desire of any angler to fish these lakes, because of uranium contamination.
   Also, the Serpent River all the way to Lake Huron will have been affected by uranium wastes with the result that people will be reluctant to use the water or the fish life therein.[16]

This process of containing waste in tailings ponds led to the significant pollution of the Serpent River watershed as some of these ponds and "dead lakes" (as they were also called) inevitably leaked as a result of dam failures from time to time.[17] As early as the 1950s, officials recognized that drainage or seepage from these sites posed a significant environmental danger. A report by the Decommissioning Review and Advisory Committee, an organization of various stakeholders concerned with the decommissioning process at Elliot Lake in the mid-1990s, noted in 2000 that "the companies were not required to take corrective measures until the mid-1960s."[18] Jurisdictional disputes between federal and provincial levels of government created significant problems for regulatory agencies because of the "over-riding authority which is assigned under the Atomic Energy control act," which resulted in delays.[19]

These jurisdictional disputes between federal and provincial agencies did not stop with the regulation, containment, and treatment of tailings.[20] Questions of federal-provincial responsibility also cast a shadow on the need to protect the drinking water of town residents, as well as those living in communities downstream.[21] Peter Johnston, an Elder who had advocated for the health of the river, recalled the effect this debate had on SRFN and the inequities inherent in the jurisdictional issue:

> I think it was through public relations through the media when the [neighbouring settler] town of Serpent River found out that the water contained high amounts of radium. And because it was a white community they went to the provincial government because they were getting their drinking water from the river. And ... they said to the provincial government, "we know our water's been contaminated by the mines. We need funding from you guys in order to find a process that will eliminate that so that it's not a danger to our health." And so in fact that's what happened: the provincial government provided them with the money to build a treatment plant. At the very same time that was happening, ... some members of our community were taking water from the river for their own use. And when we went to the federal government and said, you know, there's high radium contents in that water, and it's above the provincial drinking water standard, the federal government's response was well, I don't remember the exact, I think it was three picocuries per litre for the provincial government, but the standard for the federal government was [ten] picocuries per litre. So it wasn't okay for the white community but it was okay for the Indian community to drink the very same water ... Just because of the different jurisdictions ... We fought tooth and nail for years and years and years to get that standard lowered and eventually we embarrassed the government enough where they finally did bring it down to the provincial standard. But in the meantime, though, I mean, people drank their water.[22]

Indeed, the province of Ontario had a safety standard of 3 picocuries per litre (pCi/L, the unit of measurement for radioactivity), and samples taken from the river at the reserve measured as high as 6.2 pCi/L.[23] However, the federal government did not consider that level of radioactivity to be significantly dangerous, as its safe level was defined as being 10 pCi/L.[24] While settler communities could be protected by provincial standards, despite being vulnerable to river pollution stemming from mining operations at Elliot Lake, the Serpent River First Nation was governed by federal standards because Status Indians and lands reserved for them fall under federal jurisdiction. In an article in the *Globe and Mail*, which called attention to this inequality on the basis of ethnicity and jurisdiction, the National Indian Brotherhood's representative, Lloyd Tataryn, was paraphrased as saying "it is wrong to have different standards for whites and Indians. Indians at Serpent River reserve were allowed to ingest up to 10 picocuries per litre while upstream white cottagers were protected by the more stringent three picocurie standard."[25] It was not until the 1970s that attention was called to the fact that federal standards for radioactivity in drinking water differed from those of the provincial government, but it took lobbying on the part of SRFN and Tataryn to accomplish this.[26]

In her recollection of community concerns over drinking water safety, Gertrude Lewis also noted this jurisdictional issue: "And we complained that they didn't do anything for us. We had three families getting their water from the Serpent River up at the bridge there." When asked to clarify if families still relied on water, even at that time, she went on to name them, and continued:

> There were the three families that were living there. And they couldn't get any help to put in any protection for our water up there. They didn't do anything for them. And yet in Serpent River [neighbouring settler community] they were paying for water treatment for the people there. And that's another thing we were complaining about – how come they can do that for you know, off-reserve, and on-reserve they don't seem to care whether we have good water or not?[27]

Community members were well aware of the situation and at several points, articulated their concerns over potentially dangerous water and the inequality in water protection that resulted from federal jurisdiction over Indigenous affairs.[28] Community members did not see this as just another political struggle, even though raising these concerns was an inherently political act; they understood it to be more about a struggle for equal access to basic services and safe water. As these knowledge holders suggest, it was also understood to be more than a jurisdictional debate for the people in the community – an all too familiar story in many other areas of Indigenous history.

SRFN members felt that jurisdictional disputes and official regulatory hurdles often prevented them from realizing traditional reciprocal roles with the land and water, underscoring the politico-cultural importance of the issue. At a later point in her interview, Lewis once again returned to the idea of river pollution and the difficulty of getting answers from different levels of government, emphasizing its significance to both her own personal experience as well as that of other reserve residents:

[We] couldn't drink the water, of course. We had three families that were getting their water from there. That was, that was kind of bad. And then another thing that was that was difficult was if you had a problem, it was just like a football. Between the federal government and the provincial government: "Oh, it's not our jurisdiction." "You're under the feds, we don't have anything to do with that …"[29] That's one thing I didn't like. We were just like a football bouncing back and forth there. We didn't know what to do, you know, or where to go.[30]

Lewis also tied this historical pattern to contemporary concerns about the watershed, saying, "And look at how long they're taking to clean it up again there now. I suppose there's no money. Nobody wanted to put any money in the last time … Probably thinking the same way again. 'Oh jeez, it's an Indian Reserve, never mind.'"[31] Lewis's football simile nicely encapsulates the jurisdictional issues that continue to plague relations between the federal and provincial levels of government. In this particular case, the feeling that families and leadership had about being "bounced" back and forth is highlighted here in this Elder's memory, particularly as it led to a feeling of hopelessness and frustration.[32] From the community's perspective, the province and the federal government seemed to be squabbling, not for control, but rather to avoid this issue. The overall feeling when speaking to Elders about this point is that they were seen as "troublemakers" who had to embarrass all levels of government into action. While there is a tremendous frustration apparent in these interviews, one of the other feelings is pride in not only overcoming that sense of helplessness, but more importantly in the community's growing activism, which allowed members to reclaim their traditional role as stewards of the land.

Drinking water was not the only concern of people living in the area. Tourism was an important secondary industry along the North Shore as many communities are easily accessible via the Trans-Canada Highway, so the economic implication of the pollution of lakes and rivers became a significant concern – in addition to health and safety – for the settler communities. The management of waterways and water safety in non-reserve lands fell to the Province of Ontario. To this end, the government of Ontario had established the Ontario Water Resources Commission (OWRC) in 1956 to make water publicly available to municipalities and to manage its quality.[33] By the late 1950s, it was also responsible for monitoring the Serpent River system north of the reserve lands near the Trans-Canada Highway.[34]

In the early 1960s, public concern about radiological contamination at sites in both Elliot Lake and the Bancroft area began to mount. In 1964, political pressure in the provincial legislature from members of the Liberal opposition placed the issue before the government. Liberal leader Andrew Thompson noted the "shocking irresponsibility" of the OWRC and its failure to adequately study radiation in the area of Elliot Lake. In response, Conservative Premier John Robarts established a committee on 13 November 1964, chaired by T.R. Hilliard, the deputy minister of Energy and Resource Management, which included representatives from several provincial departments such as the deputy ministers of the Departments of Health, Mines, and Lands and Forests, as well as the manager and staff of the OWRC, to look into the matter.[35] But this did little to satisfy opposition members. Thompson criticized the composition of Robarts's committee, saying it was an "in group."[36] Stan Farquhar, Liberal Member of Provincial Parliament (MPP) for Algoma-Manitoulin, described the hand-picked task force as taking a "hurried, frenzied, farcical approach" to the situation.[37] Radiological pollution was a relatively new threat in Canada and it was an issue that provided the opposition with political hay while also posing a potential economic and health threat to members of communities on the North Shore and near Bancroft.

Robarts's government was anxious to defend its handling of the situation at Elliot Lake. Matthew B. Dymond, minister of health for the province, described the work in which his department was involved: "Radioactive pollution of public waters in uranium mine areas near Elliot Lake and Bancroft, upon which we have been keeping a watch since 1958, became a prime object of interest in 1964 and it was for this reason that the committee was set up at Deputy Minister level, charged with the task of developing remedies."[38] For Dymond, the committee would address any potential threats and pose solutions to any problem it found. But the opposition wanted facts about any pollution released to the public rather than dealt with behind closed doors. When Jim Renwick, MPP for Riverdale, asked Dymond if the committee – which involved four deputy ministers – had any reports that were "to be published or any information made available to the public in this general field," the latter dodged the question and redirected it to the Premier.[39] The Conservative majority would clearly not be served by the release of information that might implicate the government in the mishandling of radioactive pollution.

The pollution of northern Ontario lakes and rivers with radioactive waste was a topic, though, which captured the public's attention. It could not be as easily dismissed as the complaints of the Serpent River First Nation alone, and water pollution and the government's unwillingness to make the facts of the case public made national headlines in 1965. In November of that year, a front-page story in the *Globe and Mail* exposed the fact that the release of the OWRC report commissioned by the government of Ontario detailing radioactive contamination in the Elliot Lake and Bancroft areas had been delayed not once, but twice that summer.[40] Although the report had been ready for release in June, the *Globe* claimed that it was initially delayed in order to protect the tourism business in those areas.[41] Its release was delayed once more by Premier Robarts until after the federal election, as his office "didn't think it would be the gentlemanly thing to do to make this public before Nov. 8," according to Dr. J.K. Reynolds, chief executive officer of the Premier's Office.[42] The real reason behind the delays in the report's release is that it tended to contradict the government's assertions that the environmental problems related to uranium mining were minimal and that the OWRC had the situation under control. Although the report blamed the federal government for having been "delinquent by not combating radioactive pollution in the uranium mining areas of Elliot Lake and Bancroft," it nevertheless validated the opposition's arguments that the OWRC had refused to release information to the public and had failed to adequately solve the problems as Dymond promised it would do.[43]

Although the report attempted to downplay the significance of the threat – and reads in an intentionally disarming way – it provides clear evidence of the extent of the damage done to the Serpent River watershed. The report outlines several conclusions reached by the subcommittee, the first of which admitted that "low-level radiological contamination [had] occurred in certain public waters in the Elliot Lake and Bancroft mining areas as a result of waste disposal practices which have been considered to be standard in the mining industry."[44] However, in an effort to minimize fear and public outcry, the report then questioned the actual significance of the contamination. "Radiological analyses of samples of surface waters taken in both mining areas indicate that there is no danger to persons drinking the waters in question," it read, "since the concentrations of radioactivity are within acceptable limits for short-term exposure promulgated by international bodies. However, improved waste control measures are needed to reduce the levels of radioactivity for prolonged exposure."[45] This final clause is key, since well-established communities in both the Elliot Lake and Bancroft areas relied on these contaminated waters for municipal purposes, and long-term exposure to radioactivity needed to be mitigated.[46] Economic dependence on the industry would almost certainly have influenced their perception of the water quality problem.

At the same time that the report downplayed the consequences and significance of the pollution, it also admitted that a full scientific understanding of both the pollution itself and its effects were lacking. The report further called for a more "detailed investigation" into the extent of the contamination, as well as the nature of the measures taken by mining companies to address radiological pollution. Here the report's authors pointed to "the need [to develop] a schedule of maximum permissible concentrations for application to water affected by wastes from the uranium mining industry in Ontario." Regulation of seemingly inevitable radioactive contamination appeared to be the only solution and thus the report's authors recommended that safety guidelines be established for the mining industry. In its list of recommendations, the report called for the government to establish regulations initially "for the control of radioactivity in public waters arising from uranium mining and milling operations" that would generally correspond with the provincial Department of Health's broader guidelines:

a) In accordance with modern scientific knowledge and opinion, any unnecessary exposure to radioactivity should be kept to a minimum.
b) Concentrations of from 10 to 3 picocuries of radium-226 per litre of water should be adopted as the initial objectives to be attained in public drinking-waters in the Elliot Lake and Bancroft areas.
c) Concentrations of from 30 to 10 picocuries of radium-226 per litre of water should be adopted as the initial or first-level objectives to be attained in those lakes and streams where present levels are in excess of this range.[47]

The report makes special note that there should be an annual review of all of the above-described regulatory goals, and that the water monitoring programs should be expanded through a sustained, long-term multi-departmental effort. It also promoted the continuation of collaborative efforts between provincial government bodies and mining companies "to seek practical means for the control of radioactivity and to establish sound design criteria for treatment and disposal works."[48] The report's conclusions and recommendations suggest that a collaborative relationship already existed and was possible to sustain among departments and between the province and the uranium mining industry.[49] Yet at the same time it called for an increased reliance on private industry to actually safeguard the waterways while conducting its mining operations and to safely dispose of mine wastes. Even if the parties had agreed to such cooperation and regulation, it would again raise questions about jurisdiction over the acceptable limits of picocurie exposure for First Nations and settler communities in waterways that flowed through both reserve and traditional lands. In conceiving of the pollution problem within a narrowly construed political framework defined by federal and provincial responsibilities and economic considerations, the report did nothing to address the impact of the pollution upon First Nations downstream of mining sites.

The report also clearly placed ultimate responsibility for managing the problem at the feet of the federal government, bringing to mind Gertrude Lewis's image of radioactive pollution as a political football. In that vein, the report addressed the jurisdictional confusion over water and land resources in the context of federal responsibility outlined in the Atomic Energy Control Act, by calling for the clarification of "statutory authority."[50] Its recommendation that "the Province approach the Government of Canada with a view to clarifying procedure under existing legislative authority so as to assure the control of radioactive pollution of public waters resulting from the disposal of mining and milling wastes from operating and abandoned uranium mines, within limits acceptable to the Province"[51] was a direct criticism of the federal government's record when it came to water pollution. It suggests that the federal-provincial relationship as it existed in the context of the uranium industry and pollution was uneven and in need of reassessment.

It seems as though the cooperative relationship that gave birth to the Town of Elliot Lake was challenged once it became clear that the uranium industry brought with it a series of serious environmental concerns, not the least of which was about water resources. But, again, the report made no mention of the First Nations communities that were affected in these areas. Indeed, the reference to a relatively safe short-term exposure to water in its summarized conclusions addressed the tourism and cottager industry and the temporary nature of vacationers' exposure. It did not address the fact that there were Indigenous people dependent upon the river for drinking water as well as for traditional and leisure pursuits.

While compartmentalized, jurisdictional thinking was perhaps an inevitable political reality of the federal-provincial partnership in the Elliot Lake area and in uranium mining in general, the practical issues that the pollution of the Serpent River watershed raised for First Nations were shared by many local settler residents of the area as well. The report on river contamination would not have surprised local tourism business owners, for example. One camp owner, Robert Weatherley, reported that some of his guests complained of dead fish on Whiskey Lake, and another, William Webb, noticed changes in the industry for the second time since mining operations began. "There has been a marked drop in tourist registrations, and now it has become worse than it was in the uranium boom days," wrote Webb. "Between here and Espanola [a pulp and paper mill town] on the Spanish River there are hardly any fish to be caught by angling, and now that all this talk has come about the possibility of radioactive contamination it will be hard to draw in visitors."[52] James B. Vance, a tourist operator and commercial fisherman, and his son Russell worried that American tourists would not leave one polluted area just to visit and fish in another![53] They also noted that the quality of the fishing as a whole was diminishing and that the fish that were caught tasted bad.[54]

Concerns about the health of fish species in the Serpent River watershed and along the North Shore also came to the attention of the provincial government from its own employees. J.S. Ball, district forester, outlined questions about fish quality in his letter to C.F. Schenk, a supervisor at the biology branch of the OWRC: "For your interest, we have had many reports that lake trout caught in Elliot Lake and Big Quirke Lake are not fit for consumption and have a very distinctive odour associated with them when cooked," Ball wrote in 1966. "One of our commercial fishermen was in Big Quirke Lake in 1961 and caught fair poundages of lake trout. However, trout under five pounds were very rare. One of our Officers observed that even in late October and November female trout apparently had not released their eggs."[55] The local employees of the Fish and Wildlife Branch of the Ontario Department of Lands and Forests were also aware of the problems with fish in the area. George Vozeh of the Department of Lands and Forests reported that there were trout in Quirke Lake that had three-year-old eggs, a significant indication of spawning problems.[56] Spawning rates seemed to be declining, as suggested by both observation of female trout cycles (they should spawn in October) as well as the scarcity of juvenile trout under five pounds (lake trout have an average weight of about ten pounds, or 4.5 kilograms).[57] This is significant in light of the fact that trout can generally live up to twenty years and they only reach sexual maturity at approximately seven years old.[58] Along with water contamination, the main threats to lake trout were the acidification of water and oxygen-poor waters.[59] Put simply, if the number of young fish was in decline and females were not spawning as they should, ministry employees feared that the health of the population would be threatened.

The documentary evidence suggests that these concerns of members of the public, provincial employees, and experts were already well known to the members of the OWRC by the early 1960s. In a 1964 OWRC interoffice memorandum from G.M. Galimbert, the assistant general manager, to D.S. Caverly, the general manager, the concerns of a lodge owner on Whiskey Lake were discussed at length. Mr. L.J. Prior, proprietor of Redwood Lodge, had written several letters detailing his concerns about water and fish quality. One of these letters, dated 17 December 1963, told of his suspicion that contamination was harming Whiskey, Kindle, and Hook Lakes, and his concern about the safety of the drinking water and fish: "some of the fish were very thin and in some, the spawn was not normal."[60] The response described the monitoring program that was then in place and said that once information was available, the OWRC "would be in a better position to comment on the ... condition of the fish."[61] Of course, by 26 August, the Reconnaissance Survey of the OWRC had been completed but not released to the public, a fact not lost on Galimbert: "you are aware that the report we prepared on the Serpent River watershed has not been made available to the public. There are, of course, certain people who are vitally interested in the findings of the report."[62] The OWRC, which had carried out its own preliminary investigation into pollution in the watershed, was aware that many people were concerned about their livelihoods, as well as their health, before the committee's report was written. Yet this same report at once downplayed the severity and danger of the situation while emphasizing the possibility that regulation would solve most of the "minor" problems it identified.

Nevertheless, Galimbert's memorandum acknowledged that all was not well with the Serpent River watershed, and that there had been a marked change since the start of uranium mining in the area. In a second letter dated 27 January 1964, Prior wrote that "the pollution in Whiskey Lake was evident to the smell, there was considerable foam and it was black in colour, and the fish in the lakes were sterile due to radium pollution."[63] Prior was also concerned about the fact that tourists were asking pointed questions about whether the fish were suitable for consumption, as well as having noticed that the spawn were not normal.[64] The lodge owner was then told that there was no further information that could be provided to him at the time, despite the fact that he said that he might have to close his lodge if he received no answer. Galimbert's memorandum was intended to ascertain whether it would be possible to act in response to Prior's letters. But he acknowledged that a truthful reply might be devastating to the lodge owner. "You must realize that it is quite possible that his business may be affected by the information that we can now provide," he wrote. "What action he would take upon receipt of this information I do not know ... I feel that the answer cannot be delayed indefinitely because of the vital interest of Mr. Prior in the matter."[65] Galimbert seemed keenly aware that the information available to the OWRC might endanger Prior's business, but he was also constrained by the fact that the survey had not yet been released to the public. Clearly officials were weighing the competing interests of public safety and economic development in their assessment and publicization of the pollution of the Serpent River system.

By the mid-1960s, it was becoming increasing difficult for the government to refrain from acting as it learned more information from official, scientific studies of the pollution of the river system.[66] Galimbert wrote to Dr. D.J. Dewar, the senior scientific advisor of the Atomic Energy Control Board on 13 August 1964, clearly outlining the findings of the government's initial survey. Even though the results were only preliminary, they were damning. "I would like to point out that this survey was of a preliminary nature only but it did point out that in the two lakes [Quirke and Pecors][67] in which the work was carried out that there is radiological contamination beyond the tolerances that are recognized by health authorities," he wrote. "Both the Department of Health and our own group feel that a survey of more detail should be carried out but that this is secondary to an attempt to achieve some correction of conditions that have materialized."[68] Despite a desire to maintain calm and minimize the importance of the pollution, it was now impossible to ignore as public safety might be in jeopardy. Galimbert pointed out that the safety of the drinking water was clearly suspect and he wondered about its consequences for human health, particularly for infants who drank formula mixed with water from Quirke Lake.[69] This letter – which was written at about the same time as the interoffice OWRC memo discussed above – indicates that the provincial government had knowledge that at least some lakes were contaminated in the watershed and that this posed a threat not only to economic endeavours and tourism, but also to the health of the people who ate the fish and drank the water.

But some officials in the government continued to downplay these apparent threats to human health, despite the findings of their own internal studies. One October 1964 memo from G.D. Clarke of the Fish and Wildlife Branch to Frank A. MacDougall, Deputy Minister of Lands and Forests, entitled "Radioactive Pollution," contains contradictory statements made about radioactivity in the area and the health of fish and their suitability for consumption:

> I have checked with the Ontario Water Resources Commission and find that in their opinion the level of radioactivity in lakes such as Quirk and

Wiskey [sic] and as far down as Lauson [sic] is ten times what is considered tolerable for a life-time exposure. They do not consider that there is any risk in casual contact by persons coming from low-hazard areas ... Levels found in fish are lower than those in other organisms, vegetation and in the lake generally. Fish are scarce in some of the lakes with high hazard, but no objection can be seen for tourist fishing in these lakes now extensively used for that purpose. Consequently, they do not advise that we should close any lakes to angling.[70]

This summary of OWRC findings contradicts the observations of people who worked and fished in the area as well as the findings of the initial studies referred to by Galimbert. Instead, Clarke rationalizes avoiding a ban on fishing so as to protect the bourgeoning tourism industry. In doing so, he ignored the effects of long-term exposure to radiation and other toxins. While the memo seems to indicate that there was a low risk to tourists, it does not directly address the fact that many local people regularly fished in the area for both subsistence and commercial purposes. Clarke's suggestion that a fishing ban on "high hazard" lakes would be a moot point because their polluted waters lacked fish and were no longer used by tourists for sportfishing failed to consider the fact that the waters and creatures living in the Serpent River watershed were all interconnected. This reasoning also failed to account for the possibility of continued pollution through dam failures at tailings sites, not to mention the impact on traditional First Nations uses of fish, wildlife, and water. One recalls George Manuel's critique of the way the government and industry handled water pollution in the Grassy Narrows area: "When the mercury content of fish in the English and Wabigoon Rivers went up too high, southern tourists were told to 'Fish for Fun.' Native people who depend on the fish as their principal food were told nothing. Governments that were prepared to give grants to industry to locate on clean waters had no answer when native people asked, 'What are we to eat?'"[71] In the Serpent River context, the failure to acknowledge that other people depended on the resources connected to these lakes and rivers – or indeed, to understand the existence of a traditional worldview that emphasizes the intimate relationships between all aspects of Creation – was yet another way that government officials compromised SRFN community wellness in the name of promoting economic success.

Only when the pollution became bad enough to visibly threaten the health and confidence of tourists and recreational land users did the government begin to contemplate action. That same October, representatives of the US Public Health Service, the OWRC, the Ontario Department of Health, the Department of Lands and Forests, and the

Department of Mines attended a multi-departmental meeting held at Elliot Lake. The purpose of the three-day seminar was to "observe and review the extent of pollution resulting from uranium mining and milling in the area."[72] R.W. McCauley wrote a report of the meeting he attended, which he described in detail, and his alarm was apparent: "Numerous places where flimsy impounding structures had been washed out allowing tailings to enter lakes were evident from the air. Several lakes in which the colour of the water was a pronounced green from this pollution was noted. The flight over the area impressed the writer of the seriousness of the pollution in the water system."[73] McCauley paid particular attention to the dam structures and their capacity to leak, if not fail altogether. His observation of the green colour of tailings lakes was made possible by the aerial tour of the affected region, which had been arranged by the OWRC. McCauley also mentioned visits to tailings sites on the ground, especially those areas where there had been leaks. His conclusion was that "the view from the ground was more impressive than that from the air in that the depth of the tailings covering over a hundred acres also became evident."[74] On the second and third days of the seminar, the issue of tourism and the possible effect of the pollution on cottaging in the area took centre stage. Economic issues, rather than the public health of local residents, clearly continued to dominate official discourse about the consequences of uranium mining. One participant, D. Gillespie of the Department of Lands and Forests, Sudbury region, asked pointed questions: "what do we tell cottagers and anglers on a lake containing water above the maximum possible limit? What do we tell eaters of fish (and possibly clams) from the polluted waters?" It was also suggested at this time that the OWRC draft a press release and that a more comprehensive scientific study be undertaken of the area. As officials gained more knowledge about the extent of the pollution in the mid-1960s, it became increasingly difficult to justify inaction from a legal and public health standpoint.[75]

The evidence presented above makes it clear that the high levels of radioactivity in the Serpent River watershed had been known to the OWRC since 1957. Rather than raise public alarm, the government and commission allowed economic concerns about the viability of the uranium industry, and later tourism, to trump concerns about public health. But, as officials discovered, the public was not happy at being deceived. In 1964 a newspaper story in the *Globe and Mail* broke the news that the pollution of the river system had been kept a secret for more than two years by the Ontario government, thus endangering the health of all those who lived and vacationed in the area. "Although some contamination has been known to exist for at least two years, no serious effort has been made by the authorities to inform the population," wrote investigative reporter Barrie Zwicker. "The accepted long-term safe concentration of radioactivity in a litre of drinking water for much of the population in the Elliot Lake area is 10 picocuries. An OWRC report, which the commission refuses to release, shows that Elliot Lake water has reached twelve to fourteen picocuries per litre during the past year. Nearby Quirke Lake water has been measured at forty to one-hundred picocuries and plankton in the lake at thousands of picocuries."[76] Indeed, the information contained in the report was only released after extensive pressure by the *Globe and Mail*. Not surprisingly, the provincial cabinet disavowed all responsibility for suppressing the report and dealing with its contents, blaming the OWRC.[77] The latter maintained that it was a cabinet decision and fell under ministerial responsibility.[78] A *Maclean's* editorial written a month later entitled, "Since When Did the Truth Become More Dangerous than the Danger Itself?" noted the hazards of hushing up concerns about public health and drinking water safety. It also expressed dismay at the government's reaction to the publication of the story: "when the long-suppressed story was finally broken by a Toronto newspaper, the official reaction seemed at first to be more resentment than embarrassment."[79] The editorial went on to chide Elliot Lake residents for being more concerned about tourism than their own health: "neither are we consoled to learn that local residents 'knew about the situation all along' (though in fact some said they didn't) and were mainly concerned that the fishing had been spoiled in the lakes round about. Even this fact is by no means trivial, since Elliot Lake had been trying to repair its shattered fortunes by transitioning into a tourist outfitting centre. Were any tourists told that they might be fishing in radioactive lakes?"[80] It is interesting to note that "fishing" is defined here as a non-Indigenous, middle-class leisure pursuit that had economic importance only in so far as it was able to attract visitors to the area.[81] The traditional role of fishing to both settler and First Nations communities in the area in supplementing family diets was completely ignored.[82] The classist and racist implications of this statement stem from the all too common exclusion of impoverished groups and First Nations from the economic narrative of the North Shore. Even when the story broke in the national press, it continued to be dominated by a discourse that prized wilderness areas for their economic value – either for resources or tourism. Pollution was seen as a threat to the economic viability of the region, not as a destructive force that could tear apart the fabric of communities and traditional relationships to the land.

Suggested solutions included further regulation and control by government, and the editorial problematized a lack of adequate initial planning rather than the mining operations and the rapid industrialization of the region itself. "We know enough to treat it not with casual neglect but with the utmost caution," continued the *Maclean's* editorial. "The Elliot Lake incident reveals that our governments are not in fact exercising this caution. They are not policing the situation as they should, are not using what knowledge they do have to provide a machinery of protection, and even feel no obligation to warn us of the dangers we have unwittingly incurred ... it's high time we, the Canadian public, shifted the burden of proof from the poisoned to the poisoners."[83] The editors held government accountable for monitoring and prevention and attempted to demonstrate how elected officials failed the Canadian public, not just through inaction in passing adequate regulation, but also by suppressing important health and safety information. Implicit in this critique of government inaction and suppression of vital public health information is the belief that elected officials had a responsibility to the Canadians who voted for them. It was a public discourse of citizenship and rights that naturally excluded Indigenous peoples from the list of the wronged.

In 1964, Status Indians had only been enfranchised for four years.[84] In fact, the one group that indisputably depended on the government's fiduciary duty to "protect" were the very people who were hurt the most and were ignored in the public discourse. As some of the Elders noted, the two levels of government fought about who did *not* have responsibility for protecting First Nations people from the dangers of uranium and, given their lack of legal power and standing, no one else stood up to champion their cause.[85] Like their settler neighbours who also relied on fishing, the Serpent River Anishinaabek were concerned with the fact that the river pollution was impeding their livelihoods. Community members consistently voiced grievances about threats to traditional economic pursuits. In a moving account of loss in a published oral history, a member of the Serpent River First Nation, identified only as Junior, outlines his family's struggles with the effects of the pollution on their livelihood:

My grandfather had a camp at Quirke Lake. They just walked in. There goes his camp, there goes everything. This was his trapping ground. Nobody compensated him for taking his camping ground. I mean, we're talking '52, '53 when they got started. All our fish are gone. Our rivers are never ever going to come back to what they was. Never. I mean, I used to be able to go fishing down the Serpent River down by the highway over there and catch all kinds of fish. Every time you'd put the line in the water. It's nothing now.[86]

But fishing was not the only thing to suffer from the effects of pollution. As local First Nations understood from a traditional standpoint, the river and its inhabitants were only one part of a larger interconnected environmental chain. Junior went on to describe his concerns with the quality of moose meat and its effects on the health of those who ate it. "We should mention something about our moose – remember, something about the kidneys and the livers they wanted for a while there because they were contaminated? They were telling us their kidneys were contaminated and whatever else. What about the rest of it, the whole body?"[87] Junior summarized the Anishinaabe worldview of connectivity, saying: "they all drink the same water [and we eat them]."[88]

The consequences of pollution were felt long after the boom went bust. DIA officials also began to recognize the importance of advising the community about the potential risks to their food supply – but only ten years after similar concerns were first raised for the settler residents of the area and tourists. A letter from Indian and Northern Affairs to Chief and Council of SRFN dated 30 July 1974 outlined what their department was doing during this time:

> There are tests being made on pollution of the Serpent River and the water where the acid plant used to be. One of our officials had advised that they suspect that the fish taken from the Serpent River may be contaminated. It would be appreciated if you would advise us immediately as to whether it would be possible for you to catch and ship a couple of different species of fish caught in the Serpent River and we will give you the required instructions on where and how to ship these fish. In the meantime, as a safety precaution, *we would advise you not to eat these fish or to drink the water from the Serpent River until the results of the tests are obtained.*[89]

While it had been the partnership between mining companies and various levels of government that led to the contamination issue in the first place, DIA made SRFN leadership responsible for its own health and safety. It was not the DIA official who was to gather samples, but rather, community members were meant to catch these samples themselves for scientific study rather than for consumption.

By the mid-1970s, the issue of Indigenous drinking water was also receiving more attention than it had in previous public debates. At the request of the community, the National Indian Brotherhood (NIB) became involved in some of these discussions.[90] In a letter to Roméo

LeBlanc, who was then the acting federal minister of the environment, NIB President George Manuel described a list of concerns about the findings made public at a meeting held by George Kerr, the Ontario minister of the environment:

> Mr. Kerr informed the meeting that radiation levels in the Serpent River were unsafe. He also suggested that wells on the Serpent River Reserve may be contaminated with radiation ... You can appreciate our concern when we discovered that people living on the Serpent Indian Reserve are not only drinking radiation contaminated water but are also eating fish from the river system. These fish are undoubtedly contaminated with radiation. Naturally we are concerned about the health of the people living and fishing on the Serpent River System. You will note that the situation is not unlike that of White Dog and Grassy Narrows in Northwestern Ontario. There the environment which supported the Indian lifestyle was destroyed by thoughtless dumping of mercury into the English-Wabigoon-Winnipeg River system. It would appear that the thoughtless handling of mining materials in Elliot Lake has done the same thing in the Serpent River area.[91]

The letter from the NIB drew a clear comparison between the situation on the North Shore and the one taking place at Grassy Narrows, which at this time had already garnered more public attention.[92] The NIB was also becoming increasingly involved in the public discourse surrounding First Nations issues, particularly when it involved political debates and environmental concerns. In this case, SRFN asked the NIB to assist with legal representation and the lobbying of government departments.[93] The letter thus went on to request that more information about contamination be sent to SRFN residents through a formal education campaign and that clean water be provided for the community. Finally, it asked for an end to all sources of contamination. Manuel addressed the all too convenient excuse of jurisdictional problems clearly and concisely: "Mr. Kerr informed delegates that acting to alleviate the pollution problem is complicated by the fact that Indians are a Federal responsibility, and some of the people clearly in danger from the radiation contamination of the Serpent River are Indians. I trust you will not use this jurisdictional problem as an excuse for inaction."[94] Although the industries involved in the pollution of SRFN were very different than those at Grassy Narrows, Manuel clearly connected them in this letter, and portrayed them both as being ultimately responsible for inflicting similar anguish on the two communities. In other words, the disharmony between human beings and the land was not one of First

Nations' making, but was instead due to foreseeable industrial pollution that resulted in the alienation of the people from their resources.[95]

LeBlanc was unable to offer many concrete solutions. His response to Manuel's letter outlined the control measures that would be implemented to curb further environmental damage, although the rest of the letter only contained vague timelines and few details as to the actual courses of action that would be taken.[96] A waste treatment facility was to be opened the following year at the Stanrock–Can-Met property then owned by Denison.[97] At Milliken-Stanleigh, LeBlanc wrote that "contaminated seepage from the Crotch Lake tailings area and a tailings spill west of the tailings area is entering Sherriff Creek. It is my understanding that a control order to correct the situation will be issued in the near future by the Ontario Ministry of the Environment."[98] The letter went on to acknowledge and describe a disturbing fact about the health of the Serpent River and how it was directly affected by leakage: "In 1970, the Stollery dam failed, releasing precipitates into the Serpent River. These precipitates continue to dissolve in the low sulphate fresh water producing increased levels of Ra 226. Stabilization or removal of these precipitates may be required. The alternatives for their stabilization or removal will be determined so that corrective action may be taken."[99] Vague "corrective action" was also promised for other spills at the Stanrock and Panel Mines. LeBlanc wrote this letter six years after the Stollery dam failure that was responsible for radium 226 contamination in the Serpent River watershed, as well as the unnamed spills at Stanrock and Panel. But the reality was that in the 1970s almost no direct action was forthcoming.

Nevertheless, river contamination continued to pose a hazard to daily living on the reserve. In 1976, Health and Welfare Canada finally sent a letter to Chief Loreena Lewis explicitly advising that residents not drink water from the river: "According to the latest studies by the Provincial government, radioactive contamination of the Serpent River is above acceptable levels for drinking water standards. If any of the Serpent River Band members are obtaining drinking water from this source, *they should stop immediately.*"[100] However, this warning letter was written a full twelve years after the 1964 report on water contamination was first released and at least fourteen years after the OWRC first learned of the problem.

By the end of 1976 there had been some discussion among provincial and federal government officials as to the safety of fish consumption for reserve residents. By then, a decade had passed since initial fears of threats to tourism kept potential health risks from the public eye. There were several meetings to address health and environmental concerns.

Bruce Rawson, deputy minister of Health and Welfare Canada, wrote to Everett Biggs, deputy minister of the Environment for Ontario, to discuss the outcome of a meeting of representatives of both levels of government, as well as community leadership. It was agreed that further monitoring and analysis of the river system and wells would be undertaken, as well as a study of reserve residents' eating habits, especially in regard to fish. Interestingly enough, this meeting also included a demand for a solution to the acid plant contamination,[101] as it was most likely seen as a related concern to community health. But while governments continued to meet with various stakeholders, dams failed, and spillage occurred in the Serpent River system, and the studies continued. The 1976 status report was optimistic in its observation that "levels of radioactivity as reflected by radium (Ra-226) showed a significant decrease between 1970 and 1975," but continued more cautiously, "overall Ra-226 activity in the system as measured near the river mouth remained slightly above the permissible level for public surface waters."[102] The low pH as a result of leakage from contaminated lakes was still a significant concern:

> accessory data collected on lakes in the basin during 1975 indicate that the pH depression problem is much more severe in some lakes in the watershed including Pecors, Quirke, McCarthy, and Whiskey, than indicated by WQM data (stream stations). The low, continuously declining pH of these lakes is evidence of a serious ongoing problem – likely a consequence of the oxidation of sulphides present in the tailings wastes and/or the relatively long residence time of waters in the basin.[103]

As the report made clear, the low pH in several lakes within the Serpent River watershed was directly connected to mining operations and older abandoned mine sites. The study's summary concludes:

> it appears that in general, significant reductions in Ra-226 levels have occurred throughout the system and lesser decreases in concentrations of ammonia, TDS [dissolved solids] and sulphate were recorded at sites not affected by active operations. Downstream of mining and milling activity, high loadings of ammonia, TDS and sulphate continued … Drainage from the abandoned tailings area of Stanrock and Can-Met uranium mines appears to be the major contributor to radioactive contamination and pH depression in the basin while the greatest elevation of ammonia, TDS and sulphate occurs below the presently active mining and milling operations.[104]

Although Ra-226 decreased in some lakes over a five-year period, the system as a whole was still under threat from further leakage. In a letter that accompanied the 1976 *Status Report: Water Pollution in the Serpent River Basin*, R.E. Moore, Northeastern Regional Director of the Ontario Ministry of the Environment, identified the primary source of pollution for the Serpent River basin: "the major contributor to radioactive contamination and pH depression in the basin appears to be drainage from the abandoned tailings area of Stanrock and Can-Met uranium mines. The greatest elevations of ammonia, total dissolved solids and sulphate were found below presently active mining and milling operations."[105] Since those mines were still in operation, there was little hope that the situation could be improved upon. Local residents, tourists, and the Anishinaabek still depended upon the water for consumption as well as for fish and game.

A meeting was held in Toronto on 17 November 1976 to discuss the Serpent River First Nation's concerns about mining and radioactive pollution. Representatives from the Ministries of Health, Natural Resources, and the Environment, as well as the federal Departments of Indian Affairs and the Environment attended and one of the main concerns was the effect this pollution had, not just for people drawing water directly from the river, but also those who had wells nearby: "it is thought that the source of water for these wells could be the river and that there was a possibility of radiological contamination. The levels in the river for radium-226 range from 3 to 7 pc/l."[106] The concern was due not only to the wells' proximity to the river, but also to the fact that many of them were old, "poorly constructed, and ... susceptible to contamination by surface drainage." There were plans to undertake a sample study of fish in the river, and while ten fish had already been sent for radiological testing,[107] it was hoped that there could be more caught and handed over to officials in the autumn: "an attempt was to be made to obtain more fish this fall from the natives, if they were still fishing. However, it was determined that there is no collection going on this fall and that the collection will have to be done next spring."[108] It is not known why this was the case.

The representatives at the Toronto meeting also discussed an update on the state of the acid plant wreckage that continued to be a source of concern for SRFN: "Environment Canada is still looking into the Cutler C.I.L. acid plant and will take appropriate action on problems which have been created through leachate from a liquid storage lagoon. It will advise Regional MOE [Ministry of Environment] of developments in the investigation."[109] This meeting took place in 1976, but it would be twelve years before the situation would be addressed, and then only as a result of agency and political force of Serpent River First Nation leadership and community members.

Note that no one from the community had been invited to this meeting, even though its concerns were deeply felt locally, and it had voiced them at a previous meeting: "The meeting was called to deal with the concerns expressed at a recent meeting with Mr. Kerr and Mr. Biggs, which was attended by several interest groups, including the Serpent River native community and its advisors. Concern had been particularly expressed about the potential for radiological contamination in private wells and fish."[110] Frustratingly, the minutes did not identify those advisors specifically or where and when exactly that particular meeting occurred. Even in cases where there was community representation, it was listed in these minutes as an "interest group," rather than a First Nation that was facing a profound problem.

The representative from the federal Health and Welfare Department had also declined the invitation to the meeting, even though representatives were invited.[111] With only one representative from the Department of Indian and Northern Affairs, and only cursory contact with the Department of Health and Welfare, it is difficult to ascertain the effectiveness of such a meeting, particularly in the absence of any kind of representation from SRFN itself. While the community had to deal first-hand with the decline in resources, and, thus, its traditional pursuits, it continued to be excluded from many of the discussions that involved not only river pollution, but, also by extension, community health and well-being. This would change drastically by the end of the decade as community leaders demanded to be active participants in the discussions that concerned them most.

The damage to the Serpent's home had been an ongoing community issue, and along with the Cutler Acid Site, characterized the Indigenous-settler relationship along the North Shore. While it was not only Serpent River First Nation community members that were affected by uranium production, they were stewards of the watershed for centuries before the establishment of the Elliot Lake townsite. Once uranium production began, that relationship with the land and water changed profoundly, and SRFN was excluded from the dialogue surrounding the vitality of the river. The values inherent in traditional Anishinaabe relationships with the land and water were affected just as the river itself underwent rapid change in the mid-twentieth century. As resources diminished and were compromised, so too were the traditional ways in which the community interacted with the land. While tourists were simply warned not to visit, there was little concern for the traditional lifestyle of the Indigenous inhabitants of the area who had a more holistic and complete reliance on the land and water. For several decades, the Serpent River First Nation was given only partial information about the health of the river system, and attention was only paid to SRFN's concerns ten years after the initial story surfaced in 1964. Report after report described the need for departments at different levels to cooperate in the management of the water system upon which the community had been dependent since time immemorial. But it would only be a few years before rumours of the expansion of the uranium mines at Elliot Lake would present yet another level of urgency and contention. The next chapter discusses SRFN's continuous struggles to have a loud voice in these discussions.

Chapter Six

"Ooh yes, we all went up to Elliot to protest": Resilience and Resistance at Serpent River First Nation

I remember being at Indian Affairs office in Toronto at the regional office and pounding my fist on the table with the people from Indian Affairs trying to get them to understand how determined we were that there was a problem and that it was their problem, not ours.[1]

– Peter Johnston

In the summer of 1985, the *Toronto Star*'s investigative reporter Olivia Ward "broke" the story about pollution on the Serpent River First Nation to an unaware Canadian settler public. The effects of the acid plant on reserve land were said to have created a "hell on earth" in which environmental degradation had left a legacy of serious health effects for reserve residents.[2] A few days later, the paper's editorial board demanded to know how such a thing could happen only a few hundred kilometres north of Toronto. "How did this happen?" they asked. "Thirty years ago the people of Serpent River thought Ottawa was doing them a favour by allowing Noranda Mines Ltd. to build a plant on their reserve that would produce sulphuric acid for use in uranium mines – and generate jobs for the Indians. But when the plant was closed some years later, Noranda and the company that followed it, Cutler Acid Ltd., a subsidiary of Canadian Industries Ltd. (CIL), didn't clean up after themselves ... Since then, there has been nothing but stalling and government-corporate buck passing ... One wonders whether it would have been cleaned up long ago had it been anywhere but an Indian reservation."[3] By the 1980s, the Canadian public was increasingly being confronted by environmental issues as well as the physical legacy of colonialism in First Nations communities. Despite front-page media coverage – which came and went with the news cycle – it fell to community members themselves to seek redress for past wrongs and reclaim their traditional relationship with the land.

This chapter examines how members of the Serpent River First Nation protested proposed increases in mining production, sought to protect river resources, and strove to force an adequate reclamation process for the land lost to the Cutler Acid Plant. It argues that these efforts throughout the 1970s and 1980s reflect a significant shift not just in Serpent River First Nation leadership, but also in Indigenous communities across the country. This shift toward lobbying and activism on the part of community members took place at a time when local Indigenous communities were beginning to work together with national and provincial First Nations organizations such as the National Indian Brotherhood and the Ontario Union of Indians.[4] It also occurred within a larger national context in which environmental concerns in Canada were growing among the settler population. At the same time, DIA was increasingly withdrawing from direct intervention in reserve life and governance, and community leaders were demanding increased control over First Nation affairs. It was the confluence of these external and internal factors that set the stage for this new phase of the colonial relationship. Thus, the clean-up and compensation for the damage to the community was the result of the work of the First Nation itself. It represented as much a reclamation of traditional stewardship roles as it did a political and environmental victory.

By the late-1970s, uranium was again projected to be a major energy source, according to the World Energy Conference of that year.[5] Alistair Gillespie, minister of energy, mines and resources stated, "we must set aside our own reserves and maintain a 'Canada first policy.'"[6] A secret international uranium cartel was formed among Canada, Australia, South Africa, France, and Britain to "control the world price and supply of uranium through a complex scheme of price fixing, bid-rigging, and the allocation of markets."[7] Nuclear power was seen as the cure for a global energy crisis that was fuelling inflation and the cost of living.[8] In the case of Elliot Lake, this good news came hot on the heels of a renewed contract with Ontario Hydro, signed in 1976.[9] Ontario Hydro's decision to buy uranium for nuclear power rather than enter the mining business itself caused discussion and controversy, as the contract was worth $7.3 billion.[10]

The late 1970s was a hopeful time for the settlers living in the Elliot Lake region as economic expansion seemed poised to begin anew. The contracts with Hydro appeared imminent, and local news outlets reported that Rio Algom and Denison were each planning to increase production and hire more workers. Rio Algom's net earnings alone increased by more than 100 per cent in the first quarter of 1977, thanks to an increase in the export price for uranium.[11] According to George R. Albino, President and CEO of Rio Algom Ltd., "the expansion at Elliot Lake is going well and a number of programs are under way."[12] Not only could it increase production of its previously developed mines, but it could also expand their mineral reserves. This in turn led to stimulating discussion about how and when the town was going to expand to reflect the projected population increase. The mining companies started housing construction projects in 1976 and even embarked on a joint recruitment process.[13] In its year-in-review edition, the *Standard* ran a headline which reflected the community's confident anticipation of both renewed industrial expansion and social revitalization: "1976 – a very good year."[14] It was like 1955 all over again – almost.

By the mid-1970s, government officials were acutely aware of the potential hazards of unbridled economic expansion in relatively isolated areas of the province that remained dependent on a boom-bust resource economy. Any expansion of uranium mining, it was feared, might worsen the environmental problems that had plagued the tourism and recreation industries when the boom went bust in 1962.[15] It was important that any growth had a minimal environmental impact, which would require careful planning and the approval of the Ontario Environmental Assessment Board (EAB). The EAB would hold several hearings and issue a report before any expansion began.[16]

The EAB began its hearings in November 1976 and invited submissions from local stakeholders and interested third parties at several meetings held over the next few months. Most of the presentations and questions surrounding the potential for Elliot Lake's expansion centred on how expansion would impact the social, economic, and political structure of the municipality and local economy. Various stakeholders were included: the town council, mining companies, the United Steelworkers of America (the union representing employees at all mines in the area), the Province of Ontario, the Town of Blind River, St. Joseph's General Hospital, the local school boards, and, at their own insistence, members of SRFN. As revealed in the board's interim report, *The Expansion of the Uranium Mines in the Elliot Lake area: Interim Report Community Assessment*, issued in March 1979, the concerns of most stakeholders and board members centred on the long-term sustainability of economic growth and the need for economic expansion:

> The Board recognizes that the expansion of a community to the size that Elliot Lake is expected to be (a two to three-fold expansion) may be one of the most significant aspects of the expansion of the uranium mines. If

one looks beyond the life of the mines as presently envisioned, serious questions are raised as to what will ultimately happen to this community. While the closing down of the physical facilities of the mines may be achieved with minimal effort, the past indicates that the closing of a community of the size which Elliot Lake expects to become can present substantial problems.

Because of its dependence on ore reserves and market conditions, the uranium mining industry has tended to be cyclical. The Town of Elliot Lake, in its short history, has already experienced one drastic decline resulting from the closing down of most of the uranium mines in the area during the 1950s and 1960s. The evidence before the Board indicated that under the present contractual commitments, the life of the mines and consequently the life of the Town, unless other primary or secondary industries can be attracted to Elliot Lake, is expected to be between thirty and forty years. The Board hopes that the various parties including the Province of Ontario, the Town of Elliot Lake and the mining companies as well as the United Steelworkers of America will co-operate to ensure that all avenues are explored in the attempt to define alternative strategies for Elliot Lake to minimize its long term dependence on the uranium industry.[17]

In the end, the board hoped that temporary expansion of the mines would fund long-term investment in more economically sustainable and stable industries and that the various stakeholders from the settler community might work together to achieve that goal.[18] While the report briefly mentioned water quality and tailings disposal, it was only in the context of municipal infrastructure.[19] The vast majority of the fifty-page interim report dealt with social services such as education, social workers, and health care, while housing,[20] water, and sewage were discussed in ways that were consistent with any municipal planning program.[21] Tourism operators were the only settler group at the meeting to express concerns about how expansion might hurt their businesses by damaging the environment.

Serpent River First Nation leaders and members voiced their concerns the loudest, and as Betty Jacobs shared, "we all went up to Elliot to protest."[22] They were determined to prevent a repeat of the environmental devastation that had resulted from the last uranium boom. To the community's Elders, many of whom held leadership positions at the time, it was much more than an investigation into the feasibility of municipal expansion. Rather, it was their opportunity to voice objections to mining, as well as showcase their grievances before an increasingly sympathetic audience in the context of the growth of environmentalism in public discourse. This was also a time when the expansion of resource projects was affecting other First Nations communities throughout the country.[23] But First Nations were also becoming increasingly vocal in their opposition to such projects.

The Mackenzie Valley Pipeline Inquiry and Thomas Berger's subsequent 1977 report is one example of Indigenous peoples and concerned Canadians being at odds with the settler resource industry.[24] It marked one of the first times that First Nations peoples were invited to give their testimony in the preparation of a comprehensive study of the social and environmental impacts of resource development in the North.[25] Significantly, it was also one of the first times that the social and environmental costs of an oil and gas project were considered "before and not after the fact."[26] And it was also one of the first times that First Nations were successful in speaking over the voices of corporations and government. One geographer described Berger's willingness to include and acknowledge Indigenous stakeholders concerned with stewardship over the land: "Having redressed the characteristic imbalance between northern communities and southern entrepreneurs and governments, the Inquiry established a foundation for participation in which northerners' traditional ecological knowledge was recognized and became influential."[27] The Berger Inquiry's ultimate finding – that although the pipeline was feasible, there should be a decade-long moratorium on development until Indigenous claims could be addressed – was one of the first of its kind in acknowledging Indigenous land rights, and it came less than a decade after the *Calder* decision which acknowledged the existence of Indigenous title to land.[28]

The 1970s were a time of struggle for many Indigenous groups. The fight of the James Bay Cree in the 1970s, and the first modern treaty that ensued in 1975 in the form of the James Bay and Northern Quebec Agreement, is another example of First Nations protecting their rights in the face of resource development and related environmental threats.[29] The notion that a lawsuit brought forth by the Cree could result in an injunction against development was confounding to both the companies involved and the province itself. Nevertheless, 150 witnesses and an injunction later, the need for an agreement that could satisfy all parties involved – not the least of which was the James Bay Cree – was readily apparent. It ensured that development did not move forward without consultation or compensation, as Quebec Premier Robert Bourassa and his government had originally anticipated.[30]

In the post-war period, the role of DIA was changing. As Hugh Shewell has argued, "the post-war era introduced a new, intensified form of state subjugation ... Indians now required social adjustment, modern education, and opportunity."[31] DIA abandoned the term "assimilation" and replaced it with "integration." Not only did this new era in Indian Administration provide a reason for the acid plant's establishment in the first place, but it also helped to explain DIA's gradual retreat from the day-to-day administration of communities and switch to focusing on policy-related issues. Indian Affairs phased out the Indian agent model in the 1960s, but regional offices remained.[32] Policy proposals such as the Hawthorn Report[33] and the White Paper[34] advocated change in the 1960s, albeit very different types of change, respectively, from the top down.

Consequently, during this critical period of change, First Nations intensified their assertions of Indigenous rights. However, from the perspective of both government and mining officials at Elliot Lake (as well as the public), the area of the North Shore of Lake Huron had been ceded through the Robinson-Huron Treaty of 1850 and therefore Indigenous rights in the area were given minimal importance.[35] In the case of development at Elliot Lake, there were few settlers who understood the Anishinaabe view of the treaty and their desire and cultural obligation to continue to pursue a stewardship role not just within reserve boundaries, but for the Serpent River watershed as a whole. Furthermore, in both the James Bay and Mackenzie River areas, inquiries or court cases were undertaken at a crucial stage *before* large-scale resource development projects began. However, in Elliot Lake, the EAB was meeting to determine how an expansion to pre-existing mining operations would affect the surrounding communities and the mining town itself. The EAB's purpose was decidedly not to debate the merits of the uranium industry and its environmental effects, but instead to discuss how best to manage an inevitable expansion of those industries from an economic point of view. The process emphasized the economic concerns of a growing municipality over the environmental impact on First Nations land use.

The significance of the EAB hearings for Elliot Lake's expansion lies in how SRFN leaders and community members used the public forum to express their grievances and concerns. It was the first time that the community was able to participate in discussions with the wider settler community about its role in the region, independent of the interference of DIA. While the James Bay Cree and people of the Mackenzie Valley fought to stop developments that would damage their lands as SRFN had been damaged decades before, Serpent River First Nation community members now fought to have their voices heard in the debate.

Peter Johnston, who was Chief at the time, remembered the animosity and controversy surrounding the discussions about reopening the mines. "I often think about those days," he said.

> So when the uranium mines ... finally got contracts and it looked like the future of uranium was going up [in the late 1970s] and they were talking about expansion and doubling the capacity, the productivity of the mines, I mean right away we decided as a band that we had to do whatever we could to prevent that from happening. And so we engaged what was at the time, or what is now, AFN [Assembly of First Nations] and we asked them for their expertise and they sent an environmentalist that was working with them at the time. And ... we put together a paper that we presented at the Environmental Assessment Board.[36]

The paper argued against the expansion of the mines, citing the various health and environmental impacts of previous expansion. But community members did not limit themselves to submitting reports. They were determined to make their presence felt at every meeting which the board held, a fact that the EAB eventually noted in its report.[37]

Two of the advocates representing the Serpent River First Nation at these meetings were Loreena Lewis, the community's first female Chief, and Gertrude Lewis, a Councillor. When asked how their presentations were received by the board and the people there representing different stakeholders, Gertrude Lewis responded, "Well, I don't think they were received too well by some of the people." She went on to clarify that some of the responses characterized SRFN representatives as troublemakers: "You could see them looking at us when we walked in, 'oh here they come again.'"[38] This characterization of SRFN spokespersons as troublemakers is something that was echoed in an older interview in 1999 with Loreena Lewis. She simply stated that while "some people in Elliot Lake were supportive ... some were not." Gertrude agreed: "For Elliot Lake the mine expansion was a boost for them. They built new homes. For us it was being cautious and asking them not to expand until they could find a safe way to get rid of the waste. They were thinking more of the benefits of expansion."[39] Both Loreena and Gertrude were acutely aware of the controversy their work had in the area dominated by mining interests, both in terms of the companies and the people dependent on the incomes mining operations provided. Neither woman was unsympathetic to the desire for expansion, and, in fact, they understood how it echoed SRFN's initial desire for the jobs offered by the acid plant decades before: "It was probably the same way we felt about the plant when it came here, that there would be jobs and benefits."[40] However, the toxic legacy of the acid plant, as well as the threats to the river system, ensured that both women, however understanding of the impetus behind expansion and the economic benefits it would bring to the area, wanted the mining companies to proceed with caution. First and foremost, they wanted reassurances that rapid expansion would not further threaten the environment before any steps were taken in that direction.

It is also important to note that the leaders responding to how they were seen by people outside their community were women. As women, they happened to be political leaders in their communities, but their sense of responsibility and leadership stemmed from their roles as mothers and defenders when it came to both the community and the land. This was most likely lost on the members of the male-dominated panel, not to mention the mining and government representatives who were predominately male as well. The sight of several Anishinaabe *kwewag* (women) – Betty Jacobs was present at many of the meetings as well – in equal (if not dominant) speaking roles to the board, was probably an unusual sight to a panel comprised of settlers. They were there as leaders, at the table along with the men of their community, speaking to the board and the broader public.[41]

Both women were aware of how their presence confused settlers at the hearings, and their identical last names did not help matters. In the earlier interview, Gertrude recalled at an incident involving mistaken identity:

> After Loreena's term was over I went to another hearing. There was a lawyer there from Rio Algom. He was confused and kept saying "isn't that right, Chief Lewis?" He would address me as Chief Lewis and I would not answer him. He kept saying Chief. I kept saying nothing. Peter Johnston was the chief at the time. Peter said, "It's Chief Johnston. We only have one chief." That's how much they paid attention to us.[42]

Although both women share the last name Lewis, they were not physically similar, nor had Gertrude ever served as Chief of the community. Despite the fact that the Chief of a community in the area would be a stakeholder in the discussion, the lawyer of one of the two mining companies seeking permission to expand did not seem to know which woman he was dealing with. Gertrude's act of resistance in refusing to respond would have most likely been unsettling and embarrassing for the lawyer, mining company representatives, and members of the board: to be ignored by a woman whom they thought they were addressing directly in such a formal environment would have made the exchange uncomfortable. Her continued refusal to respond, even when she was repeatedly addressed by this lawyer, made it clear that she was not to be mistaken for someone entirely different. Her silence, although seemingly passive, was in fact an aggressive assertion of her identity and refusal to be mistaken as another woman from the community. Although Gertrude was a community representative, she was not the sitting Chief, and this was an important political, cultural, and respectful distinction she required the lawyer and other stakeholders to make.

The community members' attendance and presentations at the hearings were important forces in advancing a collective politically active identity. There was a sense of loneliness in being one of the only groups questioning expansion in a settler society, but it was a message that the community as a whole needed to appreciate given the past struggles of its Elders. "But we were ... one voice, the *only* voice that was against this expansion of the mines," said Johnston. "Everybody else, the City of Elliot Lake, the Chamber of Commerce, anybody that was anybody was all in favour, and we were the lone little voices in the wilderness trying to make a statement. It was a lonely – there were lonely, lonely fights, I'll tell you. People don't realize, especially our community, how much we fought and how much energy we expended trying to right what we considered wrongs."[43] When one side was not considered to be an equal player – despite the historical understanding of the treaty that allowed resource extraction to occur in the first place – any discussion about how to move forward also became uneven. Not only did community leaders assert themselves in a situation that automatically positioned them as inferior, they were also fighting an immensely unpopular battle from a regional point of view.

In the mid-1950s, when the mines were first opening and DIA proposed building an acid plant on reserve land, community members were forced to choose between jobs and their traditional relationships with the land. At the same time, that choice was largely made for them by DIA officials who saw the plant as a tool through which Anishinaabek would be made less dependent on the government and traditional lifestyles. In that situation, it was not so much a choice as an eventuality as forums for discussion and dissent were minimized. When allowed to speak and to choose how to balance personal economic interests with traditional obligations, Serpent River First Nation members called for caution. It is important to note that many of the men on the reserve worked at one time or another in a job somehow connected to the uranium industry.[44] By the late 1970s the wage economy had become the norm in the community as the local environment could no longer sustain traditional economic activities.[45] Community opposition to the expansion of the mines was, in some ways, contradictory – but only if viewed solely through an economic lens. For Serpent River First Nation members, when allowed to speak for themselves and in the absence of economic pressures, the importance of the land had to be balanced with economic activity. While the teaching that any decision made has to consider the well-being of future generations was commonly understood in the community, it was a point of view that appeared to clash loudly with uranium development.[46]

At the same time, community leaders found an unlikely ally in the local Steelworkers leadership. Some settlers also understood the devastating impact of unbridled expansion by the late 1970s. Homer Seguin, the union's local steward, voiced his concern: "We have to be completely reassured even if we have to be oversafe [sic] ... while we're in favour of expansion, it has to be based on giving the most attention to the environmental care of the water and air."[47] He also worried that expansion at the rate that was expected could be detrimental to the work that had already been completed: "A big boom could erode all the advances we've made."[48] Seguin and the Steelworkers had previously called upon the government to improve its practices to prevent water pollution, particularly in lakes surrounding the town. Their concerns stemmed from a 1976 Ontario Ministry of the Environment status report titled *Water Pollution in the Serpent River Basin* which demonstrated that the quality of local waters had only slightly improved during the period of limited mining operations between 1970 and 1975 – something which flew in the face of previous expectations.[49] "What will happen when the mines expand?" asked Seguin, "The Steelworkers do not want townspeople to pay for prosperity with their health."[50]

The environmental concerns expressed by the Steelworkers under Seguin's leadership were symbolic of a growing Canadian awareness of environmental issues. From the publication of Rachel Carson's *Silent Spring* in 1962[51] to the creation of Greenpeace in 1970,[52] the environmental movement in North America was becoming increasingly important. The founding of Earth Day in 1970 in the United States marked a growing environmental awareness, one that Pollution Probe, a group of University of Toronto students, had already introduced in Canada in their staging of a mock funeral for the Don River in 1969.[53] The environmental movement has grown since the late 1960s from a leftist fringe concern to a widespread movement in Canada, especially since the first Earth Day Canada was celebrated in 1990.[54]

In fact, when one consults newspaper letters to the editor, it is clear that the public had a growing interest in clean waterways. Readers responded with concerned interest to the *Globe and Mail*'s investigative journalism by Barrie Zwicker about the pollution at Elliot Lake and Bancroft. As J.W. Black of Sudbury wrote: "Kindly accept our thanks for your articles regarding radium-tailings seepage into the waters of the Serpent River and the Elliott [sic] Lake area ... Fish life has been affected in several of the lakes on this river system, owing to the pollution. One wonders at the Government's lack of interest in this matter. Thank the Great Manitou that we have newspapers such as the Globe and Mail."[55] It is not known whether this reader was himself Anishinaabe or if he appropriated this term for the Creator, but he was clearly concerned for the ecological integrity of the river system, on which his cottage was located.

Other letters of concern were written directly to the Ontario Water Resources Commission. One concerned taxpayer felt compelled to write a letter after the 1964 Zwicker article was published. "Public concern has been aroused recently by the disclosure that much of the water in the Elliot Lake and Bancroft districts have been contaminated," the individual noted. "As an interested tax-payer I would like to know to what extent these two areas have been contaminated and what is being done to decontaminate them. I would also like to know at what level radio-activity in water is considered dangerous and how it is detected." He went on to ask, "how are mine operators able to get away with this for so long without detection?"[56] The public outcry, evident in both government correspondence records and newspaper editorial sections, indicates a growing public concern for environmental issues, particularly water safety.

At the time of the Board hearings in the late 1970s, it was already well known that uranium had taken its toll on lakes surrounding the town. Nevertheless, visiting the sites of pollution could still elicit a shock. "When they were talking about the expansion, because we toured one of the sites and oh, it was terrible there," Gertrude Lewis recalled.

And the smell, you know. And there was a little lake there and it was a dead lake. At that that time there were ten dead lakes around Elliot Lake. That was in the paper ... And so that was one of the dead lakes that we were at. And the animals would be piled so high around that lake, all dead from this lake. Probably drinking a little bit of water that was in it. And ... the Ministry of Environment noticed that there was no sprinklers system working, like the mine should have had a sprinkler system working. And they didn't. And when we got there with the Ministry of Environment, boy did they ever run around to turn on the sprinkler system. And, and then we had noticed all those dead animals around there, rabbits, all kinds of dead animals. But we couldn't see them all because they were all around the back of the lake. And we told them, the Ministry of Environment that. We were traveling with [the Ministry of the Environment], by the way ... We were in their car. Which didn't look good, I guess to the mines. And they got their men to pick up some of those dead animals. They wanted to take them back for analysis. We never got the results of that. And the head fellow from the [Ministry of] Environment that was traveling with them that day. He never came back here again. That was his last meeting ... And he was never allowed to come back again. Next time they had another meeting up there, it was a young fellow. And oh was he ever miserable with us. He sure didn't want to talk to us at all. And they didn't even want to take us on that tour. We toured the mines that time, and they didn't want to take us. They said we couldn't go. And it ... was the head of the union in Elliot Lake and he said, "no, let the women go." So they allowed us to go.[57]

The ecological and health consequences of mining and waste disposal in the area were obvious.[58] Negative publicity was something that all pro-expansion parties were attempting to avoid, and literally chauffeuring political leaders from the nearby First Nations community to tour the dead lakes was starkly at odds with the overall aim to facilitate expansion. Nevertheless, the women were able to participate, ask questions, and report back to their community about the extent of the damage they witnessed. That said, the officials running the tour seemed ill at ease with their presence: "It seemed that they were kind of afraid of us because we were noticing everything," Gertrude Lewis recalled.[59]

During the hearings, the Serpent River First Nation leadership also invited representatives from the EAB to visit the community to see for themselves the destruction that had been left by uranium mining and the acid plant even after the first clean-up attempt had been carried out a decade before. The community wanted people to see the extent of the damage and the basis of some of their concerns. It was not only the possibility of river contamination that was an issue: children were still left to play in the contaminated bay and around the rubble of the acid plant. Once the panel members toured the area, they were invited to the community centre for a meal, but they refused all attempts to offer them beverages: "We brought those guys down here from the panel, to see the destruction around here, and we had a lunch for them at the band hall. They wouldn't drink tea or coffee!" Lewis recalled.[60] When further attempts to offer hospitality were met with hesitation, SRFN members reassured their guests that it was "not water from Elliot Lake, you know!"[61] The effort to host a meal was consistent with social expectations in the Anishinaabe community, and the humour is undercut by the board members' awareness of the issues surrounding water and ground pollution as a result of mining. In this situation, SRFN hosts, while still conforming to Anishinaabe social protocols, forced the EAB representatives to acknowledge the extent of contamination when confronted with their own health choices: they could leave and drink water elsewhere while SRFN community members had no such luxury.

In their interim report, the EAB expressed the belief that the river system would actually recover itself over time, but this too was contradicted by events at the time.[62] In fact, there had actually been another dam spill or overflow at Rio Algom during the course of the board's hearings! When asked for comment on a tailings spill on 28 March 1978, a Rio Algom official provided the following: "Quite honestly, this concerns us as much as it does anyone. The spills cost us money and we don't need the publicity that goes with it."[63] It was not, apparently, the danger posed to the river system that was seen as a main problem, but rather the cost of cleaning it up and the ensuing bad press. Another spill at Johnston Creek caused concern because the land between the creek and the Serpent River was swampy, but the potential dangers of a hundred thousand gallons of tailings waste were dispelled by Jerry LaHave, an official from the Ministry of the Environment:

The extent of the spill and any possible contamination to the Serpent River is so small that even if some radioactivity found its way into it (the river) you couldn't even measure it that far down ... we're looking at two things right now. In the short term, we're looking for ways to control the Radium 226 that has dissolved in the water. Our second concern, the long term problem, is that we get all the solid waste because if we don't, there's a chance it could gradually dissolve in the water.[64]

Spills such as this concerned the community. Not only had community members described the effects of the acid plant on reserve land, they had ongoing reasons to be concerned about mining activities at Elliot Lake.

This was the point of view expressed in the Environmental Assessment Board's final report, dated May 1979, which recorded the grievances brought forth by the Serpent River First Nation. While the board acknowledged the community's concerns, they found that there was little they could do for the community:

The Board heard a plea from the Band that the expansion be delayed until compensation for past environmental insults is received. The Board does not have the power to grant such a request. However the Board has reviewed the existing situation in the watershed, has noted the many upstream lakes which have been seriously damaged through contamination from the mines and has considered the corrective measures that are proposed. Based on this review it is the Board's opinion that the recovery of the watershed is probable with the expansion.[65]

The notion that the expansion of such mining operations would have a positive effect on the watershed simply did not make sense, but rather highlighted the fact that the EAB had little interest in actually interrogating the companies' practices and responsibility, or in evaluating the real environmental concerns that expansion would bring. From the board's perspective, river contamination and the reclamation of the Cutler Acid Site were not the responsibility of mining companies. The EAB believed that DIA should bear the brunt of responsibility for the reclamation of the acid plant land and for water concerns:

It is the Board's understanding that the Department of Indian Affairs has neither indicated a willingness to agree to the arrangement nor proposed a suitable alternative. In the Board's opinion too much time has elapsed since the plant close-out without action. On behalf of the Indian Band, the Board suggests it is incumbent on the Department of Indian Affairs to seek an expeditious solution to the Band's concerns. Early in the hearing, the Board invited the Department to participate. Unfortunately this invitation was not acted upon.[66]

It is unclear why DIA did not attend the meetings, but it could be because of the jurisdictional divide between federal and provincial responsibilities, and the fact that the EAB was meeting about natural resources rather than Indigenous issues. While this non-interventionist stance allowed SRFN community members to voice their own concerns, it also minimized federal responsibility for the environmental devastation which had been allowed to happen while DIA was still operating under the aegis of its fiduciary responsibility to the Anishinaabek. In this respect, the EAB listened to SRFN community members' voices, arguing that DIA had a responsibility to clean up its own messes: "In the Board's opinion, ... those who are responsible for the administration of the rights of the Band and the protection of the reserve should review the Band's concerns with all possible haste. Indeed the problems have been left without resolution for too long."[67] In this sense, SRFN community members were successful in bringing DIA's lack of action into the public record and making members of the public and regulatory bodies aware of their grievances.

But when it came to the issue of expansion in general, the EAB's final report supported a measured degree of expansion. "Based on the evidence heard and received in written form," it read:

> the Board is of the general opinion that the technology exists to carry out the expansion in an environmentally acceptable manner in the short term ... Based on the evidence of these experts, the Board is of the opinion that this expansion can be carried out in such a way as to ensure that the people of the area will not receive unacceptable exposures or be exposed to unacceptable risks. With respect to the long term, present day knowledge is, to a large extent, limited. It is evident to the Board that considerable effort and time is required before solutions to the long term aspects of waste management can be found.[68]

But after all of the effort that went into the hearings, the whole debate proved to be moot. While some modest expansion of housing and mining activity took place, Elliot Lake's population in this period never rose to the anticipated 27,000 people.[69] This was partly due to the fluctuation of uranium prices on the world commodities market but also the fact that during the 1980s, Saskatchewan-mined uranium seized domestic market share, eventually comprising 48.3 per cent of the Canadian uranium market by the end of the decade.[70] As a direct result, in 1991, Ontario Hydro sought to renegotiate its contract with the Elliot Lake companies, arguing that uranium from Saskatchewan was higher-grade and therefore more cost-effective.[71] But for SRFN, the decade truly did mark a new beginning. With the same spirit that underpinned their presentations to the EAB, SRFN leaders began to publicly demand that the pollution and its effects be cleaned up on their land. This led to a radicalization of community politics as leaders sought new and more forceful methods to assert their claims to compensation and restitution.

In the fall of 1979, approximately six months after the EAB issued its final report, the community began seeking external advice from academics and activists. If DIA was going to do little to help the community, then the community would help itself. The Institute for Environmental Studies at the University of Toronto conducted a study that was meant to ascertain what, if anything, could be done with the land upon which the acid plant once stood. The researchers surveyed the extent of the environmental damage and outlined some of the uses that would be safe for the community to develop on the site.[72] The report examined such land use possibilities for industry, recreation, housing, and nature parks, and ranked each possibility in terms of feasibility and the costs involved.[73] It reviewed reclamation possibilities and surveyed community members about their goals for the site. The researchers also highlighted the unusual skin rashes that reserve residents often exhibited after swimming in the bay.[74] They concluded it was "unlikely that from a description of the sores that the origin was in the swimmer's itch parasite ... the main outbreak may have [in fact] coincided with the breaking of the dam across the shoreline between the waste piles and the lake."[75]

While the cost and process of the clean-up was examined, Serpent River First Nation leadership also followed up the University of Toronto researchers' concerns, commissioning a professional study to quantify the human cost of the pollution to further support their claims.[76] Dr. Rosalie Bertell, a Grey Nun and a distinguished public health activist who had worked with United Nations projects around the world, began to study the health effects that the harsh sulphur had on residents of the area.[77] SRFN leadership had asked Bertell, a public health specialist at the Jesuit Centre for Social Faith and Justice and later founder and director of research at the International Institute of Concern for Public Health, to conduct a preliminary comparative health study between the Serpent River, Mississauga and Sagamok First Nations. Bertell designed a questionnaire which was, thanks to the help of two trained community members, "administered to most families living on the Serpent River Reserve."[78] In the early 1980s, she visited the site, along with co-investigator Dr. Michael Stogre, to speak with community members as well as health care staff; in addition, Stogre and Dr. Dermot McLaughlin provided medical context for community members' affidavits in which individuals voiced their health concerns.[79] Bertell and her team were interested in a community-based study that not only examined the health of male workers (either as plant or mine workers), but also the health of women and children in the community.

In two reports released in 1984 and 1985, Bertell's findings linked pollution on the reserve from uranium and the acid plant to severe long-term health problems among reserve members. Most significant was the unusual incidence of chronic and serious diseases in the community. In her first report titled the "Joint Health Report: Serpent River, Mississaug[a] and Spanish River [Sagamok] Reserves" released in January, 1984, the total percentage of residents reporting some type of disease was 50 per cent on the Serpent River First Nation, as compared to 45 per cent at Mississaug[a] and 39 per cent at Spanish River.[80] The report explains the reasons behind the discrepancy: "Conditions favouring health are not the same on the three reserves, with the Spanish River being most conducive to health. Since both males and females at Serpent River are reporting chronic diseases at a higher rate than at the other reserves, the problem(s) may be environmental. Generally males are reporting more chronic diseases than females, which may indicate differences related to occupation."[81] According to Bertell's study, the toxic effects of the acid plant compromised the overall health of the community.

The best empirical evidence of the health effects of the pollution was Bertell's examination of maternal and infant health. Bertell assessed reproductive patterns and drew links between the reserve's high-risk environment and her findings. The average number of pregnancies per couple was similar for each community: Serpent River had 5.7, Mississauga 4.1, and Spanish River [now Sagamok] 4.9.[82] However, Bertell found differences among the communities when examining the success rate of those pregnancies. Pregnancies on the Serpent River First Nation were approximately 6.2 times more likely to end in fetal death than on the Spanish River reserve, and approximately 4 times more likely to end in fetal death on the Mississauga reserve.[83] Bertell concluded that "just as chronic diseases were more frequent at Serpent River, so are pregnancies ending in fetal death … The loss of these pregnancies appears to be related to maternal ill health, some occupational exposures and perhaps environmental pollution."[84] The higher rate of fetal deaths among the residents of the Serpent River First Nation, in conjunction with the pattern of chronic illness in higher numbers than on neighbouring reserves, gave a strong indication that there was a pattern of health concerns attributable to the location of the Serpent River First Nation. The biggest difference between the Serpent River reserve and the other similar reserves in the area was the existence of the acid plant, which was a known source of environmental pollution.[85]

Bertell's second comparative study, which took place the following year, listed several health problems that were common among the male workers in the community and categorized them by men who worked in the acid plant, those who worked at the uranium mines at Elliot Lake, and those who were from other North Shore reserve communities and therefore had a lower degree of exposure. The study was based on a questionnaire sent to every household in the three communities, with 68 per cent of responses coming from the Serpent River reserve.[86] While the statistics are not conclusive, they nevertheless provide an indication about the plant's potential effects on the community. The data point to a higher incidence of sickness and disease on the Serpent River First Nation than in the neighbouring two communities. Bertell found that 14.3 per cent of acid plant workers suffered from chronic bronchitis, while 9.1 per cent of males in other occupations also reported the condition. Dr. Bertell reported that "sulphur, sulphuric acid, sulphur dioxide and hydrogen sulfide are all known respiratory irritants. Radon gas is associated with both non-cancerous and cancerous changes in respiratory tissues. Workers at the Print Shop located for the past 10 years on the former Cutler Acid Plant site complained of constant 'sniffles.'"[87] The respiratory problems indicated that exposure to the irritants described by Bertell were substantial and far-reaching within the community, regardless of the occupation of the male of the households.

Bertell's study also concluded that 16.2 per cent of males on the reserve who did not work at the acid plant (and were therefore classified as having medium exposure to emissions) reported eye problems, defined as blindness or poor eyesight.[88] This is in comparison to the 2.8 per cent of males from another reserve who did not work at the site (classified as having had low exposure).[89] Indeed, eye problems reported by reserve residents were so numerous that in 1974 the Algoma Health Unit requested special assistance in dealing with them.[90]

In addition to respiratory and eye problems, skin disorders were common among community residents, particularly among children who swam in Aird Bay on the North Shore of Lake Huron on the reserve near the acid site. According to the report, "As early as 1974 these rashes had been reported. Government officials at times discounted them as probably due to a parasite common on the North Shore which caused 'swimmer's itch.'"[91] The rashes, however, did not appear when children swam in other areas, and while one rash was characterized as "red blotches on arms and legs after swimming, which disappeared in an hour or an hour and a half," the other type included more serious "red spots with blisters."[92] Bertell reported that one child's condition was so difficult to diagnose that he/she was sent to Toronto for testing.

Bertell's report, which was undertaken with the cooperation of SRFN members, highlighted the disastrous consequences that uranium mining and the sulphuric acid plant had had on the community – in the type of quantifiable western terms which would be understood by government officials. In cooperating with external experts independent of DIA oversight, SRFN community members succeeded in not only drawing attention to their plight but also in obtaining the type of third-party outside advice that the community leadership had desired – but was denied – when the original acid plant lease was negotiated. The publication of these reports had its desired effect. In July 1985, just over a year after the first report was released, Olivia Ward of the *Toronto Star* broke an important story on the effects of the pollution on the Serpent River First Nation. The article recounted the community's troubled past with the acid plant, describing its acceptance so as to further employment in the late 1950s, its closure only a few years later, the destruction of the site in a Department of National Defence training exercise, and the unwillingness of any federal agency to assume responsibility for cleaning up the site – a process that was conservatively estimated to cost $1.5 million.[93] While DIA officials told the *Star* that they would "not back down on [their] responsibility for funding the proposed clean-up," they also acknowledged that the initiative and funding for an empirical study of the contamination and the cost estimate for the reclamation process came from Chief Earl Commanda.[94] When DIA officials arrived during Ward's visit to the community to talk to the Chief, he told the reporter that "Maybe we'll get something done, or maybe we'll just be one more group that gets together to talk."[95] He did not seem hopeful.

During the 1980s, DIA officials repeatedly expressed their desire to help the community while also falling back on their new policy of non-intervention in First Nation community affairs to minimize their obligation. To those involved in these discussions, a tremendous amount of frustration is evident, but so too is a real sense of determination and self-sufficiency. "We started putting pressure on the federal government for funding to do a proper clean-up," recalled Peter Johnston.

> And it must have taken us at least ten years of real hard [work] ... I remember being at Indian Affairs office in Toronto at the regional office and pounding my fist on the table with the people from Indian Affairs trying to get them to understand how determined we were that there was a problem and that it was their problem, not ours. But it was really, really hard. I mean, they were civil servants living far away from the problem. As long as it didn't affect their daily lives to the extent that it was affecting ours, it wasn't the problem as we saw it. And so it was a lot of real hard bargaining. We ended up going to using every means that we had available to us ... But it was, I'm telling you, I mean it drained us. I mean the amount of energy and time and money we spent just fighting to get the money to do the clean-up was just awful.[96]

Experience had taught community leaders that the government was not protecting their interests, and so they entered into their own negotiations. DIA was not their protector in this case: it was both the defendant and the organization that continued to block the community's goals.

As a result, community members grew weary of endless meetings and promises of studies. Serpent River First Nation leadership increasingly looked to harness public opinion to both draw attention to the problems on the reserve as well as to put pressure on the government to meet its demands for reclamation and compensation. In February 1986 Chief Commanda first threatened to block the Trans-Canada Highway, which runs through the community. "The band council passed a resolution in January stating if we don't get a meeting with the minister that the possibility of this type of action will exist," he told the Elliot Lake *Standard*, "We've talked about this type of action as a protest against the lack of response from Indian Affairs."[97] While Chief Commanda described the companies as well as the provincial Ministry of the Environment, federal bodies Environment Canada, and Health Canada as being willing to cooperate and support the clean-up, he blamed DIA for the delay: "Our own Indian Affairs ministry is where the thing gets bogged down." DIA had wanted to stall discussions and action in order to find out who was really responsible for the clean-up via the Department of Justice. He recalled the original involvement of DIA and laid the blame with the ministry: "They are in breach of trust. They broke our trust by allowing the plant to be built there."[98] Commanda was more explicit the following week: "I'm told a 24-hour blockage (of highway 17) would bring the uranium industry to its knees. In a lot of ways we could gain negative attention. You reach a point where you just don't care. We also have the CPR line running through the reserve and an Ontario Hydro line."[99] The community set a deadline for the end of May – the beginning of the tourist season.

Highway blockades organized by First Nations in response to colonial practices, now more familiar since the Oka Crisis,[100] were increasing in frequency in the 1980s. As Nicholas Blomley suggests, "the blockade in both its effects and meanings, is directed outwards; it is aimed at the dominant culture ... To the extent that the blockade speaks graphically of generations of friction, grievances, and lost opportunities, it deserves attention and analysis from whatever quarter."[101] A blockade is not simply a symbolic stance against government inaction, nor it is it only a physical representation of anger and impatience; a blockade is a direct stance against dominant culture and an assertion of Indigenous control.[102] In many cases, activists and leaders distribute pamphlets with information about the reasons for the protest and give press conferences, all in an effort to gain support from some members of the public while calling attention to official government oppression. The important function of blockades or protests generally is for First Nations to demonstrate their agency and press for change.

As Serpent River First Nation leaders renewed their efforts to get the government to address the acid plant clean-up, they had actually found a new ally in the *Standard*. Coverage of the acid plant and pollution at SRFN ebbed and flowed in tandem with the economic tides of the region. When economic expansion loomed on the horizon, environmental concerns were minimized. When the mining economy contracted, tourism and recreational land use became more important and so too did concerns about the acid plant eyesore on Highway 17 and the quality of the fishing in the area. As the uranium mining industry began to take a downward turn in the late 1980s, coverage in the local Elliot Lake newspaper began to favour Anishinaabe initiatives aimed at securing federal assistance in cleaning up the site. This included the community's threats to block the highway. The change in the *Standard*'s coverage between the 1950s and the 1980s is obvious. Both articles on the highway closures cited above described the community's concerns in sympathetic terms and noted that the report by the International Institute of Concern for Public Health was about to be released.[103] For a paper that had once described the plant as a means to move the reserve into the twentieth century economy, the plant had now become a concern to both communities. While this certainly reflected the changing economic situation in the region, it was also indicative of a larger shift in public support for both environmental concerns and Indigenous issues during the 1980s. In any case, in the local media the main actor and the driving force behind the clean-up efforts was clearly the Serpent River First Nation, not DIA.

In the spring of 1986, SRFN chose not to block the highway when federal officials offered to meet with the community. But by the end of the summer, little had been accomplished – it was more of the idle talk that Commanda had lamented about to Ward the previous year.[104] At the top of the community's immediate list of demands was the removal of 110,000 cubic metres of toxic waste from the site.[105] In a letter to Ontario Minister of the Environment James Bradley that was a follow-up to a 11 July meeting, Commanda reminded the province that its assistance was needed to "initiate high-level discussion" with Rio Algom so the waste could be managed at a site at one of its defunct mines, Pronto. Commanda was also looking for technical support with the processes required to reclaim toxic waste, and to think of alternate sites for waste disposal should Pronto not work out.[106] The letter has the following scrawled at the top with a telling description of what the response would be: "~~Send~~ Prepare letter for Minister low-key response and thanks."[107]

By the end of September, community leadership was growing increasingly impatient. Keith Lewis, the SRFN planner, told the press, "[q]uiet negotiation has brought us along to where are now [but] it's getting us nowhere and we're forced to consider other options."[108] These other options included blocking the highway and main East–West CPR line, cutting the Ontario Hydro North Shore transmission line, and moving the toxic waste to the edge of the highway itself.[109] In October,

Commanda held a press conference, announcing that the community would move the actual waste to areas outside the reserve if there was no immediate response from the government.[110] That fall, before the snow fell, the community moved "approximately 26 truckloads of waste [from the acid plant] to the edge of the Trans-Canada highway,"[111] and erected a sign outlining DIA's role in the establishment of the plant and its hesitation to provide funding for waste removal. It read:

> A Tribute to the Government of Canada – Here lie the remains of what was once the Cutler Acid Plant – 9000 truckloads of contaminated waste. Owned and operated in consecutive eras by Noranda Mines and CIL. The Plant shut down in 1963, leaving us with this great legacy. DIA negotiated the lease on behalf of the band and settled it without including us. The people of the Serpent River Indian Band dedicate this site to them in recognition of their relentless pursuit of good on our behalf. God save the Queen.[112]

The tongue-in-cheek dedication to the federal government revealed a community memory of betrayal and the long-standing sense of bitterness about the three decades it was taking for DIA to correct the situation. The words "relentless pursuit of good on our behalf" was an especially cutting commentary. Of course, "God save the Queen" not only referred to a colonial past, but also the continuing colonial patterns that defined the community's relationship to the state and sovereign. The community entered into the 1850 Robinson-Huron Treaty as a partner in negotiation, but the resulting pollution and slow action exposed the erosion of such promises and the nation-to-nation relationship.

In addition to public protest, SRFN citizens continued to express their concerns through official channels. During preparations for a 1987 presentation to the House of Commons Standing Committee on Aboriginal Affairs, Gertrude Lewis reflected on more than thirty years of struggles with the federal government.[113] "As a band member of the Serpent River Band I attended meetings in '55 with representatives of Noranda Mines and D.I.A.," she told the committee.

> I can still hear Indian Affairs people telling us we had nothing to worry about. The Band tried to request their own lawyer, but were told Indian Affairs would look after our interests very well. We've had sulphur fires flare up at any time during the summer months. On a hot, windy day the red calcine dust can be seen blowing across Highway 17 and can be smelled as you drive through our community. The health of our people is a concern to us. We are counting on you the committee to approve our endeavours.[114]

It was clear to community members that the mining industry had caused harm to them and their families both in terms of health and traditional lands. Lewis saw those two concepts as being intimately linked, if not completely inseparable. In her mind, the health of the community was tied together with the fires, dust, smells, and the larger history of the community and its colonial relationship with DIA.

The Serpent River First Nation's 1987 submission to the House Standing Committee summarized the community's claims and more than a decade of activism on the part of elected leaders. It included a history of the area, quoted Rosalie Bertell's study, and a gave a lengthy description of the ways in which the government did not represent the best interests of the community. For instance, as noted above, the history of the lease agreement, which was entered into by Noranda and DIA, was shown to be possible only through a technicality.[115] The brief outlined the issues in the area, referring to the sulphur, pyrite, calcine, concrete, rebar, and fill waste on approximately 200 hectares (or about 2 square km) of reserve land.[116] It also discussed the importance of Crown responsibility for the reclamation process. To make its case, the report also used selected quotations from the media to equate government inaction with racism. One 1969 quotation from Elmer Sopha, MPP for Sudbury, provides part of the introduction to the brief: "If such a situation existed in or near a white community, there would be such a howl of protest that the appropriate and responsible officials would be required to take steps with expedition to eliminate it. The fact that this one has been permitted to exist for so many years demonstrates once again that Canada's first citizens can be expected to suffer any indignity."[117] Further on in the brief, the community quoted from a 1985 editorial in the *Toronto Star* which followed Ward's exposé and echoed Sopha's comments almost two decades later: "According to the environmental geologist Derek Smith, 'the site is 110 cubic metres of some of the worst pollution I have seen in this Province. It should be cleaned up now.' One wonders whether it would have been cleaned up long ago had it been anywhere but an Indian reservation."[118] The quotations were chosen carefully, and they demonstrate not only the community's frustration with environmental racism, but also its willingness to hold the government accountable for its actions.

Ample quantitative and qualitative evidence clearly existed to support the community's claims. Another section of the presentation provided a case study of Ville de Lasalle, QC, which also suffered from industrial waste problems. The main difference between the two cases was that soon after a government task force was established to look at Lasalle, action was taken: "This example of rapid government action strengthens the Band's past and present frustrations, but it also offers hope."[119] Although the swift action taken when a settler community was affected by industrial waste was frustrating, it did prove that it was possible to move forward quickly if government support was forthcoming. What is clear from the community's perspective, as outlined in its brief, is that environmental racism was evident in the history of the acid plant site. Community members also referred to the length of time it took government officials to act. One section of the presentation was entitled, "Serpent River – Justice Delayed is Justice Denied." The community was suffering from "study fatigue," as no fewer than four environmental studies had been undertaken in the area to try to ascertain the level of damage and come up with reclamation processes that could work with the kind of industrial waste that was present.

The waste sat at the edge of the Trans-Canada Highway for more than a year as Serpent River First Nation continued to pursue other means of negotiation and protest.[120] Just before the Canada Day long weekend, on 29 June 1988, the community set fire to the pile of toxic waste. "The pile [of waste dedicated to the federal government] is now alight and Commanda said it could burn for days or months," reported the *Toronto Star*. "Although there are no flames or sparks, the smoke can be seen for miles and a rotten egg smell permeates the area, irritating the noses and throats of residents and Trans-Canada travellers. The burning material contains sulphur, pyrite, calcite, and cement."[121]

When asked to describe protests and other actions that were taken to call attention to the issues of land reclamation, Peter Johnston did not differentiate between political meetings in downtown Toronto and the type of visible public protest that occurred in 1988; in fact, he remembered them as being intimately linked as a coordinated effort in one instance. "We had those [discussions] ongoing," he said.

> We had one big meeting that was scheduled with – I think it was a meeting we had in Toronto. And it was with federal government departments. And … when I say the federal government, I'm not saying Indian Affairs because it involved Treasury Department, it involved Environment Canada, Justice Department, because Justice Department were the lawyers that were handling the legal work for the Department of Indian Affairs. So it involved all these departments. We had a big, big meeting scheduled in Toronto. And we decided to have a big day of protest. And we lit the fires purposely. We lit the sulphur piles. And they blew as they usually did with the westerly blow of the wind. All the material blew across Highway 17. It closed Highway 17 down. I mean motorists couldn't go by. And it became a real PR problem for the government. And we used

that to its full advantage. And when we went to that meeting in Toronto, we told them, we said, "if you turn your TV on tonight, or you turn it on right now, you'll find out how, just what our people at the community level feel about this; you're not just talking to us here as the leaders of our community. We're representing people at the community level and things are getting out of hand." I remember saying to them "you see on the news tonight where Highway 17, the Trans-Canada Highway, has been closed because of the burning of the material that is still on that site." And pretty soon, the federal government started to realize that they did have a problem. But it took us, I mean we had to fight and fight tooth and nail before they finally came up with the funding in order for us to do that.[122]

The Serpent River First Nation had found the government's weak spot. Less than a month after setting the pile of toxic waste on fire, the federal government caved.[123] On 20 July 1988, it was reported that the Treasury Board authorized a $5,777,000 funding package and it was anticipated that waste removal would begin in February. To compensate the Township of Shedden for taking over responsibility for the waste, the federal government paid for the construction of a football field-sized disposal site as well as an insurance liability policy, and it also offered to "finance other municipal improvements."[124] Once brought to the nine-metre-deep site, the waste would be neutralized by lime.[125]

As for the companies that ran the acid plant, the *Standard* announced in November that Noranda, which had originally promised a small settlement, would not contribute to the clean-up process since the government had already agreed to fund the process.[126] By the end of the year, however, CIL agreed to pay $106,500 to the community, although this was far less than what Commanda had hoped for. "We're not happy with the settlement; we're disappointed," he told a reporter. "But in contrast to Noranda Mines, which took a $50,000 offer off the table, we're pleased to get something." Chief Commanda went on to describe the community leadership's reaction to Noranda's change of heart: "We were just flabbergasted. They are still saying we have no claim against them."[127] CIL was the company that operated the plant for only eleven months as compared to Noranda's primary role in negotiating, building, and operating the plant for seven years. Nevertheless, CIL's spokesperson, Bruce Millar, when asked if the company was happy with the settlement responded: "Happy? Are we ever … We're pleased it's finally settled. Hopefully, it's at an end for us now."[128] While many other issues remained outstanding between the reserve and the government of Canada, the clean-up of the acid plant site came about as a result of community activism.

After more than three decades of struggle with both the river pollution and the threat of disaster from spills, as well as the legacy of the acid plant, the Serpent River First Nation had a long-awaited solution to one of the problems caused by the uranium industry. Its leaders had tirelessly advocated for a responsible and slow expansion to the mining operations at Elliot Lake in the 1970s, and became increasingly vocal in negotiations with various departments, as well as the press. The acid site clean-up in 1988–9 was due in no small part to the efforts of Serpent River First Nation leadership and the rest of the community. Their savvy use of the media continued the tradition of Chief William (Bill) Meawasige, who started the trend in the 1960s, but twenty years later leaders were also threatening to block the highway with plant waste in an effort to put pressure on the federal government to remediate the site. The plant had been established to facilitate the industry, but it left behind damaging effects that the community had to live with for decades. The political consciousness of the community, although not a new development itself, was made more apparent to settlers along the North Shore. Community leaders were able to appeal to widespread public environmental consciousness and health concerns to successfully lobby for the 1988 reclamation process. When this was not enough, they resorted to forcing the federal government into action. By referring to DIA's direct involvement in the origins of the plant, community leaders established the federal government's responsibility to clean it up. These "troublemakers" eventually succeeded in drawing attention to the environmental and health devastation that plagued both their reserve and traditional territory.

Conclusion

I first learned about the legacy of uranium mining and pollution as a small child. I stayed with my grandmother a lot, and she often told stories about the acid plant and the river. I have a few memories of my growing recognition of the differences between the colonial space of the reserve and the town, which accompanied my growing awareness of my own physical difference. My grandmother had an aerial photo of the acid plant on her bedroom wall, and she would tell me about what it was like to live near it and what she and others had to do to fight to clean it up. I also remember driving by a gas station demolition with my father. It was in Elliot Lake. The building and pumps had been removed, and the site was being dug up. As we drove by, he said that that was what they should have done with the plant site. I was too young to understand the complexities of what he was saying about reclamation, but I understood that in a settler town, more care was taken to remove a gas station than there was to decommission a sulphuric acid plant on the reserve. Settler colonialism was, for me, not a distant historical process but one that was ongoing and continuously affecting Indigenous lives.

More than twenty years later, the legacy of uranium remains prominent in the minds of the people of the Serpent River First Nation and was vividly recalled by the Elders I interviewed. Peter Johnston offered this emphatic response about the pollution that still plagues the area where the acid plant stood and the tailings dams that offer thin protection against further pollution in the river:

There's no question right now that the biggest legacy is what is still there. And that includes what is still here. I mean we tried to clean it up but obviously we didn't do the kind of job that should have been done and so we still have that problem. It's not as big a problem, though, as what the mines have left us. The potential for disaster is just tremendous in my estimation. I mean I predict, and I've said this all along, that sooner or later an act of nature is going to happen and one of those dams or other or dams are going to break and when they do, everybody keeps talking I mean anybody that is an environmentalist talks about the re-growth of Serpent River and how it's coming back to its original – what it was originally … I mean what's lying on the bed of the Serpent River will never … come back to its original state. But the potential that exists up there for disaster is just mind-boggling. And it's bound to happen. I can't see how it won't happen, I mean, these are man-made structures. There's no guarantee that those things are going to maintain their integrity forever.[1]

The fact that the river system has had to rely on human-made tailings dams as a solution to a problem created by humanity is disturbing to many community members. Of course, environmental reclamation technology has improved since the spills of the mid-twentieth century, but it cannot return the land and river system to its original state.

Gertrude Lewis agreed that the legacy of uranium was "the pollution that they left behind. That's the biggest thing." Her primary goal for the community was to "get the acid plant cleaned up really well! And not to have to worry about it in another twenty or thirty years. I won't be around. At least the young people should have someplace to call home."[2] The concept of homeland, one that is viable for generations to come, was at the forefront of her mind when I asked her what the community's priorities should be. The quotation also underscores her concept of community responsibility: Gertrude was politically and socially involved in these struggles and wanted to ensure that the homeland will be around for future generations once she is gone. Her words are particularly prescient now that she has passed on, as it really is up to a new generation to ensure that the traditional responsibility of stewardship continues in perpetuity.

Terry Jacobs echoed this sentiment about the land: "As far as reclamation was concerned, that's the part we're concerned about."[3] It is clear that community Elders did not want to have to be worried that there would be yet another political negotiation to stall a proper reclamation process. They want the land returned to the community in a good way and to be able to move forward as a nation.

Betty Jacobs recalled rapid and extensive change brought by the plant and the mines: "A lot of big changes, eh? It felt like a big change."[4] Arnelda Jacobs described the rapid changes brought by the wage economy, however short-lived, in the ways the community interacted with the land and with each other. These changes were more than economic, as they also had an effect on social relationships that were sustained and renewed by community gardening, fishing, hunting, and living with the land in general.[5] There were, of course, people who lost family members as a result of the acid plant and mining operations. Valerie Commanda not only lost her spouse, but she also had to go through a decade of struggle before it was acknowledged that his occupation had contributed to his death.[6]

In all of these stories, Elders shared a sense of profound loss that emphasized the fundamental changes brought on by the uranium industry, both to the community and to the environment. This is not surprising given the holistic Anishinaabe worldview that emphasizes connectivity and the centrality of land and water to *mino bimaadiziwin*, a good life. These changes, however, brought a new reliance on steady wage employment, the depletion of resources that had been used and protected for years, and the subsequent reliance on store-bought goods. Traditional pursuits such as fishing, hunting, and trapping were no longer tenable and new opportunities for waged labour were both fleeting and unsafe.

While the confines of settler colonialism complicated Indigenous dissent, this is nevertheless a story of resilience and reclamation. Elders were enthusiastic in their recollections of their protests, their roles at the EAB hearings, and their meetings with various government officials. This was an empowering time for them in their lives, and it was an honour to listen to their stories, which they told with fiery honesty and humour. Community leaders asserted their roles as stewards in a time of transition: there were changing dynamics both in terms of media attention and government policy, coupled with Indigenous activism, which provide the backdrop for their individual stories.

The legacies of uranium extraction continue along with the stories. SRFN's struggle with reclamation of the acid plant site did not end in 1988. Although $5.8 million was spent removing the debris from the reserve and containing it in lime, it was not just the refuse that posed an obstacle to reclamation. It has since become clear that the water and bottom of Aird Bay continue to be polluted by the site. In the fall of 2009, Chief Isadore Day and Serpent River First Nation filed a specific land claim to address the need for compensation for continued contamination of the Cutler Acid Site. Clearly the process is far from over.

The story of uranium mining and the Serpent River Anishinaabek challenges efforts to historicize colonialism or to suggest that the ongoing trauma of the colonial relationship has somehow lessened over time. The United Nations Declaration on the Rights of Indigenous Peoples (UNDRIP), issued in 2007 but not adopted in Canada until 2016, emphasizes the need for the free, prior, and informed consent of Indigenous peoples in the context of land development, among many other aspects of Indigenous experiences.[7] Canada is now responsible for implementing changes as a result of UNDRIP and the Truth and Reconciliation Commission of Canada, which culminated in its 2015 report and ninety-four calls to action.[8] However, in this same context, Canadians have witnessed the 2012 passage of Bill C-45, an omnibus bill which removed environmental protections for waterways, and helped galvanize Indigenous people across the country in the #Idlenomore movement. More recently, the Trudeau government purchased Kinder Morgan's Trans Mountain pipeline for $4.5 billion in order to ensure the project moves forward, despite environmentalist and Indigenous dissent. While this book is about the Cold War period, today's practices are still colonial, and Indigenous people remain vigilant in our assertion of Indigenous rights and our roles as land and water defenders both within and without the DIA framework. Despite efforts to make it appear kinder and gentler, colonialism is still pervasive.

The Cold War brought a new global imperative to the country, and while this is a local study of the effects the new atomic economy had on the Indigenous people of the area, it is also important to locate it within its larger international and national context. The lucrative and short-lived uranium contract with the United States would have the power to both create and destroy the livelihoods of settler families who moved to the area to live and work. In an effort to avoid the ghost towns that populated some areas of northern Ontario, it was decided that a modern townsite would be "carved from the rock," a phrase indicative of a local settler memory celebrating man's manipulation and victory over natural resources. This image serves to commemorate a particular way of seeing the world and its resources: for settlers, the rock was key to an important resource. It brought prosperity at some points and worry at others, but here the rock is seen as both the foundation of and impediment to development in the area. The rock was what housed uranium and thus needed to be disturbed and manipulated.

This narrative excludes both the Anishinaabe worldview and the nature of the historical relationship between the two communities. When these interactions are acknowledged, it is often confined to a quick nod to the original inhabitants of the area prior to contact and during the fur trade before the narrative moves on to the central "more important" history of the area. On the other hand, the history of the Anishinaabek, both in terms of worldview and their relationships with subsequent settler intrusions, has been defined by interactions with the land and water. Uranium was not the first resource that was sought in the area. Rather, as Europeans encroached further into the Great Lakes area in search of furs and souls, the Anishinaabek continued to live as they had and adapted to cultural and linguistic changes that suited them while disregarding others. They also resisted encroachments and sought to protect their territory. When Euro-Canadians came for minerals, this subsequent intrusion necessitated a nation-to-nation agreement in the form of the Robinson-Huron Treaty in 1850. By the late nineteenth century, lumber companies sought trees and built mills as they had in other Anishinaabe territories in the United States, and the Macdonald government required land for its railway, so DIA facilitated lease agreements in order to secure Indigenous territory. Even though Serpent River First Nation leaders proactively bought part of their land back after the mills closed, the transaction – a process largely controlled by DIA – was never finalized in accordance with the Indian Act. This meant that when it came time to negotiate the lease for the Noranda Acid Plant, the land was conveniently available for such purposes, with disastrous consequences in the Cold War period.

This new Cold War colonialism brought about a new settler town through careful planning and the tripartite relationship between mining companies, the federal government, and the Province of Ontario. What is more, the town's boom-bust history would prove that the success of uranium mining was dependent on the international market, but crucially, it would be the federal government's responsibility to ensure that there would be stockpiling and mortgage schemes to assist where economic forces could not. At the same time, DIA presented the idea of the acid plant to the community as a way to mitigate the economic disparity that was apparent as more settlers moved into the area in search of jobs in the uranium industry. The plant operated for fewer than ten years, but its environmental and health consequences were far-reaching. In short, the jobs were fleeting, but the legacy of the acid plant was not. As for the river and the Serpent for which it is named, the legacy of uranium changed its ability to care for the community and for the community's ability to interact with the land as they once had. Community members could no longer safely draw drinking water from the river and the traditional pursuits of hunting and fishing changed as people were asked to do so with caution.

As colonial relationships changed throughout the twentieth century, and the legacies of uranium became more apparent and long lasting, Serpent River First Nation leaders continued patterns of resistance and grew ever more assertive in voicing their concerns. Community members were resilient, and their lobbying during the Environmental Assessment Board hearings in the late 1970s was a political and conscious act of dissent against rapid and thoughtless mining development. Asking for assistance from the National Indian Brotherhood in demanding a voice at the negotiating table marked another act of political consciousness and reflected the larger Red Power movement happening across Turtle Island. Whether it was to question rapid and extensive expansion of uranium production at Elliot Lake, to attend meetings in Toronto or Ottawa, or to threaten to block the highway if DIA continued to impede a clean-up process of the acid site, SRFN community members resorted to creative and consistent means of asserting Indigenous rights.

The struggle and stories of the people of the Serpent River are the legacy of Cold War colonialism and they challenge the idea that Canada is in a post-colonial period, as well as the assumptions that underpin that convenient and comforting idea. Many of the processes, experiences, and traumas that historians traditionally associate with the late nineteenth or early twentieth centuries in fact played out again after the Second World War, albeit in different ways. Territorial encroachment, settlement, agreement making and breaking, efforts to assimilate or Westernize, and the imperative of "progress" all characterized a process in which the impetus was no longer nation-building, as it once had been, but economic development in accordance with global strategic aims. The community responded to these challenges and rapid period of change in a variety of ways, eventually galvanizing around resistance and resilience, narratives that dominate the community's memory of those years today. Environmental degradation as a result of industrial economic development was not a new story in Canada, nor is Serpent River First Nation the only Indigenous community to have suffered as a result of it. The choices made by the Serpent River First Nation were shaped by paternalistic colonial circumstances that continue to have a presence in the community. But this was also not one-sided: when the community was faced with a dominant power that privileged economic gain and a narrow view of resource development that clashed with the importance it placed upon its social relationship with the land, SRFN sought ways to assert Anishinaabe worldviews.

The story is likely not over as the City of Elliot Lake's interest in mining continues. A company known as Pele Mountain Resources Inc. recently looked into renewing mining activity in the area, potentially to exploit rare earth minerals through its Eco Ridge Mine Rare Earth and Uranium Project. In May 2018, it renewed a sustainable energy agreement with the City of Elliot Lake to be the exclusive "developer of energy and energy storage projects on City lands until May 1, 2020." Pele and Elliot Lake, according to Mayor Dan Marchisella, were to focus on "renewable energy, energy storage, and reduced dependence on the regional power grid in Elliot Lake," a departure from previous mining interest in the area.[9] Meanwhile, Denison maintains a presence in the community, restyled as Denison Environmental under which it oversees a monitoring program to ensure the viability of the river system.[10] As the company changed its focus from uranium extraction to responsible and transparent stewardship, Serpent River First Nation leadership worked collaboratively with the company to oversee joint stewardship of the watershed. It is chilling that new mining developments are being contemplated while the local Indigenous and settler communities have only recently begun to deal with the legacy of early boom periods.

There is hope though, because there is also evidence that the efforts of community Elders and leaders to assert their rights and demand a voice in decision-making have changed the dynamics of development in the region. The City of Elliot Lake recently pursued cottage lot development, which brought both Elliot Lake and Serpent River First Nation to the table. In April 2015, the *Standard* reported that a draft agreement had been negotiated between SRFN and Elliot Lake which allowed development to begin.[11] Importantly, the subcommittee in charge of reaching the agreement was comprised of three Elliot Lake members and six SRFN representatives. There appeared to be a better understanding of Indigenous rights, Anishinaabe territory, and, according to the *Standard*, "the draft agreement mentions the Robinson-Huron Treaty of 1850 and how obligations have not always been implemented correctly. With the city and SRFN working together however, the agreement covers consultation, accommodation, benefits and relationship between the two communities, which were concerns voiced by SRFN in 2012."[12] The agreement also mentioned a profit-sharing scheme as well as a process for environmental impact assessments.[13] This marked an important departure from the earlier stages of the Indigenous-settler relationship in the region and it demonstrates the power of asserting and renewing the role of Indigenous knowledge in the community's interactions with the land. Responsible and accountable resource development depends upon the assertion of the Anishinaabe worldview that privileges Indigenous knowledge and stewardship responsibilities, and it remains to be seen how this partnership will function in the future.

Relationship-building began largely after the closure of the last uranium mine in 1996 and has subsequently brought the Indigenous and settler communities closer together in a spirit of reconciliation. In June 2018, both communities agreed to establish closer working relationships, particularly on economic and land use issues.[14] On 21 June 2018, the City of Elliot Lake raised the SRFN flag at the Miner's Memorial Park to symbolically renew the relationship.[15] The Miner's Memorial Park is located in Elliot Lake, on a beautiful site overlooking Horne Lake, and serves as a physical space to remember workers who died as a result of mining accidents or occupational diseases. This act served to recognize not only the relationship between the two communities but also acknowledged the suffering of Indigenous miners and community members as a result of mining. It was indeed a hopeful development that to celebrate National Indigenous Peoples Day, Chief Elaine Johnston and Mayor Dan Marchisella, the leaders of each community, stood together in a ceremony marked by Anishinaabe prayer and song at the site that commemorates the human cost of uranium development.

Yet even as the relationship between the Indigenous community and settlers evolves in positive ways, conflict remains possible where development and environmental stewardship clash. In 2015, the City of Elliot Lake entered a competitive process to become one of the long-term nuclear storage sites operated by the Nuclear Waste Management Organization (NWMO), a development that would have brought an influx of capital into a struggling local economy but would have potentially had disastrous environmental consequences.[16] The question of building a new underground hazardous waste storage site was a divisive one, especially considering that the management of existing tailings ponds and waste sites remains an ongoing problem and new mineral development is always possible.[17] Area First Nations, including Serpent River First Nation, were concerned not only about the overall environmental effects such a site might have on the Great Lakes region, but also the process through which the sites would be chosen. In a letter to Ontario Premier Kathleen Wynne, Isadore Day, Chief at the time, urged her government to seek meaningful input from First Nations, reminding them that "the actual sites being looked at are on treaty lands and municipalities have no say about what happens on those lands. This matter is a discussion that must take place between treaty partners."[18] While the NWMO ultimately excluded Elliot Lake as a potential repository site in December 2017, this was not the community's decision.[19] Once again, environmental concerns clashed with economic development and may do so again in future. For Serpent River First Nation, Rooster Rock continues to be a sacred site, regardless of what has been carved from it and the legacy brought upon it by mining. What the process will bring to the Great Lakes area in general, and to what extent the federal government's duty to consult will impact these discussions, remains to be seen.

Notes

1. Introduction

1 *Uranium*, directed by Magnus Isacsson (Montreal: National Film Board of Canada, 1990). Thanks to Carmella Gray-Cosgrove for reminding me of this quotation. In accordance with Anishinaabe ethics, I am only sharing general stories that have been shared with me during interviews for this project. The Serpent has also been written about in non-Indigenous sources: Tom Haddow, "Serpent River Home of Giant Reptile: Ojibway," *Standard*, 29 March 1983. Theresa S. Smith, *The Island of the Anishnaabeg: Thunderers and Water Monsters in the Traditional Ojibwe Life-World* (Idaho: University of Idaho Press, 1995), 112. Andrea Gutsche, Barbara Chisholm and Russell Floren, *The North Channel and St. Mary's River: A Guide to the History* (Toronto: Lynx Images Inc., 2008), 119–22.
2 Smith, *The Island*, 112.
3 Janice Gamble and Elder Tea, *Connected to the Land: Stories from the Serpent's Band* (Serpent River First Nation Education Department, 2013).
4 Ibid., 24–5. Interview with Arnelda Jacobs by Author, 8 July 2009, Serpent River First Nation.
5 This term is used to denote a specific place in the Great Lakes region: the North Shore of Lake Huron.
6 Sean Fine, "Chief Justice Says Canada Attempted 'Cultural Genocide' on Aboriginals," *Globe and Mail*, 28 May 2015, accessed 20 June 2015, http://www.theglobeandmail.com/news/national/chief-justice-says-canada-attempted-cultural-genocide-on-aboriginals/article24688854/. Gloria Galloway and Bill Curry, "Residential Schools Amounted to 'Cultural Genocide,' Report Says," *Globe and Mail*, 2 June 2015, accessed 20 June 2015, http://www.theglobeandmail.com/news/politics/residential-schools-amounted-to-cultural-genocide-says-report/article24740605/.

7 National Inquiry into Missing and Murdered Indigenous Women and
  Girls, *Reclaiming Power and Place: The Final Report of the National Inquiry into
  Missing and Murdered Indigenous Women and Girls*, 2019, accessed 17 July
  2020, https://www.mmiwg-ffada.ca/wp-content/uploads/2019/06
  /Final_Report_Vol_1a-1.pdf, 50.
8 James Daschuk, *Clearing the Plains: Disease, Politics of Starvation, and the
  Loss of Aboriginal Life* (Regina: University of Regina Press, 2012). For an
  overview of the Canadian literature see Ken Coates, "Writing First Nations
  History into Canadian History: A Review of Recent Scholarly Works,"
  Canadian Historical Review 81, no. 1 (2000): 99–114; Keith Thor Carlson,
  Melinda Marie Jette, and Kenichi Matsui, "An Annotated Bibliography of
  Major Writings in Aboriginal History, 1990–99," *Canadian Historical Review*
  82, no. 1 (2001): 122–71; Dimitry Anastakis, Mary-Ellen Kelm, and Suzanne
  Morton, "New Approaches to Indigenous History," *Canadian Historical
  Review* 98, no. 1 (2017): 60–3; Mary Jane Logan McCallum, "Starvation,
  Experimentation, Segregation, and Trauma: Words for Reading Indigenous
  Health History," *Canadian Historical Review* 98, no. 1 (2017): 96–113;
  John Borrows, "Challenging Historical Frameworks: Aboriginal Rights,
  The Trickster, and Originalism," *Canadian Historical Review* 98, no. 1
  (2017): 114–35; Brenda Macdougall, "Space and Place within Aboriginal
  Epistemological Traditions: Recent Trends in Historical Scholarship,"
  Canadian Historical Review 98, no. 1 (2017): 64–82; Lianne C. Leddy,
  "Intersections of Indigenous and Environmental History in Canada,"
  Canadian Historical Review 98, no. 1 (2017): 83–95.
9 J.R. Miller, *Shingwauk's Vision* (Toronto: University of Toronto Press,
  1996) and Sarah Carter, *Lost Harvests: Prairie Indian Reserve Farmers and
  Government Policy* (Montreal: McGill-Queen's University Press, 1990). See
  also John Leslie and Ron Maguire, *The Historical Development of the Indian
  Act* (Ottawa: Indian and Northern Affairs, 1978). Helen Buckley, *From
  Wooden Ploughs to Welfare: Why Indian Policy Failed in the Prairie Provinces*
  (Montreal: McGill–Queen's University Press, 1992); Bruce Dawson,
  "The Roots of Agriculture: A Historiographical Review of First Nations
  Agriculture and Government Indian Policy," *Prairie Forum* 28, no. 1 (Spring
  2003): 99–115. On education see Miller above and John S. Milloy, *A National
  Crime: The Canadian Government and the Residential School System* (Winnipeg:
  University of Manitoba Press, 1999).
10 John L. Tobias, "Protection, Civilization, Assimilation: An Outline History
  of Canada's Indian Policy," in *As Long as the Sun Shines and the Water Flows:
  A Reader in Canadian Native Studies*, ed. Ian A.L. Getty and Antoine S.
  Lussier (Vancouver: University of British Columbia Press, 1995), 39–55;
  E. Brian Titley, *A Narrow Vision: Duncan Campbell Scott and the
  Administration of Indian Affairs in Canada* (Vancouver: University of British

Columbia Press, 1986) and *The Indian Commissioners: Agents of the State and Indian Policy in Canada's Prairie West, 1873–1932* (Edmonton: University of Alberta Press, 2009).

11 Robin Jarvis Brownlie, *A Fatherly Eye: Indian Agents, Government Power, and Aboriginal Resistance in Ontario, 1918–1939* (Don Mills: Oxford University Press, 2003), xii.

12 Paulette Regan, *Unsettling the Settler Within: Indian Residential Schools, Truth Telling, and Reconciliation in Canada* (Vancouver: University of British Columbia Press, 2010), 4.

13 Regan, *Unsettling*, 4.

14 Adam J. Barker, "The Contemporary Reality of Canadian Imperialism: Settler Colonialism and the Hybrid Colonial State," *American Indian Quarterly* 33, no. 3 (2009): 325. See also Cole Harris, *The Resettlement of British Columbia* (Vancouver: University of British Columbia Press, 1997); for a more recent theoretical discussion of the concept see Evelyn Nakano Glenn, "Settler Colonialism as Structure: A Framework for Comparative Studies of US Race and Gender Formation," *Sociology of Race and Ethnicity* 1, no. 1 (2015): 52–72. See also Keith Thor Carlson, *The Power of Place, The Problem of Time: Aboriginal Identity and Historical Consciousness in the Cauldron of Colonialism* (Toronto: University of Toronto Press, 2010).

15 Arn Keeling and John Sandlos, "The Complex Legacy of Mining in Northern Canada," in *Mining and Communities in Northern Canada: History, Politics, and Memory* (Calgary: University of Calgary Press, 2015), 5–12; early works in the field viewed resource extraction as a positive nation-building force. See Harold Adams Innis, *The Fur Trade in Canada: An Introduction to Canadian Economic History*, rev. ed. (Toronto: University of Toronto Press, 1956) and Harold Adam Innis, *Settlement and the Mining Frontier* (Toronto: Macmillan, 1936); for a post-colonial critique of Innis see Jody Berland, "Space at the Margins: Critical Theory and Colonial Space after Innis," in *Harold Innis in the New Century*, ed. Charles R. Acland and William J. Buxton (Montreal: McGill-Queen's University Press, 1999), 281–309. Later interpretations focused on the legacy of mining and the development and decline of resource boom towns including John H. Bradbury, "Towards an Alternative Theory of Resource-Based Town Development in Canada," *Economic Geography* 55, no. 2 (1979): 147–66, and Mary Louise McAllister, "Shifting Foundations in a Mature Staples Industry: A Political Economic History of Canadian Mineral Policy," *Canadian Political Science Review* 1 (June 2007): 73–90. For a discussion of Indigenous experiences in British Columbia see Harris, *Resettlement*, 194–218, and Kerry Abel and Jean Friesen, eds., *Aboriginal Resource Use in Canada: Historical and Legal Aspects* (Winnipeg: University of Manitoba Press, 1991).

16 In chronological order see Arthur J. Ray, *Indians in the Fur Trade, 1660–1870* (Toronto: University of Toronto Press, 1974); Bruce G. Trigger, *The Children of Aataentsic: A History of the Huron People to 1660* (Montreal: McGill Queen's University Press, 1976); Robin Fisher, *Contact and Conflict: Indian-European Relations in British Columbia, 1774–1890* (Vancouver: University of British Columbia Press, 1977); Jennifer S.H. Brown, *Strangers in Blood: Fur Trade Company Families in Indian Country* (Vancouver: University of British Columbia Press, 1980); Sylvia Van Kirk, *Many Tender Ties: Women in Fur-Trade Society 1660–1870* (Winnipeg: Watson and Dwyer, 1980); J.R. Miller, *Skyscrapers Hide the Heavens: A History of Indian-White Relations in Canada* (Toronto: University of Toronto Press, 1989); Richard White, *The Middle Ground: Indians, Empires, and Republics in the Great Lakes Region, 1650–1815* (Cambridge: Cambridge University Press, 1991).

17 Daschuk, *Clearing the Plains*; Gerhard Ens, *Homeland to Hinterland: The Changing Worlds of the Red River Metis in the Nineteenth Century* (Toronto: University of Toronto Press, 1996); Paige Raibmon, *Authentic Indians: Episodes of Encounter from the Late-Nineteenth-Century Northwest Coast* (Durham: Duke University Press, 2005); Arthur J. Ray, Jim Miller, and Frank Tough, *Bounty and Benevolence: A History of Saskatchewan Treaties* (Montreal: McGill-Queen's University Press, 2000); John S. Milloy, *The Plains Cree: Trade, Diplomacy, and War, 1780–1870* (Winnipeg: University of Manitoba Press, 1990); John L. Tobias, "Canada's Subjugation of the Plains Cree, 1879–1885," *Canadian Historical Review* 64 (1983): 519–48; on mining and resource extraction in particular see Frank Tough, *"As Their Natural Resources Fail": Native Peoples and the Economic History of Northern Manitoba, 1870–1930* (Vancouver: University of British Columbia Press, 1996); Janet E. Chute, "Pursuing the Great Spirit's Plan: Nineteenth-Century Ojibwa Attitudes Towards the Future of Logging and Mining on Unsurrendered Indian Lands North of Lakes Huron and Superior," in *Social Relations in Resource Hinterlands: Papers from the 27th Annual Meeting of the Western Association of Sociology and Anthropology*, ed. Thomas W. Dunk (Thunder Bay: Lakehead University Centre for Northern and Regional Studies, 1991), 173–203; Nancy M. Wightman and W. Robert Wightman, "The Mica Bay Affair: Conflict on the Upper Lakes Mining Frontier, 1840–1850," *Ontario History* 83 (1991): 193–208 and Rhonda Telford, "Aboriginal Resistance in the Mid-Nineteenth Century: The Anishinabe, Their Allies, and the Closing of the Mining Operations at Mica Bay and Michipicoten Island," in *Blockades and Resistance: Studies in Actions of Peace and the Temagami Blockades of 1988–89*, ed. Bruce W. Hodgins, Ute Lischke, and David T. McNab (Waterloo: Wilfrid Laurier University Press, 2003), 71–84.

18 Brownlie, *A Fatherly Eye*, 61.

19 See, for example, J.R. Miller, "Owen Glendower, Hotspur and Canadian
Indian Policy," in *Sweet Promises: A Reader on Indian-White Relations
in Canada*, ed. J.R. Miller (Toronto: University of Toronto Press, 1991),
323–52. Janet E. Chute, *The Legacy of Shingwaukonse: A Century of Native
Leadership* (Toronto: University of Toronto Press, 1998). For an examination
of Indigenous agency in religious encounters see Susan Neylan, *The
Heavens are Changing: Nineteenth-Century Protestant Missions and Tsimshian
Christianity* (Montreal: McGill-Queen's University Press, 2003). Robin
Jarvis Brownlie and Mary-Ellen Kelm caution against this historiographical
trend in "Desperately Seeking Absolution: Native Agency as Colonialist
Alibi?" *Canadian Historical Review* 75, no. 4 (1994): 543–56.

20 Truth and Reconciliation Commission of Canada, "The History, Part 1 –
Origins to 1939" and "The History, Part 2–1939–2000," 2015, accessed
17 July 2020, http://www.trc.ca/assets/pdf/Volume_1_History_Part_1
_English_Web.pdf.

21 On Indigenous work see Mary Jane Logan McCallum, *Indigenous Women,
Work, and History, 1940–1980* (Winnipeg: University of Manitoba Press,
2014); Bonita Lawrence, *"Real" Indians and Others: Mixed-Blood Urban
Native Peoples and Indigenous Nationhood* (Vancouver: University of British
Columbia Press, 2004); on organization and activism see Nancy Janovicek,
"'Assisting our own': Urban Migration, Self-Governance, and Native
Women's Organizing in Thunder Bay, Ontario, 1972–1989," *American Indian
Quarterly* 27, nos. 3–4 (2003): 548–65 and Heather Howard-Bobiwash,
"Women's Class Strategies as Activism in Native Community Building
in Toronto, 1950–1975," *American Indian Quarterly* 27, nos. 3–4 (2003):
566–82; Sarah Marie Wiebe, *Everyday Exposure: Indigenous Mobilization and
Environmental Justice in Canada's Chemical Valley* (Vancouver: University of
British Columbia Press, 2016); on health see Patricia Jasen, "Race, Culture,
and the Colonization of Childbirth in Northern Canada," *Social History
of Medicine* 10, no. 3 (1997): 383–400; Mary-Ellen Kelm, *Colonizing Bodies:
Aboriginal Health and Healing in British Columbia, 1900–50* (Vancouver:
University of British Columbia Press, 1998); Maureen K. Lux, *Medicine
That Walks: Disease, Medicine and Canadian Plains Native People* (Toronto:
University of Toronto Press, 2001); Maureen K. Lux, *Separate Beds: A History
of Indian Hospitals in Canada, 1920s-1980s* (Toronto: University of Toronto
Press, 2016); Kathryn McPherson, "Nursing and Colonization: The Work of
Indian Health Services Nurses in Manitoba, 1945–1970," in *Women, Health
and Nation: Canada and the United States since 1945*, ed. Georgina Feldberg
(Montreal: McGill-Queen's University Press, 2003), 223–46; Krista Walters,
"'A National Priority': Nutrition Canada's Survey and the Disciplining of
Aboriginal Bodies, 1964–1975," in *Edible Histories, Cultural Politics: Towards
a Canadian Food History*, ed. Franca Iacovetta, Valerie J. Korinek and

Marlene Epp (Toronto: University of Toronto Press, 2012), 433–52; on social programs and policy see Hugh Shewell, *"Enough to Keep Them Alive": Indian Welfare in Canada, 1873–1965* (Toronto: University of Toronto Press, 2004); Sherene Razack, *Dying from Improvement: Inquests and Inquiries into Indigenous Deaths in Custody* (Toronto: University of Toronto Press, 2015); and on experimentation see Ian Mosby, "Administering Colonial Science: Nutrition Research and Human Biomedical Experimentation in Aboriginal Communities and Residential Schools, 1942–1952," *Histoire sociale/Social History* 91 (2013): 145–92.

22 Robert Bothwell, *Alliance and Illusion: Canada and the World, 1945–1984* (Vancouver: University of British Columbia Press, 2007); Robert Bothwell, *The Big Chill: Canada and the Cold War* (Concord: Irwin, 1998); Robert Bothwell, Ian Drummond, and John English, *Canada since 1945: Power, Politics, and Provincialism*, rev. ed. (Toronto: University of Toronto Press, 1993); Philip Buckner and R.D. Francis, eds., *Canada and the British World: Culture, Migration, and Identity* (Vancouver: University of British Columbia Press, 2006); Greg Donaghy, ed., *Canada and the Early Cold War, 1943–1957* (Ottawa: Department of Foreign Affairs and International Trade, 1988); Andrew Richter, *Avoiding Armageddon: Canadian Military Strategy and Nuclear Weapons, 1950–1963* (Vancouver: University of British Columbia Press, 2002); Reg Whitaker and Gary Marcuse, *Cold War Canada: The Making of a National Insecurity State, 1945–1957* (Toronto: University of Toronto Press, 1994); Reg Whitaker and Steve Hewitt, *Canada and the Cold War* (Toronto: James Lorimer, 2003).

23 Valerie Korinek, *Roughing It in the Suburbs: Reading Chatelaine Magazine in the Fifties and Sixties* (Toronto: University of Toronto Press, 2000); Veronica Strong-Boag, "Canada's Wage-Earning Wives and the Construction of the Middle Class, 1945–60," *Journal of Canadian Studies* 29, no. 3 (1994): 5–25; Veronica Strong-Boag, "Home Dreams: Women and the Suburban Experiment in Canada, 1945–60," *Canadian Historical Review* 72, no. 4 (December 1991): 471–504.

24 Doug Owram, *Born at the Right Time: A History of the Baby Boom Generation* (Toronto: University of Toronto Press, 1996); Dimitry Anastakis (ed.), *The Sixties: Passion, Politics, and Style* (Montreal: McGill-Queen's University Press, 2008); Stuart Henderson, *Making the Scene: Yorkville and Hip Toronto in the 1960s* (Toronto: University of Toronto Press, 2011).

25 Nancy Adamson, "Feminists, Libbers, Lefties, and Radicals: The Emergence of the Women's Liberation Movement," in *A Diversity of Women: Ontario, 1945–1980*, ed. Joy Parr (Toronto: University of Toronto Press, 1995), 252–80; Jennifer Bonnell, *Reclaiming the Don: An Environmental History of Toronto's Don River Valley* (Toronto: University of Toronto Press, 2014); Tarah Brookfield, *Cold War Comforts: Canadian Women, Child Safety,*

and Global Insecurity (Waterloo: Wilfrid Laurier University Press, 2012);
Magda Fahrni and Robert Rutherdale, eds., *Creating Postwar Canada:
Community, Diversity, and Dissent, 1945–75* (Vancouver: University of
British Columbia Press, 2008); Ryan O'Connor, *The First Green Wave:
Pollution Probe and the Origins of Environmental Activism in Ontario*
(Vancouver: University of British Columbia Press, 2015); Joan Sangster,
"Radical Ruptures: Feminism, Labor, and the Left in the Long Sixties in
Canada," *American Review of Canadian Studies* 40, no. 1 (March 2010): 1–21.

26 Nancy Christie and Michael Gauvreau, eds., *Cultures of Citizenship in Post-
war Canada, 1940–1955* (Montreal: McGill-Queen's University Press, 2003);
Frank K. Clarke, "'Keep Communism Out of Our Schools': Cold War
Anti-Communism at the Toronto Board of Education, 1948–1951," *Labour/
Le Travail* 49 (Spring 2002): 93–120; Franca Iacovetta, *Gatekeepers: Reshaping
Immigrant Lives in Cold War Canada* (Toronto: Between the Lines, 2006);
Ninette Kelley and Michael Trebilcock, *The Making of the Mosaic: A History
of Canadian Immigration Policy* (Toronto: University of Toronto Press, 1998);
Gary Kinsman and Patrizia Gentile, *The Canadian War on Queers: National
Security in Sexual Regulation* (Vancouver: University of British Columbia
Press, 2009); Gary Kinsman, Dieter K. Buse, and Mercedes Steedman,
eds., *Whose National Security? Canadian State Surveillance and the Creation
of Enemies* (Toronto: Between the Lines, 2000); Dominique Marshall, *The
Social Origins of the Welfare State: Québec Families, Compulsory Education, and
Family Allowances, 1940–1955* (Waterloo: Wilfrid Laurier University Press,
2006); Lara Campbell, Dominique Clement and Gregory S. Kealey, eds.,
Debating Dissent: Canada and the Sixties (Toronto: University of Toronto
Press, 2012).

27 Mary Louise Adams, *The Trouble with Normal: Postwar Youth and the Making
of Heterosexuality* (Toronto: University of Toronto Press, 1997); Mary
Louise Adams, "Youth, Corruptibility, and English-Canadian Postwar
Campaigns against Indecency, 1948–1955," *Journal of the History of Sexuality*
6, no. 1 (July 1995): 89–117; Denyse Baillargeon, *Babies for the Nation:
The Medicalization of Motherhood in Quebec, 1910–1970* (Waterloo: Wilfrid
Laurier University Press, 2009); Mona Gleason, "Disciplining Children,
Disciplining Parents: The Nature and Meaning of Advice to Canadian
Parents, 1945–1955," *Histoire sociale/Social History* 29, no. 57 (1996): 187–209;
Mona Gleason, *Normalizing the Ideal: Psychology, Schooling, and the Family in
Postwar Canada* (Toronto: University of Toronto Press, 1999); Bryan Palmer,
Canada's 1960s: The Ironies of Identity in a Rebellious Era (Toronto: University
of Toronto Press, 2009).

28 For mining, see Saleem Ali, *Mining, the Environment, and Indigenous
Development Conflicts* (Tucson: University of Arizona Press, 2003); Ellen
Bielawski, *Rogue Diamonds: The Rush for Northern Riches on Dene Land*

(Toronto: Douglas and McIntyre, 2003); Ginger Gibson and Deanna
Kemp, "Corporate Engagement with Indigenous Women in the Minerals
Industry: Making Space for Theory," in *Earth Matters: Indigenous Peoples,
the Extractive Industries and Corporate Social Responsibility*, ed. Ciaran
O'Faircheallaigh and Saleem Ali (Sheffield: Greenleaf Publishing Ltd.,
2008), 104–22; Ginger Gibson and Jason Klinck, "Canada's Resilient North:
The Impact of Mining on Aboriginal Communities," *Pimatisiwin*, 3, no. 1
(2005): 114–40; Kerry Abel, *Drum Songs: Glimpses of Dene History* (Montreal:
McGill Queen's University Press, 2005); Arn Keeling and John Sandlos,
"Environmental Justice Goes Underground? Historical Notes from
Canada's Northern Mining Frontier," *Environmental Justice* 2, no. 3 (2009):
117–25 and "Claiming the New North: Development and Colonialism at
the Pine Point Mine, Northwest Territories, Canada," *Environment and
History* 18, no. 1 (2012) 5–34; Shirley Tsetta, Ginger Gibson, Linda McDevitt
and Sarah Plotner, "Telling a Story of Change the Dene Way: Indicators
for Monitoring in Diamond Impacted Communities," *Pimatisiwin* 3, no. 1
(2005): 59–69; Liza Piper, *The Industrial Transformation of Subarctic Canada*
(Vancouver: University of British Columbia Press, 2008). For military
presence, see P. Whitney Lackenbauer and Matthew Farish, "The Cold War
on Canadian Soil: Militarizing a Northern Environment," *Environmental
History* 12, no. 4 (2007): 920–50.

29 For hydroelectricity and its impact on Indigenous lands and peoples,
see Hans Carlson, *Home Is the Hunter: The James Bay Cree and Their
Land* (Vancouver: University of British Columbia Press, 2008); Caroline
Desbiens, *Power from the North: Territory, Identity, and Culture of
Hydroelectricity in Quebec* (Vancouver: University of British Columbia Press,
2013); James. F. Hornig, ed., *Social and Environmental Impacts of the James
Bay Hydroelectric Project* (Montreal: McGill-Queen's University Press, 1999);
Brittany Luby, "From Milk-Medicine to Public (Re)Education Programs:
An Examination of Anishinabek Mothers' Responses to Hydroelectric
Flooding in the Treaty #3 District, 1900–1975," *Canadian Bulletin of Medical
History* 32, no. 2 (2015): 363–89; and Jean L. Manore, *Cross-Currents: Hydro-
electricity and the Engineering of Northern Ontario* (Waterloo: Wilfrid Laurier
University Press, 1999).

30 Arn Keeling has compared Elliot Lake to Uranium City in "'Born in an
Atomic Test Tube': Landscapes of cyclonic development at Uranium City,
Saskatchewan." *The Canadian Geographer* 54, no. 2 (Summer 2010),
228–52. See also Michael A. Amundson, *Yellowcake Towns: Uranium
Mining Communities in the American West* (Boulder: University Press of
Colorado, 2002).

31 Keeling and Sandlos, "The Complex Legacy of Mining in Northern
Canada," 6–7. For some exceptions see Ginger Gibson and Jason
Klinck, "Canada's Resilient North: The Impact of Mining on Aboriginal

Communities," *Pimatisiwin*, 3, no. 1 (2005): 114–40; Arn Keeling and John Sandlos, "Environmental Justice Goes Underground? Historical Notes from Canada's Northern Mining Frontier," *Environmental Justice* 2, no. 3 (2009): 117–25; John Sandlos and Arn Keeling, "Zombie Mines and the (Over)burden of History," *Solutions Journal* 4, no. 3 (2013): 80–3; Lianne C. Leddy, "Poisoning the Serpent: Uranium Exploitation and the Serpent River First Nation, 1953–1988," in *The Nature of Empires and Empires of Nature*, ed. Karl Hele. (Waterloo, ON: Wilfrid Laurier University Press, 2013), 125–47.

32 Leddy, "Intersections of Indigenous and Environmental History in Canada," 84–5. For critiques of the idea of the "ecological Indian" see Shepard Krech III, *The Ecological Indian: Myth and History* (New York: W.W. Norton, 1999); see also Robert F. Berkhofer, *The White Man's Indian: Images of the American Indian from Columbus to the Present* (New York: Vintage, 1979); Finis Dunaway, "Gas Masks, Pogo, and the Ecological Indian: Earth Day and the Visual Politics of American Environmentalism," *American Quarterly* 60, no. 1 (2008): 67–99; Gregory D. Smithers, "Beyond the 'Ecological Indian': Environmental Politics and Traditional Ecological Knowledge in Modern North America," *Environmental History* 20 (2015): 83–111.

33 James D. Rice, "Beyond 'the Ecological Indian' and 'Virgin Soil Epidemics': New Perspectives on Native Americans and the Environment," *History Compass* 12, no. 9 (2014): 745–57.

34 For a methodological discussion see Linda Tuhiwai Smith, *Decolonizing Methodologies: Research and Indigenous Peoples* (London: Zed Books, 1999). See also Kathleen E. Absolon (Minogiizhigokwe), *Kaandossiwin: How We Come to Know* (Winnipeg: Fernwood Press, 2011); Kathy Absolon and Cam Willett, "Putting Ourselves Forward: Location in Aboriginal Research," in *Research as Resistance: Critical, Indigenous, and Anti-Oppressive Approaches*, ed. Leslie Brown and Susan Strega (Toronto: Canadian Scholars' Press/ Women's Press, 2005); Jo-ann Archibald, *Indigenous Storywork: Educating the Heart, Mind, Body, and Spirit* (Vancouver: University of British Columbia Press, 2008); Pam Colorado, "Bridging Native and Western Science," *Convergence* 21, no. 2 (1988): 49–68; Charles R. Menzies and Caroline Butler, "Introduction: Understanding Ecological Knowledge," in *Traditional Ecological Knowledge and Natural Resource Management*, ed. Charles R. Menzies (Lincoln: University of Nebraska Press, 2006), 10–12. Julie Cruikshank, "Uses and Abuses of 'Traditional Knowledge': Perspectives from the Yukon Territory," in *Cultivating Arctic Landscapes: Knowing and Managing Animals in the Circumpolar North*, ed. David G. Anderson and Mark Nuttall (New York: Berghahn Books, 2004), 17–32; Margaret Kovach, *Indigenous Methodologies: Characteristics, Conversations, and Contexts* (Toronto: University of Toronto Press, 2009); Lianne C. Leddy,

"Interviewing Nookomis and Other Reflections of an Indigenous
Historian," *Oral History Forum/d'histoire orale* 30 (Special Issue–2010): 1–18;
Winona Wheeler, "Reflections on the Social Relations of Indigenous Oral
Histories," in *Walking a Tightrope: Aboriginal People and Their Representations*,
ed. Ute Lischke and David T. McNab (Waterloo: University of Waterloo
Press, 2005), 189–213; Sean Wilson, *Research Is Ceremony: Indigenous
Research Methods* (Winnipeg: Fernwood, 2008).

35 Kerry Abel, *Drum Songs: Glimpses of Dene History* (Montreal: McGill-
Queen's University Press, 2005); James T. Angus, "How the Dokis Indians
Protected Their Timber," *Ontario History* 81 (1989): 181–99; Rosemary
Brown, "The Exploitation of the Oil and Gas Frontier: Its Impact on
Lubicon Lake Cree Women," in *Women of the First Nations: Power, Wisdom,
and Strength*, ed. Christine Miller and Patricia Chuchryk (Winnipeg:
University of Manitoba Press, 1997), 151–65; Keith Thor Carlson and
Jonathan Clapperton, "Introduction. Special Places and Protected
Spaces: Historical and Global Perspectives on Non-National Parks in
Canada and Abroad," *Environment and History* 18 (2012): 475–96; Hans
M. Carlson, "A Watershed of Words: Litigating and Negotiating Nature
in Eastern James Bay, 1971–1975," *Canadian Historical Review* 85, no. 1
(2004): 63–84; Katsi Cook, "Powerful Like a River: Reweaving the Web
of Our Lives in Defense of Environmental and Reproductive Justice,"
in *Original Instructions: Indigenous Teachings for a Sustainable Future*, ed.
Melissa K. Nelson (Rochester: Bear and Company, 2008), 154–67; Julie
Cruikshank, *Do Glaciers Listen? Local Knowledge, Colonial Encounters, and
Social Imagination* (Vancouver: University of British Columbia Press, 2005);
Carly A. Dokis, *Where the Rivers Meet: Pipelines, Participatory Resource
Management, and Aboriginal-State Relations in the Northwest Territories*
(Vancouver: University of British Columbia Press, 2015); James F. Hornig,
ed., *Social and Environmental Impacts of the James Bay Hydroelectric Project*
(Montreal: McGill-Queen's University Press, 1999); Igor Krupnik and
Dyanna Jolly, eds., *The Earth Is Faster Now: Indigenous Observations of Arctic
Environmental Change*, 2nd ed. (Fairbanks: Arctic Research Consortium
of the United States, 2010); Mark Kuhlberg, "'Nothing It Seems Can Be
Done about It': Charlie Cox, Indian Affairs Timber Policy, and the Long
Lac Reserve, 1924–40," *Canadian Historical Review* 84, no. 1 (2003): 33–64;
Timothy B. Leduc, *Climate Culture Change: Inuit and Western Dialogues with
a Warming North* (Ottawa: University of Ottawa Press, 2010); Deborah
McGregor, "Coming Full Circle: Indigenous Knowledge, Environment,
and Our Future," *American Indian Quarterly* 28, no. 3 and 4 (2004): 386;
Paul Nadasdy, *Hunters and Bureaucrats: Power, Knowledge, and Aboriginal-
State Relations in the Southwest Yukon* (Vancouver: University of British
Columbia Press, 2003); Liza Piper, *The Industrial Transformation of Subarctic*

Canada (Vancouver: University of British Columbia Press, 2008); Richard F. Salisbury, *A Homeland for the Cree: Regional Development in James Bay, 1971–1981* (Montreal: McGill-Queen's University Press, 1986); Anastasia M. Shkilnyk, *A Poison Stronger Than Love: The Destruction of an Ojibwa Community* (New Haven: Yale University Press, 1985); Jocelyn Thorpe, *Temagami's Tangled Wild: Race, Gender, and the Making of Canadian Nature* (Vancouver: University of British Columbia Press, 2012); Nancy Turner and Helen Clifton, "'It's So Different Today': Climate Change and Indigenous Lifeways in British Columbia, Canada," *Global Environmental Change* 19 (2009): 180–90; Christopher Vecsey, "Grassy Narrows Reserve: Mercury Pollution, Social Disruption, and Natural Resources: A Question of Autonomy," *American Indian Quarterly* 11, no. 4 (1987): 287–314.

36 Leddy, "Intersections of Indigenous and Environmental History in Canada," 92.

37 For more on the development of Elliot Lake, see Catharine Dixon, *The Power and the Promise: The Elliot Lake Story* (Elliot Lake: Gillidix Publishing Inc., 1996). Dixon also wrote a history of the local high school, *As It Happened: the Founding of Elliot Lake Secondary School* (Elliot Lake: Gillidix Publishing Inc., 2001). Two local historical collaborations are *Jewel in the Wilderness: A History of Elliot Lake 1957–1980* (Elliot Lake: Elliot Lake Secondary School, 1980) and *Dawn of a New Setting, 1980–1997* (Elliot Lake: Elliot Lake Secondary School, 1997). These two volumes were written by high school students in partnership with some community members and are largely commemorative pieces, however, they are useful for a popular and general history of the area. For an exception to this narrative trend, see Sharon Gow, "Respect and Responsibility: Community-Based Options for Perpetual Care in the Serpent River Watershed," in *Boom Town Blues, Elliot Lake: Collapse and Revival in a Single-Industry Community*, ed. Anne-Marie Mawhiney and Jane Pitblado (Toronto: Dundurn Press, 1999), 318–30.

38 Anna Stanley, "Marginalization and Challenge: The Production of Knowledge and Landscape in Canadian Nuclear Waste Management Making" (PhD diss., University of Guelph, 2006). See also Anna Stanley, "Citizenship and the Production of Landscape and Knowledge in Contemporary Canadian Nuclear Fuel Waste Management," *The Canadian Geographer* 52 (2008): 64–82.

39 Lorraine Rekmans, Keith Lewis and Anabel Dwyer, eds. *This Is My Homeland: Stories of the Effects of Nuclear Industries by People of the Serpent River First Nation and the North Shore of Lake Huron* (Cutler: Serpent River First Nation, 2003).

40 Janice Gamble and Elder Tea, eds., *Connected to the Land: Stories from the Serpent's Band* (Serpent River First Nation Education Department, 2013).

41 For a review of Indigenous environmental history see Lianne C. Leddy, "Intersections of Indigenous and Environmental History in Canada."

42 Alistair MacLeod chose it for the setting of his award-winning 1999 novel *No Great Mischief* (Toronto: McClelland and Stewart, 1999). Now that the mines have closed, the town has rebranded itself as "the Jewel in the Wilderness" and is marketed in southern Ontario as a retirement community. Nevertheless, whenever uranium and rare earth prices rise so too does speculation that the mines will one-day reopen. See for example "Pele Mountain Reports Progress at Eco Ridge Mine Site," Marketwatch, 12 November 2010, http://www.marketwatch.com/story/pele-mountain -resources-excellent-leverage-to-uranium-rare-earth-elements-2010–11–12 –84500?reflink=MW_news_stmp.

43 For a case study of traditional land use and differing understandings of treaties and "ownership," see Jean L. Manore, "Indian Reserves v. Indian Lands: Reserves, Crown Lands, and Natural Resource Use in Northeastern Ontario," in *Ontario since Confederation: A Reader*, ed. Edgar-André Montigny and Lori Chambers (Toronto: University of Toronto Press, 2000), 195–213.

44 Throughout this book, I use the terms First Nations and Indigenous when talking about Indigenous peoples generally. When talking about our specific territory, I use "Anishinaabek" to refer to the Ojibway, Odawa, and Potawatomi peoples. "Anishinaabe" is the adjective used throughout. Readers may note that the spelling of these words vary from one author to another, and one community to another, which is a reflection of the oral nature of our language. For consistency, I have adopted this spelling. See chapter two for more information.

45 See Map 2: Serpent River First Nation and the Elliot Lake Region and Map 3: Serpent River First Nation. The current village site is located just to the west of Aird Bay at what is now called Cutler, Ontario but which has also been known as Kenabutch in the past. The reserve itself is also known as *Genabaajing*.

46 For more on colonial power relations, resources, and conservation, see John Sandlos, *Hunters at the Margin: Native People and Wildlife Conservation in the Northwest Territories* (Vancouver: University of British Columbia Press, 2007) and Paul Nadasdy, *Hunters and Bureaucrats: Power, Knowledge, and Aboriginal-State Relations in the Southwest Yukon* (Vancouver: University of British Columbia Press, 2004).

47 Kathy Absolon and Cam Willett, "Putting Ourselves Forward: Location in Aboriginal Research," in *Research as Resistance: Critical, Indigenous, and Anti-Oppressive Approaches*, ed. Leslie Brown and Susan Strega (Toronto: Canadian Scholars' Press/Women's Press, 2005), 97–125. A larger methodological and location reflection appears in Lianne C.

Leddy, "Interviewing Nookomis and Other Reflections of an Indigenous Historian," *Oral History Forum/d'histoire orale*, 30 (Special Issue–2010): 1–18. Some of the text from the next few pages originally appeared there.

48 For more on this interplay between types of sources, see Lianne C. Leddy, "*Dibaajimowinan* as method: Environmental history, Indigenous scholarship, and balancing sources," in *Methodological Challenges in Nature-Culture and Environmental History Research*, ed. Jocelyn Thorpe, Stephanie Rutherford, and Anders L. Sandberg (New York: Routledge, 2017), 93–104.

49 Linda Tuhiwai Smith, *Decolonizing Methodologies: Research and Indigenous Peoples* (London: Zed Books, 1999), 34–5.

50 Winona LaDuke, *All Our Relations: Native Struggles for Land and Life* (Cambridge: South End Press, 1999); Deborah McGregor, "Honouring our Relations: An Anishnaabe Perspective on Environmental Justice," in *Speaking for Ourselves: Environmental Justice in Canada* ed. Julian Agyeman (Vancouver: University of British Columbia Press, 2009), 27–41; Melissa K. Nelson, ed., *Original Instructions: Indigenous Teachings for a Sustainable Future* (Rochester: Bear and Company, 2008); Leanne Simpson, *Dancing on Our Turtle's Back: Stories of Nishnaabeg Re-Creation, Resurgence and a New Emergence* (Winnipeg: Arbeiter Ring Publishing, 2011).

51 Leanne Simpson, *Dancing on Our Turtle's Back*, 32; Deborah McGregor, "Coming Full Circle" and "Indigenous Women, Water Justice and Zaagidowin (love)" *Canadian Woman Studies* 30, no. 2–3 (Summer/Fall 2013): 71–8.

52 Kathleen E. Absolon (Minogiizhigokwe), *Kaandossiwin: How We Come to Know* (Black Point and Winnipeg: Fernwood Press, 2011); Kim Anderson, *Life Stages and Native Women: Memory, Teachings, and Story Medicine* (Winnipeg: University of Manitoba Press, 2011); Jo-ann Archibald, *Indigenous Storywork*; Margaret Kovach, *Indigenous Methodologies*; Shawn Wilson, *Research Is Ceremony*.

53 Julie Cruikshank has examined the differences in the ways in which First Nations and settlers view environmental surroundings. See Cruikshank, *Do Glaciers Listen*. See also Dene Cultural Institute, "Traditional Ecological Knowledge and Environmental Assessment" and Milton M.R. Freeman, "The Nature and Utility of Traditional Ecological Knowledge," *Northern Perspectives* 20, no. 1 (1992): 9–12, accessed 23 April 2011, http://www.carc.org/pubs/v20no1/utility.htm. See also John Borrows, "Living Between the Water and the Rocks: First Nations, Environmental Planning and Democracy," *University of Toronto Law Journal* 47 (1997): 417–66; Deborah McGregor, "Linking Traditional Knowledge and Environmental Practice in Ontario," *Journal of Canadian Studies* 43, no. 3 (Fall 2009): 69–100. For a controversial critique of IK, see Frances Widdowson and Albert Howard,

Disrobing the Aboriginal Industry: The Deception Behind Indigenous Cultural Preservation (Montreal: McGill-Queen's University Press, 2008).

54 Shepard Krech III, *The Ecological Indian*; Michael E. Harkin and David Rich Lewis, eds., *Native Americans and the Environment: Perspectives on the Ecological Indian* (Lincoln: University of Nebraska Press, 2007); Richard White and William Cronon, "Ecological Change and Indian-White Relations," in *Handbook of North American Indians*, vol. 4, ed. William Washburn (Washington: Smithsonian Institution Press, 1989), 417–29; Paul Nadasdy, "Transcending the Debate over the Ecologically Noble Indian: Indigenous Peoples and Environmentalism," *Ethnohistory* 52, no. 2 (2005): 291–331.

55 For more on Traditional Environmental Knowledge (TEK), see Stephen Bocking, "Indigenous Knowledge and the History of Science, Race, and Colonial Authority in Northern Canada," in *Rethinking the Great White North: Race, Nature, and the Historical Geographies of Whiteness in Canada*, ed. A. Baldwin, L. Cameron, and A. Kobayashi (University of British Columbia Press, 2011), 39–61. See also Keith Thor Carlson, ed., *You Are Asked to Witness: The Sto:lo in Canada's Pacific Coast History* (Chilliwack: Sto:lo Heritage Trust, 1997) in addition to the works by the Dene Cultural Institute and Freeman, listed in an above endnote. Ciaran O'Faircheallaigh's call for more Indigenous participation in environmental policies and agreements is an example of the importance of TEK. Ciaran O'Faircheallaigh, *Environmental Agreements in Canada: Aboriginal Participation, EIA Follow-Up and Environmental Management of Major Projects* (Calgary: Canadian Institute of Resources Law, 2006); Igor Krupnik and Dyanna Jolly, eds., *The Earth Is Faster Now*; Timothy B. Leduc, *Climate Culture Change*.

56 An excellent article that describes the importance of IK is Deborah McGregor, "Coming Full Circle."

57 Lianne C. Leddy, "*Dibaajimowinan* as method."

58 This term is from *Carved from Rock: The Story of Elliot Lake* (National Dream Production, 2005). It is a commemorative film that celebrated the town's 50th anniversary. Jocelyn Thorpe deconstructs the settler view of Indigenous homelands as "wild" in *Temagami's Tangled Wild*.

2. The Serpent River Anishinaabek before 1950

1 Quoted in Felix Atencio-Gonzales, "URANIUM: It has industry 'close to meltdown,'" *Windspeaker*, 7 June 1991, 9.

2 John L. Tobias, "Protection, Civilization, Assimilation: An Outline History of Canada's Indian Policy," in *As Long as the Sun Shines and the Water Flows: A Reader in Canadian Native Studies*, ed. Ian A.L. Getty and Antoine S. Lussier (Vancouver: University of British Columbia Press, 1995), 39–55; John S. Milloy,

"The Early Indian Acts: Developmental Strategy and Constitutional Change," in *Sweet Promises: A Reader on Indian-White Relations*, ed. J.R. Miller (Toronto: University of Toronto Press, 1991), 145–54.

3 Patricia M. Ningewance, *Talking Gookum's Language: Learning Ojibwe* (Winnipeg: Mazinaate Press, 2007), xvii.

4 Patricia M. Ningewance, xvii–xviii.

5 Ningewance, xviii.

6 Deborah McGregor, "Honouring Our Relations: An Anishnaabe Perspective on Environmental Justice," in *Speaking for Ourselves: Environmental Justice in Canada*, ed. Julian Agyeman (Vancouver: University of British Columbia Press, 2009), 27.

7 Basil Johnston, *Ojibway Heritage* (Toronto: McClelland and Stewart, 2008), 14. Johnston's version mentions that the original island formed by the turtle and small amount of soil was Mishee Mackinakong (Michilimackinac). See also Edward Benton-Banai, *The Mishomis Book: The Voice of the Ojibway* (Minneapolis: University of Minnesota Press and Indian Country Communications, Inc., 2010), 29–34.

8 Johnston, *Ojibway Heritage*, 15.

9 Johnston, *Ojibway Heritage*, 14.

10 Johnston, *Ojibway Heritage*, 20.

11 Johnston, *Ojibway Heritage*, 16.

12 John Borrows, *Recovering Canada: The Resurgence of Indigenous Law* (University of Toronto Press, 2002), 16–20.

13 Basil Johnston supplies a list of place names, including Lakes Superior, Michigan, St. Clair, as well as important meeting places like Bawating (Sault. Ste. Marie, Ontario) and Michilimackinac. See *Ojibway Ceremonies* (Toronto: McClelland and Stewart, 2008), "List of Place Names," ix. See also Ningewance, *Talking Gookum's Language*, especially the glossary from pages 221–365.

14 Robert E. Ritzenthaler, "Southwestern Chippewa," *Handbook of North American Indians*, vol. 15, ed. Bruce G, Trigger, General Editor William C. Sturtevant (Washington: Smithsonian Institution, 1978), 741.

15 Brenda J. Child, *Holding Our World Together: Ojibwe Women and the Survival of Community* (Toronto: Viking, 2012), xvi.

16 Benton-Banai, 98–9.

17 Donald L. Fixico, "The Alliance of the Three Fires in Trade and War, 1630–1812," *Michigan Historical Review* 20, no. 2 (1994): 1–23.

18 Olive Patricia Dickason, *Canada's First Nations: A History of Founding Peoples from Earliest Times*, 4th ed. with David T. McNab (Don Mills: Oxford University Press, 2009), 104.

19 See, for example, Peter S. Schmalz, *The Ojibwa of Southern Ontario* (Toronto: University of Toronto Press, 1991); D. Peter MacLeod, "The *Anishinabeg*

Point of View: The History of the Great Lakes Region to 1800 in Nineteenth-Century Mississauga, Odawa, and Ojibwa Historiography," *Canadian Historical Review* 73, no. 2 (1992): 194–210; Leroy Eid, "The Ojibwa-Iroquois War: The War the Five Nations did not Win," *Ethnohistory* 36, no. 4 (Fall 1979): 297–324. Both articles cite the mid-nineteenth century works of Ojibway writers George Copway (1850) and Peter Jones (1861), among others. George Copway, *The Traditional History and Characteristic Sketches of the Ojibway Nation* (Toronto: Coles, 1972); Peter Jones, *History of the Ojebway Indians* (London: A.W. Bennett, 1861).

20　Susan M. Hill, *The Clay We Are Made Of* (University of Manitoba Press, 2017), 42–3; Leanne Simpson, "Looking After the *Gdoo-naaganinaa*: Precolonial Nishnaabeg Diplomatic Relationships," *Wicazo Sa Review* 23, no. 2 (Fall 2008): 29–42.

21　These stories are from oral histories collected for the Union of Ontario Indians by the late Perry Shawana at SRFN in 1984. The histories were collected as part of a research project into the Trans-Canada Highway that runs through the community. At present, they are held at the SRFN library where they are publicly available. Interview with Mr. Louis Meawasige and Mrs. Alice Meawasige (née Bisaillon), conducted by Perry Shawana, Serpent River First Nation, 1984. Mr. Meawasige is speaking. Interview with Mr. Bill McLeod conducted by Perry Shawana, Serpent River First Nation, 1984. See also Tom Haddow, "Rooster Rock Sacred Site," *Standard*, 29 March 1983, 29. The latter spelling, *Bakakwehngenda* comes from Elder Tea, 29.

22　Interview with Mr. Bill McLeod conducted by Perry Shawana, Serpent River First Nation, 1984.

23　Tom Haddow, "Village Was Located on Sylvah Island," *Standard*, 29 March 1983, 22. See also Elder Tea, 130–31; 38.

24　The historical analysis of economic development can be seen in the works of Harold Adam Innis, *The Fur Trade in Canada: An Introduction to Canadian Economic History* (Toronto: University of Toronto Press, 1999).

25　W.L. Morton, *The Kingdom of Canada* (Toronto: McClelland and Stewart, 1963), 29.

26　Claire Campbell, "'Behold Me a Sojourner in the Wilderness': Early Encounters with the Georgian Bay," *Michigan Historical Review* 28, no. 1 (Spring 2002), 34. Campbell examines the history of European encounters with the 'sixth lake.'

27　Gilles Havard, *The Great Peace of Montreal of 1701: French-Native Diplomacy in the Seventeenth Century*, trans. Phyllis Aronoff and Howard Scott (Montreal: McGill-Queen's University Press, 2001), 31. See also Helen Hornbeck Tanner, ed., *Atlas of Great Lakes Indian History* (Norman and London: University of Oklahoma Press, 1987), 32–3.

28 Denys Delâge, *Bitter Feast: Amerindians and Europeans in Northeastern North America, 1600–64* (Vancouver: University of British Columbia Press, 1993), 64.

29 Reuben Gold Thwaites, ed., *Jesuit Relations and Allied Documents*, vol. 33 (Cleveland: The Burrows Brothers Company, 1898), 155. See also E.S. Rogers, "Southeastern Ojibwa," *Handbook of North American Indians*, vol. 15, ed. Bruce G. Trigger, General Editor William C. Sturtevant (Washington: Smithsonian Institution, 1978), 760; Schmalz, *The Ojibwa of Southern Ontario*, 4.

30 Tanner, 36–7.

31 Bruce G. Trigger, "Jesuits and the Fur Trade," in *Sweet Promises: A Reader on Indian-White Relations in Canada*, ed. J.R. Miller (Toronto: University of Toronto Press, 1991), 3–18.

32 Studies of the fur trade include Harold A. Innis, *The Fur Trade in Canada: An Introduction to Canadian Economic History* (Toronto: University of Toronto Press, 1999 reprint); E.E. Rich, *The Fur Trade and the Northwest to 1857* (Toronto: McClelland and Stewart, 1967); A.J. Ray, *Indians and the Fur Trade: Their Roles as Trappers, Hunters, and Middlemen in the Lands Southwest of Hudson Bay, 1660–1870* (Toronto: University of Toronto Press, 1998); Robin Fisher, *Contact and Conflict: Indian-European Relations in British Columbia, 1774–1890* (Vancouver: University of British Columbia Press, 1977); Sylvia Van Kirk, *Many Tender Ties: Women in Fur Trade Society, 1670–1870* (Winnipeg: Watson and Dwyer, 1980); Jennifer S.H. Brown, *Strangers in Blood: Fur Trade Indian Families in Indian Country* (Vancouver: University of British Columbia Press, 1980). A more recent and multidisciplinary collection is Carolyn Podruchny and Laura Peers, eds., *Gathering Places: Aboriginal and Fur Trade Histories* (Vancouver: University of British Columbia Press, 2010).

33 Tanner, 29.

34 For a more complete list of fur trade posts in the central Great Lakes region, see Ernest Voorhis, *Historic Forts and Trading Posts of the French Regime and of the English Fur Trading Company* (Ottawa: Department of the Interior, 1930), map enclosure.

35 Michael Witgen, *An Infinity of Nations: How the Native New World Shaped Early North America* (Philadelphia: University of Pennsylvania Press, 2012), 69–74.

36 Michael Witgen, "The Rituals of Possession: Native Identity and the Invention of Empire in Seventeenth-Century Western North America," *Ethnohistory* 54, no. 4 (Fall 2007): 639.

37 John Borrows, "Wampum at Niagara: The Royal Proclamation, Canadian Legal History, and Self-Government," in *Aboriginal and Treaty Rights in Canada: Essays on Law, Equity, and Respect for Difference* ed. Michael Asch (Vancouver: University of British Columbia Press, 1997), 155–72.

38 Schmalz, 97–105; Phil Bellfy, *Three Fires Unity: The Anishnaabeg of the Lake Huron Borderlands* (Lincoln: Nebraska University Press, 2011), 43. Bellfy uses the estimates provided by American Indian agent Henry Rowe Schoolcraft, who had married into an Indigenous family.

39 Schmalz, 97–105.

40 "John Baptist Askin to Colonel William Claus," in Cruikshank, *Invasion of Canada* 67, 73 quoted in Schmalz, 111.

41 Schmalz, 114.

42 Cory Silverstein and Zeek Cywink, "From Fireside to TV Screen: Self-Determination and Anishnaabe Storytelling Traditions," *Canadian Journal of Native Studies*, 20, no. 1 (2000): 42.

43 Gamble and Elder Tea, 16.

44 Tanner, ed., *Atlas of Great Lakes Indian History*, 125.

45 Dickason with McNab, *Canada's First Nations*, 200–4.

46 Robert J. Surtees, *Manitoulin Island Treaties* (Ottawa: Indian and Northern Affairs Canada, 1986), np. Crown-Indigenous Relations and Northern Affairs Canada, accessed 20 July 2020, https://www.rcaanc-cirnac.gc.ca /eng/1100100028959/1564583230395.

47 Theodore Binnema and Kevin Hutchings, "The Emigrant and the Noble Savage: Sir Francis Bond Head's Romantic Approach to Aboriginal Policy in Upper Canada, 1836–1838," *Journal of Canadian Studies* 39, no. 1 (2005) 115–38.

48 Robert J. Surtees, *Manitoulin Island Treaties* (Ottawa: Indian and Northern Affairs Canada, 1986), np.

49 Ibid. The 1836 treaty was abrogated by a later agreement in 1862 whereby much of the island (with the exception of Wikwemikong) was appropriated for fishing and farming imperatives. See David Shanahan, "The Manitoulin Treaties, 1836 and 1862: The Indian Department and Indian Destiny," *Ontario History* 86, no. 1 (1994): 13–32.

50 Nancy M. Wightman and W. Robert Wightman, "The Mica Bay Affair: Conflict on the Upper Lakes Mining Frontier, 1840–1850," *Ontario History* 83, no. 3 (1991): 193.

51 Janet E. Chute, "Pursuing the Great Spirit's Plan: Nineteenth-Century Ojibwa Attitudes Towards the Future of Logging and Mining on Unsurrendered Indian Lands North of Lakes Huron and Superior," in *Social Relations in Resource Hinterlands: Papers from the 27th Annual Meeting of the Western Association of Sociology and Anthropology*, ed. Thomas W. Dunk (Thunder Bay: Lakehead University Centre for Northern and Regional Studies, 1991), 173–203. See also Nancy M. Wightman and W. Robert Wightman, "The Mica Bay Affair: Conflict on the Upper Lakes Mining Frontier, 1840–1850" *Ontario History* 83, no. 3 (1991): 193–208 and

Rhonda Telford, "Aboriginal Resistance in the Mid-Nineteenth Century: The *Anishinabe*, Their Allies, and the Closing of the Mining Operations at Mica Bay and Michipicoten Island," in *Blockades and Resistance: Studies in Actions of Peace and the Temagami Blockades of 1988–89*, ed. Bruce W. Hodgins, Ute Lischke, and David T. McNab (Waterloo: Wilfrid Laurier University Press, 2003), 71–84.

52 Nancy M. Wightman and W. Robert Wightman, "Mica Bay," 199. Chute, "Pursuing the Great Spirit's Plan," 181.

53 LAC, RG 10, vol. 612, "Letter from Chinquak to Ironside," 116–7 and LAC RG 10, vol. 123, Petition no. 225 cited in Rhonda Telford, "Aboriginal Resistance," 73.

54 Telford, 78.

55 Telford, 78–80.

56 Robert J. Surtees, *The Robinson Treaties 1850* (Ottawa: Treaties and Historical Research Centre: Indian and Northern Affairs Canada, 1986), Crown-Indigenous Relations and Northern Affairs Canada, accessed 17 July 2020, https://www.rcaanc-cirnac.gc.ca/eng/1100100028974/1564412549270.

57 Julia Jarvis, "William Benjamin Robinson," *Dictionary of Canadian Biography Online* (Toronto and Quebec: University of Toronto and Université Laval, 2000), accessed 17 July 2020, http://www.biographi.ca/009004-119.01-e.php?id_nbr=5234.

58 Robert J. Surtees, *The Robinson Treaties 1850*.

59 See, for example, "Opening Statement of the Robinson-Huron Treaty Plaintiffs," accessed 20 July 2020, https://www.robinsonhurontreaty1850.com/litigation-1.

60 *Copy of the Robinson Treaty Made in the Year 1850 with the Ojibewa Indians of Lake Huron Conveying Certain Lands to the Crown*, Crown-Indigenous Relations and Northern Affairs Canada, accessed 17 July 2020, https://www.rcaanc-cirnac.gc.ca/eng/1100100028984/1581293724401.

61 Ibid.

62 Surtees divides the territory by treaty: 35,700 square miles in the Robinson-Huron Treaty (from a population of 1,240 First Nations people), and 16,700 square miles in the Robinson-Superior Treaty (from a population of 1,422 First Nations people).

63 Ibid.

64 Crown-Indigenous Relations, *Copy of the Robinson Treaty*.

65 Canada Indian Affairs, *Report of the Special Commissioners Appointed on the 8th of September, 1856, to Investigate Indian Affairs in Canada*, Sessional Papers, Appendix 21 (Toronto: Stewart Derbishire and George Desbarats, 1858), A21–5.

66 Canada Indian Affairs, Sessional Papers, Appendix 21, A21–69.

67 Canada Indian Affairs, Sessional Papers, 1858, A21–72.
68 Canada Indian Affairs, Sessional Papers, 1858, Appendix 21, Internal Appendix 26, "Report to Commissioners by Revd. J. Hannipeaux and Revd. Ferard," August 1857, A21–227.
69 Canada Indian Affairs, Sessional Papers, 1858, Appendix 21, A21–72.
70 Canada Indian Affairs, Sessional Papers, 1858, Appendix 21, A21–72 and 73.
71 See Milloy and Tobias, as well as Hugh Shewell, *"Enough to Keep Them Alive": Indian Welfare in Canada, 1873–1965* (Toronto: University of Toronto Press, 2004).
72 Annual Report of the Department of the Interior for the Year Ended 30th June 1874. J.C. Phipps, Visiting Superintendent. part 2, page 32. The amount for land, rents, and timber was $442 for this year. See part 2, page 96.
73 Mary-Ellen Kelm, "Diagnosing the Discursive Indian: Medicine, Gender, and the 'Dying Race.'" *Ethnohistory* 52, no. 2 (Spring 2005): 371–406.
74 Dominion of Canada Annual Report of the Department of Indian Affairs for the Year Ended 31st December 1884, J.C. Phipps, Visiting Superintendent, Northern Superintendency (Parry Sound) 84–5.
75 LAC, RG 10, vol. 2116, File 22,036, "CPR surrender," 30 January 1882. See also Dominion of Canada, Annual Report for the Department of Indian Affairs for the Year Ended 31st December 1882, J.C. Phipps, Visiting Superintendent, p. 3
76 LAC, RG 10M 78903/78, "C.P.R. Kenabutch Station. Extra land for station grounds in Serpent River Indian Reserve," 1 August 1888.
77 Elders from Perry Shawana's study. Ningewance provides "ganabach" as the translation for maybe.
78 As told by Julia Recollet to Perry Shawana, 17 December 1984, SRFN, using the spelling "Paypamash." Elder Tea also uses Pahbemosh and Babamosh as alternate spellings, see pages 26 and 34, respectively, and in keeping with the family tree at the Serpent River Trading Post, I use Babamosh.
79 Dominion of Canada Annual Report of the Department of Indian Affairs for the Year Ended 30th June 1896, "serpent River Indians, Ont. (No. 32)," 505.
80 LAC, RG 10, vol. 2116, File 22,036, "Letter from Samuel Hagan to the Secretary of Indian Affairs," 6 April 1904.
81 LAC, RG 10, vol. 2116, File 22,036, "Letter from Samuel Hagan to J.D. McLean, Secretary of Indian Affairs," 11 August 1904.
82 The CPR, for their part, maintained that they had never refused reasonable compensation for lost animals due to the railway. See LAC, RG 10, vol. 2116, File 22, 036, "Letter from J.D. McLean to Samuel Hagan," 27 June 1904.
83 LAC, RG 10, vol. 2116, File 22,036, "Letter from Chas. Drinkwater, Esq. to S. Stewart, Assistant Secretary," 14 November 1904.

84 LAC, RG 10, vol. 2116, File 22,036, "Letter from Chief William Nahmawan to J.D. McLean," 7 August 1912. The chief's last name appears as "Nahnawan," "Nahmiwan", "Nahmawan," and "Namawan" in records held at LAC and the Serpent River First Nation. Elder Tea uses the Nahmiwan spelling, which is why I have used it in the text consistently. Elder Tea, 38–9.

85 LAC, RG 10, vol. 2116, File 22,036, "Letters from Samuel Hagan, J.D. McLean," August 1912.

86 LAC, RG 10, vol. 2116, File 22,036, "Letter from Wm Namawan," 17 October 1912.

87 LAC, RG 10, vol. 2116, File 22,036, "Letter from Samuel Hagan to J.D. McLean," 5 December 1912.

88 LAC, RG 10, vol. 2116, File 22,036, "Letter from Chief of Serpent River to CPR," 3 December 1912; LAC, RG 10, vol. 2116, File 22,036, "Letter from Nahmawan to Indian Affairs," 4 December 1912.

89 John L. Tobias, "Protection, Civilization, Assimilation: An Outline History of Canada's Indian Policy," in *As Long as the Sun Shines and the Water Flows: A Reader in Canadian Native Studies*, ed. Ian A.L. Getty and Antoine S. Lussier (Vancouver: University of British Columbia Press, 1995), 39–55.

90 Olive P. Dickason with David T. McNab, *Canada's First Nations: A History of Founding Peoples from Earliest Times*, 4th ed. (Don Mills: Oxford University Press, 2009), 289.

91 LAC, RG 10, vol. 2116, File 22,036, "Letter from J. Simpson, J. Metigwab, and W. Nahmawan," January 1913; LAC, RG 10, vol. 2116, File 22,036, "Letter from J.D. McLean to S. Hagan," 3 February 1913.

92 The name "Cutler" is still the community name in the mailing address for the First Nation and is sometimes used to denote the village where the Anishinaabek now live.

93 Elders from Perry Shawana's study, 1984. The Anishinaabemowin name, *Mooshmazaagiing*, comes from Elder Tea, 58.

94 Elder Tea, 56–8.

95 Dominion of Canada Annual Report of the Department of Indian Affairs for the Year Ended 30th June, 1872, 56.

96 AANDC, Indian Lands Registry, "Surrender," Registration number X12685, 17 March 1894.

97 AANDC, Indian Lands Registry, "Assignment of Lease," Registration number 47658, 27 October 1894.

98 John William Leonard, *The Industries of Detroit* (Detroit: J.M. Elstner and Co., 1887), 238. It described Mr. Cutler, the president of the company, as "a man of affairs, being Vice-President of the Chippewa Lumber Company, head of the firm of Cutler, White & Boyce, of Chicago, proprietor of the

Cutler House at Grand Haven, and otherwise prominently identified with important business enterprises," 238.

99 Dominion of Canada Annual Report of the Department of Indian Affairs for the Year Ended 30th June 1896, 25.

100 LAC, RG 10, vol. 7793, File 29013–7-2, part 1, Reel 12071, "Memo from W.A. Orr to Deputy Minister," 20 March 1906.

101 AANDC, Indian Lands Registry, "Assignment of Lease," Registration number 47659, 16 December 1901.

102 LAC, Microfiche NMC9390, R6990–287–8-E, "Map of Cutler, Ontario, Algoma District," June 1903.

103 AANDC, Indian Lands Registry, "Assignment of Lease," Registration number 47660, 27 October 1903.

104 LAC, RG 10, vol. 7793, File 29013–7-2, pt.1, Reel C-12071, "Letter from Samuel Hagan to Frank Pedley, Deputy Superintendent General," 23 December 1904.

105 LAC, RG 10, vol. 7793, File 29013–7-2, pt.1, Reel C-12071, "Letter from Dyment to Pedley," 4 January 1905.

106 Parliament of Canada, "Albert Edward Dyment, M.P." accessed 17 July 2020, https://lop.parl.ca/sites/ParlInfo/default/en_CA/People/Profile?personId=155. Marion Albert, *Trade History, North Shore of Lake Huron: A Review of Events That Shaped the Economy of the North Shore* (Blind River: Town of Blind River, 1996), 37.

107 LAC, RG 10, vol. 7793, File 29013–7-2, pt.1, Reel C-12071, "Letter from Samuel Hagan to Frank Pedley, Deputy Superintendent General," 23 December 1904.

108 LAC, RG 10, vol. 7793, File 29013–7-2, pt.1, Reel C-12071, "Letter from Samuel Hagan to the Secretary of DIA," 25 February 1905.

109 LAC, RG 10, vol. 7793, File 29013–7-2, pt.1, Reel C-12071, "Letter from Secretary to Hagan," 28 February 1905.

110 LAC, RG 10, vol. 7793, File 29013–7-2, pt.1, Reel C-12071, "Telegraph from Oshowskuheke," 5 February 1906.

111 LAC, RG 10, vol. 7793, File 29013–7-2, pt.1, Reel C-12071, "Letter from Hagan to Secretary," 5 February 1906.

112 AANDC, Indian Lands Registry, "Surrender," Registration number X12687, 10 February 1906.

113 LAC, RG 10, vol. 7793, File 29013–7-2, pt.1, Reel C-12071, "Letter from Hagan to Secretary," 10 February 1906.

114 LAC, RG 10, vol. 7793, File 29013–7-2, pt.1, Reel C-12071, "Letter from Pedley to Frank Oliver, Superintendent General of Indian Affairs," 22 March 1905.

115 LAC, RG 10, vol. 7793, File 29013–7-2, pt.1, Reel C-12071, "Letter from J.D. McLean, Secretary, to Samuel Hagan," 9 June 1906.

116 LAC, RG 10, vol. 7793, File 29013–7-2, pt.1, Reel C-12071, "Letter from J.D. McLean to Hagan," 28 August 1909.

117 LAC, RG 10, vol. 7793, File 29013–7-2, pt.1, Reel C-12071, "Letter from Hagan to McLean," 30 August 1909.

118 According to Olive P. Dickason, the ban on the sun dance, which was first enacted in 1895, was extended to all traditional dances in 1906. See Dickason, *Canada's First Nations*, 274.

119 LAC, RG 10, vol. 7793, File 29013–7-2, pt.1, Reel C-12071, "Letter from McLean to Hagan," 7 September 1909.

120 LAC, RG 10, vol. 7793, File 29013–7-2, pt.1, Reel C-12071, "Letter from Chief Nahmawon to DIA," 8 April 1912 and "Letter from Assistant Deputy and Secretary to Chief Nahmawon," 12 April 1912.

121 LAC, RG 10, vol. 7539 File 29013–7-3, pt.1, Reel C-14810, "Letter from A.J. McDonell, Superintendent of Spanish Mills Ltd to DIA," dated 21 May 1918.

122 John Kijadjiwan (Lewis) was my great-grandfather, and alternate spellings include Kijadgewan and Kahzadgawon. In the documentation, the name appears as Kahzadgawon but I have chosen to use the community spelling from the family tree held at the Serpent River Trading Post.

123 LAC, RG 10, vol. 7539 File 29013–7-3, pt.1, Reel C-14810, "Letter from Chief Kahzadgawon to DIA," 8 January 1920. This was not the first time Hagan was accused of inappropriate conduct as an Indian Agent. Several people complained to Bishop J.D. Scollard about alcohol and resource related incidents in 1907 (including allegedly buying whiskey for a Chief in order to entice him to surrender land for lumber development). Each allegation was explained away due to a lack of evidence, overzealousness, or as a result of a mistake by the accuser. Hagan was warned in each instance to ensure that it did not happen again, or to avoid acting in such a way as could be perceived in such a negative light in the future. See RG 10, vol. 3088, File 280, 620 Reel C-11322.

124 LAC, RG 10, vol. 7539 File 29013–7-3, pt.1, Reel C-14810, "Letter from McLean to Kahzadgawon," 10 January 1920.

125 LAC, RG 10, vol. 7539 File 29013–7-3, pt.1, Reel C-14810, "Letter from Kahzadgawon to DIA," 11 January 1920.

126 LAC, RG 10, vol. 7539 File 29013–7-3, pt.1, Reel C-14810, "Letter from Kahzadgawon to DIA," 6 March 1920.

127 LAC, RG 10, vol. 7539 File 29013–7-3, pt.1, Reel C-14810, "Voters' list for Serpent River Band," 8 September 1920.

128 AANDC, Indian Lands Registry, "Surrender," Registration number X12690, dated 5 October 1920.

129 LAC, RG 10, vol. 7539 File 29013–7-3, pt.1, Reel C-14810, "Statutory Declaration by George Shaw," 21 October 1920.

130 Elder Tea, 69. Marion Albert gives 1923 as the year it was destroyed by fire, p. 40.

131 LAC, RG 10, vol. 779, File 29013–7-2, pt. 1 Reel 12071, "Letter from Cooper and Landreville," 2 March 1945.

132 Andrea Gutsche, Barbara Chisholm, and Russell Floren, *The North Channel and St. Mary's River: A Guide to the History* (Toronto: Lynx Images, 2008), 105–7.

133 LAC, RG 10, vol. 7539 File 29013–7-3, pt.1, Reel C-14810, "Letter from William Nahmawon to DIA," 16 May 1925.

134 LAC, RG 10, vol. 7539 File 29013–7-3, pt.1, Reel C-14810, "Letter from Spanish River Lumber Co Limited to Chas. Rothers," 30 May 1925.

135 LAC, RG 10, vol. 7539 File 29013–7-3, pt.1, Reel C-14810, "Letter from John Lewis (Kahzadgawon) to DIA," 9 August 1930.

136 LAC, RG 10, vol. 7539 File 29013–7-3, pt.1, Reel C-14810, "Letter from Chief Alex Meawasige to DIA," 26 August 1933.

137 LAC, RG 10, vol. 7539 File 29013–7-3, pt.1, Reel C-14810, "Letter from Chief Alex Meawasige to DIA," 1 June 1938.

138 LAC, RG 10, vol. 7793, File 29013–7-2, pt. 1, Reel C-14810, "Band Council Resolution," 6 August 1943.

139 LAC, RG 10, vol. 7539 File 29013–7-3, pt.1, Reel C-14810, "Letter from D.J. Allan, Superintendent of Reserves and Trusts, to Spanish River Lumber Company," 6 April 1944. The band requested the funds to buy the land back on 26 April 1944 and the Treasury Board approved the transaction on 26 July 1944. See Aboriginal Affairs and Northern Development Canada, Indian Lands Registry, accessed 10 February 2013, http://pse5 -esd5.ainc-inac.gc.ca/ILRS/Instruments/InstrumentResults.aspx.

140 Most of the interviews conducted by Perry Shawana mentioned at least one of these activities.

3. Carving a "Jewel in the Wilderness": The Establishment of Elliot Lake

  1 Laurentian University Archives [LUL], USWA Local 5417, PO 24, Box 61, M43, 1 File 22, "Transcription of Scoping Session, Federal Environmental Assessment Review Panel on the Decommissioning of Uranium Mine Tailings Management Areas in Elliot Lake, Ontario," Serpent River First Nation, 1993. This quotation is from Angela Lewis's (Kijadjiwan) presentation to the Decommissioning review panel, and I am grateful for her permission to quote her here.

  2 I purposely use the term "settler" rather than alternatives such as "newcomer" or "non-Indigenous" in this context. It is meant to underline the fact that the invasion of First Nations territory is decidedly not a

phenomenon that is relegated to the past, but rather one that persistently challenges communication and cooperation between nations. See, for example, Paulette Regan, *Unsettling the Settler Within: Indian Residential Schools, Truth Telling, and Reconciliation in Canada* (Vancouver: University of British Columbia Press, 2010), 4. Elizabeth Furniss also interrogates settler myths in *The Burden of History: Colonialism and the Frontier Myth in a Rural Canadian Community* (Vancouver: University of British Columbia Press, 1999). An international comparative approach is taken in Daiva Stasiulis and Nira Yuval-Davis, eds., *Unsettling Settler Societies: Articulations of Gender, Race, Ethnicity and Class* (London: SAGE Publications Ltd., 1995).

3 Ramsay Cook, ed., *The Voyages of Jacques Cartier* (Toronto: University of Toronto Press, 1993), 97–9.

4 The 1849 Mica Bay incident precipitated the 1850 Robinson Treaties. Chief Shingwaukonse and others had resented mining in Anishinaabe territory, as they were neither consulted nor offered royalties. They requested a profit-sharing agreement and a land settlement, and when their concerns were ignored, they occupied the Lake Superior Mining Company at Mica Bay in an effort to stop mining there. Janet E. Chute, *The Legacy of Shingwakonse: A Century of Native Leadership* (Toronto: University of Toronto Press, 1998). See also Janet E. Chute, "Pursuing the Great Spirit's Plan: Nineteenth-Century Ojibwa Attitudes Towards the Future of Logging and Mining on Unsurrendered Indian Lands North of Lakes Huron and Superior," in *Social Relations in Resource Hinterlands: Papers from the 27th Annual Meeting of the Western Association of Sociology and Anthropology*, ed. Thomas W. Dunk (Thunder Bay: Lakehead University Centre for Northern and Regional Studies, 1991).

5 There are still concerns about mining development in northern Ontario in areas further north than Elliot Lake. The Ring of Fire development is controversial, and governments and First Nations are still negotiating how mining will unfold. See Josh Hjartarson, Liam McGuinty, and Scott Boutilier, *Beneath the Surface: Uncovering the Economic Potential of Ontario's Ring of Fire* (Toronto: Ontario Chamber of Commerce, 2014). Jody Porter, "Ring of Fire: First Nations scold Mines Minister Michael Gravelle, First Nations 'grow weary' of being shut out of decisions," CBC News, accessed 24 November 2014, http://www.cbc.ca/news/canada/thunder-bay /ring-of-fire-first-nations-scold-mines-minister-michael-gravelle -1.2760725.

6 On the resource use in the area by settlers and SRFN before the uranium industry see on timber LAC, RG 10, vol. 11352, File 13/20–7-8 parts 1 and 2, on mining LAC RG 10, vol. 13102, File 493/20–5-7, and on fishing rights LAC RG 10, 11347, File 13/20–2-8.

7 The railway was extended to Serpent River First Nation in the 1880s with the right of way surrendered on 22 June 1982 by the Band. See "Memorandum from DIA to Privy Council," 22 June 1882, LAC, RG 10, vol. 2116, File 22036. Negotiations about the right of way continued on and off until the First World War.

8 For more information about the development of Sudbury, see C.M. Wallace and Ashley Thomson, eds., *Sudbury: Rail Town to Regional Capital* (Toronto: Dundurn Press, 1993).

9 Michael Barnes, *Great Northern Ontario Mines* (Burnstown: General Store Publishing House, 1998), 1–2. See also Kerry Abel, *Changing Places: History, Community, and Identity in Northeastern Ontario* (Montreal: McGill-Queen's University Press, 2006) for identity formation in northern Ontario communities.

10 Barnes, *Great Northern Ontario Mines*, 51–2. See also the same author's *Kirkland Lake: On the Mile of Gold* (Kirkland Lake: Economic Development and Tourism Department, 1994).

11 "Increase in Value Canadian Mining Industry Output," *Sault Daily Star*, 12 January 1950, 2.

12 On the economic history of the North Shore see Marion Albert, *Trade History, North Shore of Lake Huron: A Review of Events That Shaped the Economy of the North Shore, 1600–1996* (Blind River: Town of Blind River, 1996) and Andrea Gutsche, Barbara Chisholm, and Russell Floren, *The North Channel and St. Mary's River: A Guide to the History* (Toronto: Lynx Images, 2008).

13 Robert Bothwell, *Eldorado: Canada's National Uranium Company* (Toronto: University of Toronto Press, 1984), 28–32. See also "Gilbert A. LaBine," Canadian Mining Hall of Fame, accessed 7 July 2021, https://www.mininghalloffame.ca/gilbert-a-labine.

14 Ibid., 128, 149.

15 Ibid., 292.

16 A good, succinct overview of developments in nuclear weapons technology is found in Joseph Levitt, *Pearson and Canada's Role in Nuclear Disarmament and Arms Control Negotiations* (Montreal: McGill-Queen's University Press, 1993), 23–30; see also Bothwell, *Alliance and Illusion*, 160–8; Eayrs, *In Defence of Canada, Peacemaking and Deterrence*, 260–74; and Maloney, 68ff.

17 "Uranium Claims Staked in Quebec," *Sault Daily Star*, 3 February 1950, 15.

18 "Uranium Deposit Found in Quebec," *Sault Daily Star*, 2 February 1950, 1.

19 "Step Up Quest for West Uranium," *Sault Daily Star*, 21 March 1950, 11.

20 "Find High-Grade Uranium Deposit," *Sault Daily Star*, 25 March 1950, 11.

21 "Increase in Value of Uranium to Aid 3 Sask. Deposits," *Sault Daily Star*, 28 April 1950, 3.

22 Ibid.

23 Mann, 13.

24 H.S. Spence with F.N. Senftle, *Prospectors' Guide for Uranium and Thorium Minerals in Canada* (Ottawa: Bureau of Mines, Department of Mines and Resources, 1949). See also "More Prospectors Join Uranium Hunt," *Sault Daily Star*, 13 May 1950, 11.

25 "More Prospectors Join Uranium Hunt," *Sault Daily Star*, 13 May 1950, 11.

26 "Prospectors' Class Starts," *Sault Daily Star*, 23 January 1950, 4.

27 "Increase in Uranium Price Brightens Algoma's Future," *Sault Daily Star*, 20 April 1950, 5.

28 Ibid.

29 "Happy Hunting in Ontario … For Uranium," *Bruce Mines Spectator*, 28 July 1955, 3.

30 Ibid.

31 SRFN's Band Council also tried to make good use of the excitement. In 1955 they asked DIA for permission to allow limited staking of claims on a portion of the SRFN. DIA informed council that staking could not take place on reserve land and the instead the reserve would have to cede its mineral rights to the Crown. Mineral rights on the reserve were ceded in somewhat dubious circumstances on 29 June 1955. A later Council tried to rescind the earlier transaction but were not allowed to do so by DIA. The compromise was that DIA would not actively grant extraction rights without Band permission. See various correspondence in LAC, RG 10, vol. 13102, File 493/20–5-7.

32 "Uranium Exploration in the U.S.," *Bulletin of the Atomic Scientists* VI, 6 (June 1950): 177.

33 "Algoma Uranium Finds of Commercial Value," *Sault Daily Star*, 12 January 1950, 1.

34 "Spring Development Boom in Algoma Uranium Fields," *Sault Daily Star*, 22 March 1950, 5.

35 Catharine Dixon, *The Power and the Promise: The Elliot Lake Story* (Elliot Lake: Gillidix Publishing Inc., 1996), 8ff.

36 LUL Archives, Catharine Dixon Fonds, P103, File: Maclean's Article, Star Weekly and Karl Lehlm Article, "Elliot Lake: Uranium Capital of the World."

37 LUL Archives, Catharine Dixon Fonds, P103, File: Elliot Lake: The 1960s, "Brief History of Elliot Lake," 1.

38 A diamond drill is a type of coring drill used to sample an ore body.

39 Dixon, 28–30.

40 Dixon, 20.

41 Terrence James Downey, *The Political Economy of Uranium: Elliot Lake, 1948–1970* (Master's thesis, The University of Western Ontario, 1972),

63 and 174. Downey's thesis provides a lengthy overview of government involvement in the development of the Elliot Lake area.

42 Shawn Heard, "The City of Elliot Lake to 1991: Before the Roof Fell In," in *Boom Town Blues, Elliot Lake: Collapse and Revival in a Single-Industry Community*, ed. Anne-Marie Mawhiney and Jane Pitblado (Toronto: Dundurn Press, 1999), 22–37.

43 "Uranium Surplus Forecast U.S. Produces Her Own," *Standard*, 14 July 1951, 1. See also Robert Bothwell, *Alliance and Illusion: Canada and the World, 1945–1984* (Vancouver: University of British Columbia Press, 2007). The extraction of uranium for the purposes of power generation did not become a factor until the early to mid-1960s. For an examination of Canada's interest in nuclear power beginning in the 1950s and the move toward implementing that technology, see Wilfrid Eggleston, *Canada's Nuclear Story* (Toronto: Clarke, Irwin and Company, 1965), 321–41. Rio Algom signed a contract with Ontario Hydro in 1966 and both Denison and Rio signed contracts with Japan in 1967: Catharine Dixon, *The Power and the Promise: the Elliot Lake Story* (Elliot Lake: Gillidix Publishing, 1996), 262.

44 Pearson addressed the audience on 15 October 1956 and the local media paid heed. "Weapons Too Horrible – 96 Per Cent Uranium Going War Production," *Spectator*, 18 October 1956, 1.

45 John English, *The Life of Lester Pearson: The Worldly Years, 1949–1972* (Toronto: A.A. Knopf Canada, 1992), 107ff.

46 "Weapons Too Horrible – 96 Per Cent Uranium Going War Production," *Spectator*, 18 October 1956, 1.

47 Ibid.

48 "High Cost Bars Atomic Powered Cars," *Leader-Spectator* 14 February 1957, 7.

49 Bothwell, *Eldorado*, 149.

50 Bothwell, *Eldorado*, 292.

51 "Canadian Uranium Production Heading Toward World Lead," *Bruce Mines Spectator*, 13 January 1955, 1.

52 "Pearson Indicts Government," *Standard*, 9 November 1959, 1 and 3.

53 *Carved from the Rock: The Story of Elliot Lake* (Toronto: National Dream Production, 2005).

54 For a case study approach to male workers in the Thunder Bay area, see Thomas W. Dunk, *It's a Working Man's Town: Male Working Class Culture in Northwestern Ontario* (Montreal: McGill-Queen's University Press, 1991).

55 Male miners often left their wives and families in other towns until housing was available at Elliot Lake. For a fictional account of the mining industry at Elliot Lake, see Alistair MacLeod's *No Great Mischief* (Toronto: McClelland and Stewart, 1999), especially chapters 20 through 22.

"Sometimes those of us who were off during the days or evenings would sit on benches outside our bunkhouse doors. We would engage in desultory games of horseshoes or talk with the Irish or Newfoundlanders. Many of them were older married men with families who, on paydays, lined up at the small temporary bank to purchase money orders or international bank draughts to send to their distant loved ones. Sometimes they would sit on the benches unconsciously rubbing themselves between their legs. 'In Ireland,' said the red-haired Irishman, 'I have a home but I have no money. Here I have lots of money but I have no home.' We raised our eyebrows in unison to indicate we understood." MacLeod, 147.

56 "'Gone Far Enough,' Mancini Says Steel Will 'Insist on Clean-Up,'" *Standard*, 6 June 1957.

57 "'Gone Far Enough,' Mancini Says Steel Will 'Insist on Clean-Up,'" *Standard*, 6 June 1957.

58 Ibid.

59 "A Good Beef – But Some Agitating Involved in Lake Nordic Protest," *Standard*, 13 June 1957, 11.

60 Ibid.

61 For a direct comparison see Arn Keeling, "Born in an Atomic Test Tube: Landscapes of cyclonic development at Uranium City, Saskatchewan," and B.G. McIntyre, *Uranium City: The Last Boom Town* (N.p.: Driftwood Publications, 1993); See also the several case studies in Matt Bray and Ashley Thomson, eds., *At the End of the Shift: Mines and Single-Industry Towns in Northern Ontario* (Sudbury: Dundurn Press/Laurentian University, 1992). For four American case studies of uranium mining towns, see Michael A. Amundson, *Yellowcake Towns: Uranium Mining Communities in the American West* (Boulder: University Press of Colorado, 2004).

62 LUL Archives, Catharine Dixon Fonds, P103, Box 3, "Brief to Ontario Municipal Board, 20 June 1955"; AO, RG 19, Box 3, D-8, "Brief for Ontario Municipal Board." I have given both citations where the files are originally from a different archive.

63 Robert Robson, "Building Resource Towns: Government Intervention in Ontario in the 1950s," in *At the End of the Shift: Mines and Single-Industry Towns in Northern Ontario*, ed. Matt Bray and Ashley Thomson (Sudbury: Dundurn Press/Laurentian University, 1992), 98. The literature on company towns is fairly large. In addition to those works cited above see Rex A. Lucas, *Minetown, Milltown, Railtown: Life in Canadian Communities of Single Industry* (Toronto: University of Toronto Press, 1971) and more recent works including Robert Robson, "Manitoba's Resource Towns: the Twentieth Century Frontier," *Manitoba History* 16 (September 1988): 2–16; Robert Robson, "Strike in the Single Enterprise Community: Flin Flon, Manitoba–1934," *Labour* 12 (Autumn 1983): 63–86; Robert Robson,

"Wilderness Suburbs: Boom and Gloom on the Prairies, 1945–1986," *Prairie Forum* 13, no. 2 (September 1988): 191–219; Robert Robson, *The Politics of Resource Town Development: Ontario's Resource Communities, 1883–1970* (PhD diss., University of Guelph, 1986); James Mochoruk, "Oral History in a Company Town: Flin Flon, 1926–1946," *Canadian Oral History Association* 7 (1984): 5–12; John Kendrick, *The People of the Snow: The Story of Kitimat* (Chapel Hill: University of North Carolina Press, 1987).

64 LUL Archives, Catharine Dixon Fonds, P103, Box 3, "Improvement District of Elliot Lake," 1.

65 LUL Archives, Catharine Dixon Fonds, P103, Box 3, "Improvement District of Elliot Lake," submitted by J.W.P. Carter, 2 February 1956.; AO, RG 19, Box 3, D-8, "Improvement District of Elliot Lake."

66 See Robert Robson, "Building Resource Towns: Government Intervention in Ontario in the 1950s," in *At the End of the Shift: Mines and Single-Industry Towns in Northern Ontario*, ed. Matt Bray and Ashley Thomson (Sudbury: Dundurn Press/Laurentian University, 1992), 97–9.

67 LUL Archives, Catharine Dixon Fonds, P103, Box 3, "Improvement District of Elliot Lake," submitted by J.W.P. Carter, 2 February 1956; AO, RG 19, Box 3, D-8, "Improvement District of Elliot Lake", 2–3.

68 Ibid., 3.

69 Robson, 98–102.

70 LUL Archives, Catharine Dixon Fonds, P103, Box 3, "Elliot Lake: Uranium Capital of the World."

71 LUL Archives, Catharine Dixon Fonds, P103, Box 3, "Ontario Government Press Release Issued by the Department of Planning and Development dated 22 June 1955"; AO, RG 19, Box 2, D-8, "Press Release."

72 LUL Archives, Catharine Dixon Fonds, P103, Box 3, "Improvement District of Elliot Lake," submitted by J.W.P. Carter, 2 February 1956.; AO, RG 19, Box 3, D-8, "Improvement District of Elliot Lake."

73 Ibid.

74 Robson, 97.

75 LUL Archives, Catharine Dixon Fonds, P103, Box 3, "Improvement District of Elliot Lake," submitted by J.W.P. Carter, 2 February 1956.; AO, RG 19, Box 3, D-8, "Improvement District of Elliot Lake," 6.

76 Ibid., 6.

77 LUL Archives, Catharine Dixon Fonds, P103, Box 3, "Letter from Joubin to W.M. Nickle dated 23 January 1956"; AO, RG 19, Box 3, D-8, "Letter to Hon. Nickle Jan. 23/1956."

78 "Rio Tinto Alone Plans – 700 More New Homes," *Standard*, 13 December, 1956, 1.

79 "Model of Modern Design – Promises 'Canada's Finest Town' Will Have Diversified Industry," *Bruce Mines Spectator*, 17 February 1955, 1.

80 Ibid.
81 See Doug Owram, *Born at the Right Time: A History of the Baby Boom Generation* (Toronto: University of Toronto Press, 1996), especially 84–111.
82 "From all Across Canada to Build City: $1 Million Spent House Building Alone, Already," *Bruce Mines Spectator*, 25 October 1956, 1.
83 "Townsite Officials Move against Shacks: 14 People in a Room," *Standard*, 9 May 1957, 1. Mobile homes had flooded into the area, and along with the shack-builders, there was one woman who called a bus a home for herself and her four children. See Dixon, 76–7.
84 "Townsite Officials Move against Shacks: 14 People in a Room," *Standard*, 9 May 1957, 1.
85 "Board of Trustees Decide – All Shacks Must Go," *Standard*, 16 May 1957, 1.
86 Ibid.
87 LUL Archives, Catharine Dixon Fonds, P103, Box 3, "Letter from Joubin to W.M. Nickle dated 23 January 1956"; AO, RG 19, Box 3, D-8, "Letter to Hon. Nickle Jan. 23/1956."
88 "1050 Housing Units Scheduled for Neighbourhoods One, Two and Three," *Standard*, 13 June 1957, 1.
89 Ibid.
90 LUL Archives, Catharine Dixon Fonds, P103, Box 6, "Brief History of Elliot Lake."
91 Robson, 110–12.
92 Richard Harris, *Creeping Conformity: How Canada Became Suburban, 1900–1960* (Toronto: University of Toronto Press, 2004), 129–54.
93 "From all Across Canada to Build a City, continued," *Bruce Mines Spectator*, 25 October 1956, 8.
94 "Work on School Being Rushed," *Standard*, 3 January 1957, 4.
95 "Catholic Church," *Standard*, 3 January 1957, 5.
96 "United Church," *Standard*, 3 January 1957, 5.
97 "Lady of Fatima Auxiliary Formed Good Turnout," and "Eighteen Present at Meeting of Anglican Guild," *Standard*, 16 May 1957, 8.
98 Ibid.
99 LUL Archives, "Improvement District of Elliot Lake," 6.
100 LUL Archives, Catharine Dixon Fonds, P103, Box 3, "Letter from Bouck and Derry to Hon. Kelly," dated 11 April 1955. Also AO, RG 19, Box 2, D-8, Kelly, 11 April 1955.
101 The letter also outlines the benefits of the mining operations on page 4, linking the development of the improvement district, of which road construction was an essential part, with national interests. LUL Archives, Catharine Dixon Fonds, P103, Box 3, "Letter from Bouck and Derry to Hon. Kelly," dated 11 April 1955. Also AO, RG 19, Box 2, D-8, Kelly, 11 April 1955.

102 LUL Archives, Catharine Dixon Fonds, P103, Box 3, "Letter from Bouck and Derry to Hon. Kelly," dated 11 April 1955. Also AO, RG 19, Box 2, D-8, Kelly, 11 April 1955.

103 LUL Archives, Catharine Dixon Fonds, P103, Box 3, "Ontario Government Press Release Issued by the Department of Planning and Development," 15 June 1955; AO, RG 19, Box 2, D-8 Press Release, "Ontario Government Press Release Issued by the Department of Planning and Development," 15 June 1955. The press release was to be timed for 22 June 1955.

104 LUL Archives, Catharine Dixon Fonds, P103, Box 3, "Letter to P.T. Kelly from Franc R. Joubin dated 6 April 1955"; AO, RG 19, Box 2, D-8, "Kelly April 6, 1955."

105 Ibid.

106 "Delegates Ontario C. of C. Tour Area This Week," *Standard*, 9 May 1957, 1.

107 "Governor General Massey Will Tour Mine Area and Attend Reception Saturday," *Standard*, 16 May 1957, 8. Massey was quoted in the *Sudbury Star* as having lauded Elliot Lake: "Your community will play a role of great significance in the coming Atomic Age. You are living in exciting times and your area is making a great contribution to the growing prosperity of Canada." Quoted in Dixon, 111.

108 For more on the planning of Elliot Lake as a model community, see Robson, 109–112.

109 "Problems Existing in Elliot Lake to be Presented to MLAs Friday" *Standard*, 25 July 1957, 1, 8.

110 "S.R. Kurisko Outlines Problems of Elliot Lake to Visiting MLAs," *Standard*, 29 August 1957, 5. The newspaper compared this meeting to one earlier in the spring where Lester B. Pearson, the area's MP and guest of honour at the Chamber's inaugural dinner, was cornered without warning about the availability of federally insured housing loans. One newspaper columnist described the later presentation to provincial MLAs as "anaemic" in comparison. Ken Romain, "Hed to Cum…" *Standard* 29 August 1957, 5.

111 "To Have Model of Elliot Lake," *Standard*, 22 August 1957, 1.

112 LAC, RG 2, vol. 2746, "Closing down of uranium mines; Elliot Lake area," Cabinet Conclusions, 9 February, 1960, 9 (Prime Minister Diefenbaker).

113 The Women's Delegation to Ottawa was comprised of women concerned about the fact that they had uprooted their families to Elliot Lake in the late 1950s because they had been told that the "city of the future" held a great deal of promise for them. They signed a petition and travelled to Ottawa where they met with Diefenbaker and Churchill. Helen Marshall, "Report from a Delegate to Ottawa on the Talk with Mr. Diefenbaker" and "Gals Gloomy Following Visit with Churchill," *Standard*, 3 March 1960, 1. Anna Stanley describes women's mobilization and the construction of

Elliot Lake as a domestic town as "reference points with which to order and maintain possession of the lands of the Serpent River watershed as a singular, white, Canadian, nuclear space." See Anna Stanley, "Labours of Land: Domesticity, Wilderness and Dispossession in the Development of Canadian Uranium Markets," *Gender, Place & Culture* 20, no. 2 (2013): 198.

114 "M. Diefenbaker envoie un comité d'enquête," *Standard*, 9 March 1960, 7. "Notre Page" was a section of the paper that communicated news in French for the significant Francophone population in Elliot Lake.

115 LAC, RG 2, vol. 2746, "Closing down of uranium mines; Elliot Lake area," Cabinet Conclusions, 9 February, 1960, 9 (Mr. Churchill).

116 Ibid.

117 LAC, RG 2, vol. 2746, "Elliot Lake: Present Situation," Cabinet Conclusions, 10 May 1960, 5.

118 Library of Parliament, "Stanley James Korchinski, M.P." accessed 17 July 2020, https://lop.parl.ca/sites/ParlInfo/default/en_CA/People /Profile?personId=13510.

119 LAC, RG 2, vol. 2745, "Report of the Uranium Committee," Cabinet Conclusions, 3 December 1959, 7.

120 LAC, RG 2, vol. 2746, "Closing Down of Uranium Mines; Elliot Lake Area," Cabinet Conclusions, 9 February 1960, 9–10.

121 LAC, RG 2, vol. 2746, "Report of Uranium Committee on proposed transfer of Stanleigh and Stanrock contracts to Rio Algom," Cabinet Conclusions, 7 June 1960, 3 (Mr. Churchill).

122 LAC, RG 2, vol. 2746, "Report of Uranium Committee on proposed transfer of Stanleigh and Stanrock contracts to Rio Algom," Cabinet Conclusions, 7 June 1960, 3 (Mr. Walker). Algom Uranium Mines Limited had merged with other mining companies in the 1950s. By 1960, it was known as Rio Algom.

123 LAC, RG 2, vol. 2746, "Elliot Lake: Present Situation," Cabinet Conclusions, 10 May 1960, 5–6.

124 Ibid.

125 Pearson oversaw a stockpiling initiative within his first few months in office. The Cabinet agreed that "the proposed contract between Eldorado Mining and Refining, Limited, and Rio Algom Mines, Limited for the purchase of uranium mines to keep the mine operating during the eleven month period ending June 30th, 1964, be further negotiated with the company." LAC, RG 2, vol. 6253, "Maintenance of Employment at Elliott [*sic*] Lake through purchase of Uranium from Rio Algom Mines Limited," Cabinet Conclusions, 23 July 1963, 5. On 1 August 1963, Rio's proposed changes to the contract were accepted. LAC, RG 2, vol. 6254, "Purchase of Uranium from Rio Algom Mines to maintain employment at Elliot Lake," 1 August 1963, 3.

126 LAC, RG 2, vol. 6271, "Uranium Policy," Cabinet Conclusions, 20 May 1965, 3 (Mr. Martin).
127 See chapter six for discussions about the Environmental Assessment Board and how SRFN inserted itself into the discussion surrounding the possibility of expansion.
128 Robson, 109.

4. "It took all the trees": The Cutler Acid Plant and Its Toxic Legacy

1 Interview with Gertrude Lewis by Author, 22 February 2008, Serpent River First Nation.
2 For a comparison of Indigenous mining labour and modernization, see Arn Keeling and Patricia Boulter, "From Igloo to Mine Shaft: Inuit Labour and Memory at the Rankin Inlet Nickel Mine," in *Mining and Communities in Northern Canada: History, Politics, and Memory*, ed. Arn Keeling and John Sandlos (Calgary: University of Calgary Press, 2015), 35–58.
3 See various documents in LAC, RG 10, vol. 11352, File 13/20–7-8 Pts 1 and 2 which outline timber use on the reserve from the 1920s to the early 1960s.
4 Right of ways for the highway and telephone lines were ceded in 1914. See LAC RG 10, vol. 2879, File 177/991–2.
5 Noranda's annual reports for the period in question are available at Library and Archives Canada in LAC, RG 20, vol. 775, File 23–100-N17.
6 In 1959, for example, Noranda had $33 million in profits from its production operations alone. The Cutler Acid Plant contributed to those profits. See "Noranda Mines Limited 1959–37th Annual Report: Statement of Operations for the Year Ended December 31, 1959," LAC, RG 20, vol. 775, File 23–100-N17, 5.
7 Centers for Disease Control and Prevention, "NIOSH [National Institute for Occupational Safety and Health] Pocket Guide to Chemical Hazards – Sulfuric Acid," accessed 26 February 2011, http://www.cdc.gov/niosh/npg/npgd0577.html.
8 "New Acid Plant Cost $3,000,000," *Standard*, 13 December 1956, 1. The title of the article refers to the construction of an acid plant in the Sudbury area.
9 "Blind River Area Prominent Recent Issue Financial Post: New Acid Leach Mill and Pulp Paper Mill Subject of Article," *Leader-Spectator*, 23 June 1955, 1.
10 See LAC, RG 20, vol. 775, File 23–100-N17.
11 "Blind River Area Prominent Recent Issue Financial Post: New Acid Leach Mill and Pulp Paper Mill Subject of Article," *Leader-Spectator*, 23 June 1955, 1.

12 Ibid.

13 Ibid.

14 "Noranda Acid Plant at Cutler to Supply Entire Area Will Be Largest in Canada," *Standard*, 4 July 1957, 7.

15 Leslie Roberts, *Noranda* (Toronto: Clarke Irwin, 1956), 199.

16 Robert Robson, "Building Resource Towns: Government Intervention in Ontario in the 1950s," in *At the End of the Shift: Mines and Single-Industry Towns in Northern Ontario*, ed. Matt Bray and Ashley Thomson (Sudbury: Dundurn Press/Laurentian University, 1992), 100.

17 Andrea Gutsche, Barbara Chisholm, and Russell Floren, *The North Channel and St. Mary's River: A Guide to the History* (Toronto: Lynx Images, 2008).

18 Robson, 100.

19 LAC, RG 2, vol. 2746, "New Wharf at Cutler," Cabinet Conclusions, 6 June 1960, 4.

20 Robson, 100.

21 Government of Canada. *Department of Citizenship and Immigration Report of Indian Affairs Branch for the Fiscal Year Ended March 31, 1959* (Ottawa: Queen's Printer, 1960), 37.

22 Ibid.

23 Government of Canada. *Canada Department of Citizenship and Immigration Report of Indian Affairs Branch 1956–57* (Ottawa: Queen's Printer, 1957), 31.

24 LAC, RG 10, vol. 11367, File 493/28–7-17493, "Letter from Indian Agent to District Supervisor."

25 Shewell, *"Enough to Keep Them Alive,"* and John F. Leslie, "Assimilation, Integration, or Termination: The Development of Canadian Indian Policy, 1943–1963" (PhD diss., Carleton University, 1999).

26 On the resource use in the area by settlers and SRFN before the uranium industry see on timber LAC, RG 10, vol. 11352, File 13/20–7-8 parts 1 and 2, on mining LAC RG 10, vol. 13102, File 493/20–5-7, and on fishing rights LAC, RG 10, 11347, File 13/20–2-8.

27 "Spanish Indians Collected Maple Syrup Here," *Standard*, 16 April 1959, 6. Emphasis added.

28 See various documents in RG 10, vol. 11367 File 493/28–7-17493.

29 "Spanish Indians Collected Maple Syrup Here," *Standard*, 16 April 1959, 6.

30 See DIA publications, for example, *The Indian in Transition* (Ottawa: Government of Canada, 1961). For an examination of how DIA functioned within the Department of Citizenship and Immigration, see Heidi Bohaker and Franca Iacovetta, "Making Aboriginal People 'Immigrants Too': A Comparison of Citizenship Programs for Newcomers and Indigenous Peoples in Postwar Canada, 1940s–1960s," *Canadian Historical Review* 90, no. 3 (September 2009): 427–61.

31 Robson, 100.

32 LAC, RG 10, vol. 11367, File 493/28/7/17493, "J.T. O'Neill to Indian Affairs Branch, Dept. of Citizenship and Immigration," 6 April 1956.

33 Ibid.

34 Many community members seem to recall the lure of jobs when the plant was discussed in 1955–6. This has been consistent over time. In addition to the interviews conducted for this study, see Anna Stanley, "The Experiences of the Serpent River First Nation of the Nuclear Industry," held in the SRFN Library, Cutler, Ontario.

35 Gertrude Lewis and Peter Johnston both recalled the desire to hire independent legal representation.

36 Brownlie, *A Fatherly Eye*, 104–23. Hugh Shewell also documents this concern for Indigenous "self-support," 95–6.

37 LAC, RG 10, vol. 11326, File 7–33, DIA Memoranda dated 8 March 1939 and 17 April 1940.

38 For mineral right surrender, which the next Council tried to rescind, see LAC, RG 10, vol. 13102, File 493/20-5-7.

39 BCR, dated 22 June 1955, Aboriginal Affairs and Northern Development Canada, Indian Lands Registry, accessed 10 February 2013, http://pse5 -esd5.ainc-inac.gc.ca/ILRS/Instruments/InstrumentResults.aspx.

40 Interview with Peter Johnston by Author, 7 July 2009, Serpent River First Nation.

41 Interview with Gertrude Lewis by Author, 22 February 2008, Serpent River First Nation.

42 LAC, MG31 K39 R6847, vol. 36, Serpent River First Nation, "Background Information: Highlights of the History of the Cutler Acid Site," 1986, 1. Author unknown.

43 AANDC, Indian Lands Registry, "Minutes of the Meeting of the Committee of the Privy Council," Registration number 12703, dated 2 February 1956. Author's emphasis.

44 AANDC, Indian Lands Registry, "Order in Council P.C. 53/5770," Registration number X12697, dated 26 July 1944.

45 Ibid.

46 The company changed names several times but the lease he was talking about was clearly to the Spanish River Lumber Company.

47 This quotation is from an interview with Chief Commanda, transcribed in Lorraine Rekmans, Keith Lewis, and Anabel Dwyer, eds., *This Is My Homeland: Stories of the Effects of Nuclear Industries by People of the Serpent River First Nation and the North Shore of Lake Huron* (Cutler: Serpent River First Nation, 2003), 2. See also page xv, where it is stated by one of the authors, "DIAND used an old lease from the Cutler Salvage and Lumber Company on Anishnabe land to host a sulphuric acid plant to provide acid for leaching uranium at Elliot Lake. DIAND hoped this would

provide a 'better' standard of living for people at Serpent River First Nation. Instead this site left a legacy of waste and contamination in the community."

48 Interview with Peter Johnston by Author, 7 July 2009, Serpent River First Nation. From the perspective of the community, the issue of consent was very important, and Johnston's words are echoed by a report issued by the Serpent River First Nation in 1986: "The Indian Act requires that the members of a Band consent to the lease of reserve land. Indian Affairs officials were afraid that the Band members would not approve the lease with Noranda, so the government relied on a technicality to approve the lease without the formal consent of the Band." LAC, MG31 K39 R6847, File: Serpent River, "Background Information: Highlights of the History of the Cutler Acid Site," 1986, 1.

49 AANDC, Indian Lands Registry, "Lease between Her Majesty represented by the Minister of Citizenship and Immigration and Noranda Mines, Limited," 10 April 1956.

50 Olive Patricia Dickason with David T. McNab, *Canada's First Nations: A History of Founding Peoples from Earliest Times*, 4th edition (Don Mills: Oxford University Press, 2009), 289.

51 Interview with Peter Johnston by Author, 7 July 2009, Serpent River First Nation.

52 AANDC, Indian Lands Registry, "Lease between Her Majesty represented by the Minister of Citizenship and Immigration and Noranda Mines, Limited," Registration number X12704, 10 April 1956.

53 LAC, RG 10, vol. 11367, File 493/28/7/17493, "Letter from J.T. O'Neill to Indian Affairs Branch, Dept. of Citizenship and Immigration," 6 April 1956.

54 On the reacquisition of mineral rights see "H.M. Jones to J.T. O'Neill," 18 September 1958, LAC, RG 10, vol. 13102, File 493/20–5-7; on early claims of damage to property see various correspondence in LAC, RG 10, vol. 11336 Files 493/3–11–7 and 493/3–8-7.

55 LAC, RG 10, vol. 11364, File. 493/28–7-17493, "Letter from A.R. Aquin to Superintendent," Sault Ste. Marie Agency, 9 January 1964.

56 LAC, RG 10, vol. 13102, File 493/20–5-7, "Letter to A.B. Irwin, Superintendent Mineral Resources, Indian Affairs Branch," 21 April 1964.

57 Interview with Gertrude Lewis by Author, 22 February 2008, Serpent River First Nation.

58 Interview with Terry Jacobs by Author, 8 December 2008, Serpent River First Nation.

59 See on timber LAC, RG 10, vol. 11352, File 13/20–7-8 parts 1 and 2, on mining LAC RG 10, vol. 13102, File 493/20–5-7, and on fishing rights RG 10, 11347, File 13/20–2-8.

60 For a good definition of "moditional," see John Lutz, *Makúk: A New History of Aboriginal-White Relations* (Vancouver: University of British Columbia Press, 2008), 9, 23–4.

61 Government of Canada. *Department of Citizenship and Immigration Report of Indian Affairs Branch for the Fiscal Year Ended March 31, 1959* (Ottawa: Queen's Printer, 1960), 37.

62 The interviews conducted by this author as well as those undertaken by Anna Stanley suggest that poverty was the motivating factor for many. See the interviews cited elsewhere here as well as Anna Stanley, "The Experiences of the Serpent River First Nation of the Nuclear Industry," held in the SRFN Library, Cutler, Ontario.

63 Environmental concerns for non-Indigenous views of development did not exist at this time. Places such as Sudbury and Sault Ste. Marie, for example, had industrial economies that had compromised the land, as did Elliot Lake. C.M. Wallace and Ashley Thomson, *Sudbury: Railtown to Regional Capital* (Dundurn Press, 1993); See other company histories that make little mention of environmental consequences of industry: Terrence J. Downey, "The Political Economy of Uranium, 1948–1970" (Master's thesis, University of Western Ontario, 1972); Jim Lyon, *Dome Petroleum: The Inside Story of Its Rise and Fall* (New York: Beaufort Books, 1983) ix-xi, 142–65; Peter Foster, *Rags to Riches: The Story of Bow Valley Industries Ltd.* (Calgary: Bow Valley Industries, 1985), 9. An even more popular example of a corporate-sponsored company history is Peter McKenzie-Brown, *The Richness of Discovery: Amoco's First 50 Years in Canada, 1948–1998* (Calgary: Amoco Canada Petroleum Co., 1998). It was written to commemorate the company's fiftieth anniversary.

64 Other First Nations communities entering the workforce or engaging in the wage economy suffered similar consequences, whereby short-term economic gains had long term health and socio-economic consequences. There is a growing literature on Indigenous peoples and labour. See, for example, John Lutz, "After the Fur Trade: The Aboriginal Labouring Class of British Columbia, 1849–90," in *Canadian Working-Class History: Selected Readings*, 3rd edition, ed. Laurel Sefton MacDowell and Ian Radforth (Toronto: Canadian Scholars' Press, 2006), 125–48; Rolf Knight, *Indians at Work: An Informal History of Native Labour in British Columbia, 1848–1930* (Vancouver: New Star Books, 1996); Mary Jane Logan McCallum, *Indigenous Women, Work, and History, 1940–1980* (Winnipeg: University of Manitoba Press, 2014); Frank Tough, *"As their Natural Resources Fail": Native Peoples and the Economic History of Northern Manitoba, 1870–1930* (Vancouver: University of British Columbia Press, 1996); Toby Morantz, The *White Man's Gonna Getcha: The Colonial Challenge to the Crees in Quebec* (Montreal: McGill-Queen's University Press, 2002); Diane Newell, *Tangled*

Webs of History: Indians and the Law in Canada's Pacific Coast Fisheries (Toronto: University of Toronto Press, 1989); Henry Pennier, *"Call Me Hank": A Sto:lo Man's Reflections on Logging, Living, and Growing Old*, ed. Keith Thor Carlson and Kristina Fagan (Toronto: University of Toronto Press, 2006); John Lutz and Keith Thor Carlson, "Sto:lo People and the Development of the B.C. Wage Economy," in *You Are Asked to Witness*, ed. Keith Thor Carlson, 109–24; Paige Raibmon, *Authentic Indians*, especially chapter four: "Picking, Posing, Performing"; Robin Jarvis Brownlie, "'Living the same as the white people': Mohawk and Anishinabe Women's Labour in Southern Ontario in the 1920s and 30s," *Labour/ Le Travail* 61 (Spring 2008): 41–68. Paige Raibmon, "Theaters of Contact: The Kwakwaka'wakw Meet Colonialism in British Columbia and at the Chicago World's Fair," *Canadian Historical Review* 81, no. 2 (June 2000): 157–90. Charles R. Menzies and Caroline F. Butler, "The Indigenous Foundation of the Resource Economy of BC's North Coast," *Labour/Le Travail* 61 (Spring 2008): 131–49. For a collection that documents Indigenous ways of using resources and how they changed over time, see Kerry Abel and Jean Friesen, eds., *Aboriginal Resource Use in Canada*; For an examination of the effects of game regulations on First Nations in Saskatchewan, see Anthony G. Gulig, "'We Beg The Government:' Native People and Game Regulation in Northern Saskatchewan, 1900–1940," *Prairie Forum* 28, no. 1 (Spring 2003): 81–98.

65 Interview with Gertrude Lewis by Author, 22 February 2008, Serpent River First Nation.

66 Rekmans, Lewis, and Dwyer, eds., *This Is My Homeland*, 45.

67 Interview with Terry Jacobs by Author, 8 December 2008, Serpent River First Nation.

68 Several young families were able to connect electricity to their homes in 1956–7, for example. See LAC, RG10, File 13/8–8-8.

69 Community members remember other employees who died at a relatively young age due to work in the acid plant, but it is complicated to prove a causal relationship. There was a high correlation between smoking and working in the mining industry, making claims for occupational exposure to lung diseases difficult to prove.

70 Interview with Valerie Commanda by Author, 7 July 2009, Serpent River First Nation. Workplace Safety and Insurance Appeals Tribunal Decision, 2002. One detail that is referred to in several places is that Mr. Commanda was a non-smoker, making his claim about lung cancer slightly easier to prove. The author wishes to thank Mrs. Commanda for sharing her experience of the WSIB and the outcome of her claim.

71 Interview with Frank Lewis by Author, 16 May 2014, Serpent River First Nation. See also Lianne C. Leddy, "'Are you only interviewing women for

this?': Indigenous Feminism and Oral History," in *Beyond Women's Words: Feminisms and the Practices of Oral History in the Twenty-First Century*, ed. Katrina Srigley, Stacey Zembrzycki, and Franca Iacovetta (New York: Routledge, 2018), 104–5. I conducted this interview with Frank Lewis in 2014 and am grateful for his permission to use it here.

72 On the health effects of workplace surroundings in this period, see Ontario, *Royal Commission on the Health and Safety of Workers in Mines* (Toronto: Ministry of the Attorney General, 1976). See also Laurel Sefton MacDowell, "The Elliot Lake Uranium Miners' Battle to Gain Occupational Health and Safety Improvements, 1950–80," *Labour/Le Travail* 69 (Spring 2012): 91–117.

73 Interview with Betty Jacobs by Author, 8 December 2008, Serpent River First Nation.

74 Interview with Terry Jacobs by Author, 8 December 2008, Serpent River First Nation.

75 Interview with Arnelda Jacobs by Author, 8 July 2009, Serpent River First Nation.

76 Interview with Valerie Commanda by Author, 7 July 2009, Serpent River First Nation.

77 Interview with Terry Jacobs by Author, 8 December 2008, Serpent River First Nation.

78 Interview with Peter Johnston by Author, 7 July 2009, Serpent River First Nation.

79 There are more concerns with the fish and game associated with the river system, but that will be discussed in the next chapter.

80 A discussion of the work of Dr. Rosalie Bertell and other studies undertaken by the community will follow in chapter six.

81 Interview with Arnelda Jacobs by Author, 8 July 2009, Serpent River First Nation.

82 LAC, RG 10, vol. 11353, File 493/20–11–7, "Agreement between Noranda Mines and Chief and Council, Serpent River Band," 19 October 1959.

83 LAC, RG 10, vol. 11353, File 493/20–11–7.

84 LAC, RG 10, vol. 11353, File 493/20–11–7, "Letter from G.S. Lapp, Regional Supervisor of Indian Agencies to Noranda Mines," 15 April 1964.

85 LAC, RG 10, vol. 11353, File 493/20–11–7, "Letter from J.O. Hinds to G.S. Lapp," 8 June 1964.

86 LAC, RG 10, vol. 11353, File 493/20–11–7, "Letter from J.O. Hinds to G.S. Lapp," 8 June 1964 and "copy of letter from J.O. Hinds to Chief William Meawasige," 5 June 1964.

87 LAC, RG 10, vol. 11353, File 493/20–11–7, "Memorandum from G.S. Lapp to the Superintendent, Sault Ste. Marie Agency Re: Noranda Mine Agreement," 10 March 1965.

88 LAC, RG 10, vol. 11353, File 493/20–11–7, "Sulphur Fumes – Serpent River Reserve," 24 May 1964.

89 Ibid.

90 Ibid.

91 LAC, RG 10, vol. 11353, File 493/20–11–7, "Sulphur Fumes – Serpent River Reserve," 24 May 1964.

92 This idea will be discussed further in reference to calls for decommissioning of the site later in the decade.

93 The mention of the community's centennial in the memo is puzzling. The treaty was signed in 1850 and so the reserve centennial had already passed. If instead it was a reference to Canada's centennial, the passing phrase demonstrates DIA's insensitivity to the larger issues at hand: that perhaps celebrating the state's birthday was not a high priority for a reserve that was so damaged by its commercial exploits.

94 It appears that the Department of Lands and Forests supplied the nursery stock. LAC, RG10, vol. 11353, File 493/20–11–7, "Letter from J.O. Hinds, Assistant Secretary at Noranda Mines to G.S. Lapp, Regional Supervisor of Indian Agents."

95 As per the researcher's agreement I signed with LAC to access these files, the name of the family will not be divulged in the interests of protecting its privacy.

96 LAC, RG 10, vol. 11336, File 493/3–11–7, "Letter to J. O'Neill, Superintendent from T.R. Wearing, Plant Manager, Sulphuric Acid Division, Noranda Mines," 26 September 1960.

97 Ibid.

98 According to an online CPI calculator, $500 in 1960 had the same purchasing power as $4,300 today. Consumer Price Inflation Calculator, accessed 24 July 2018, http://data.bls.gov/cgi-bin/cpicalc.pl.

99 LAC, RG 10, vol. 11336, File 493/3–11–7, "Letter to J. O'Neill from J.O. Hinds," 25 May 1961.

100 LAC, RG 10, vol. 11336, File 493/3–11–7, "Letter from A.R. Aquin to J.O. Hinds," 7 June 1961.

101 LAC, RG 10, vol. 11336, File 493/3–11–7, "Letter to A.R. Aquin, Superintendent of Sault Ste. Marie Agency from J.O. Hinds, Assistant Secretary for Noranda Mines," 26 June 1961.

102 Interview with Valerie Commanda by Author, 7 July 2009, Serpent River First Nation. Cars had only recently made their appearance on the reserve and were considered a luxury item by most families at the time.

103 Interview with Gertrude Lewis by Author, 22 February 2008, Serpent River First Nation.

104 Interview with Terry Jacobs by Author, 8 December 2008, Serpent River First Nation.

105 Rekmans, Lewis, and Dwyer, eds., *This Is My Homeland*, 45.
106 It should be noted that just because there is laughter on a topic, that does not mean that residents find the topic amusing in a positive way. For more on the topic of First Nations humour, see the works of Drew Hayden Taylor, Thomas King, as well as the Author's own article, "Interviewing Nookomis and Other Reflections," *Oral History Forum/ d'histoire orale* (Special Issue–2010): 1–18. http://www.oralhistoryforum .ca/index.php/ohf/article/view/386.
107 Interview with Gertrude Lewis by Author, 22 February 2008, Serpent River First Nation.
108 Interview with Terry Jacobs by Author, 8 December 2008, Serpent River First Nation.
109 Interview with Valerie Commanda by Author, 7 July 2009, Serpent River First Nation.
110 Interview with Gertrude Lewis by Author, 22 February 2008, Serpent River First Nation. More on the effects of water pollution from the mining industry in the Serpent River basin will follow in the next chapter.
111 LAC, MG 31 K39 vol. 36, "Serpent River Report, 1985," by the International Institute of Concern for Public Health, 17. For a lengthy discussion of this report see chapter five.
112 LAC, RG 10, vol. 13102, File 493/20–5-7, "Chief to A.B. Irwin, Superintendent Mineral Resources, Indian Affairs Branch," 21 April 1964,
113 Ibid.
114 LAC, RG 20, vol. 775, File 23–100-N17, "A Report on Progress: Noranda Mines, Limited, 1959," and LAC, RG 2, vol. 2746, "New Wharf at Cutler," Cabinet Conclusions, 6 June 1960, 4.
115 LAC, RG 20, Industry, Trade, and Commerce, vol. 775, File 23–100-N17, "A Report on Progress: Noranda Mines, Limited, 1961."
116 Ibid.
117 AANDC, Indian Lands Registry, "Assignment of Lease Transfer to Cutler Acid Limited," Registration number X12723, 31 October 1962.
118 Interview with Terry Jacobs by Author, 8 December 2008, Serpent River First Nation.
119 "Two Earth-Shaking Explosions Launch Acid Plant Demolition," *Standard*, 28 August 1969, p.1.
120 "'Like Stalingrad After the Siege': Ojibway Chief Doesn't Have Solution," *Standard*, 2 February 1967.
121 Ibid.
122 LAC, RG22, vol. 1196, File 2/493–1-837 vol. 1, "1 Field Squadron RCE Exercise Powder Serpent."
123 "Embarrassed" is one of the sub-headings of the article, since the first attempt did not result in the building's collapse. "Chief Tells Story Behind

Story of Cutler Acid Plant Demolition," *Standard*, 4 September 1969, 1. Peter Johnston recalls watching the demolition, witnessing the initial failure, and hearing someone shout, "bring in the Air Force!" Interview with Peter Johnston by Author, 7 July 2009, Serpent River First Nation.

124 LAC, RG 22, vol. 1196, File 2/493–1-837 vol 1, "Letter from N. Long to W. Terentiuk," 24 February 1970.

125 "Chief Tells Story Behind Story of Cutler Acid Plant Demolition," *Standard*, 4 September 1969, 1.

126 LAC, RG 22, vol. 1196, File 2/493–1-837 vol. 1, "Serpent River Band Council Resolution," 19 February 1970.

5. "We weren't supposed to use that water at all!"
Uranium Mining and the Serpent River

1 Interview with Terry and Betty Jacobs by Author, 8 December 2008, Serpent River First Nation.

2 Elder Tea, 29.

3 Interview with Terry and Betty Jacobs by Author, 8 December 2008, Serpent River First Nation.

4 Interview with Terry and Betty Jacobs by Author, 8 December 2008, Serpent River First Nation.

5 Interview with Terry and Betty Jacobs by Author, 8 December 2008, Serpent River First Nation.

6 Terry's exact wording of the river pollution differed from that of Gertrude Lewis, who recalled that the water was cleaner than that of Aird Bay, which is why she chose to have her children swim there. This probably has to do with Terry comparing the river before and after the establishment of uranium mining, while Gertrude was comparing the river to the obviously polluted Aird Bay, where the acid plant was.

7 Interview with Terry and Betty Jacobs by Author, 8 December 2008, Serpent River First Nation.

8 AO, RG 1–282–4-56 File: Serpent River 1964–67, A.E. Armstrong, 9 February 1967.

9 "Study Uranium Mine Area Water Disposal Problems," *Leader Spectator*, 30 May 1957, 7.

10 Ibid.

11 The most readable and concise description of the leaching process is as follows: "operations at uranium mines and mills are based on the underground mining of uranium-bearing ore and followed by crushing, grinding and extraction to recover it as uranium oxide. The ore is then crushed, ground, and leached with sulphuric acid to dissolve the uranium. The waste rock after leaching is separated and discharged to

waste as tailings. The liquid portion, containing the uranium in solution, is fed to ion exchange resin columns where the uranium is extracted by the solution by the resin and is, in turn, stripped from the resin by nitric acid. It is then precipitated, filtered, and dried in yellow cake form for shipping. The ion exchange feed solution, having been stripped of its uranium, is neutralized with lime and discharged with the tailings to the disposal area." Deputy Minister's Committee, "Report on Radiological Water Pollution in the Elliot Lake and Bancroft Areas" (Government of Ontario, 1965), 45. See Appendix IV: Methods of Waste Disposal and Treatment and Recommended Control Measures for Uranium Milling and Milling Procedures.

12 "Study Uranium Mine Area Water Disposal Problems," *Leader Spectator*, 30 May 1957, 7.

13 Ibid.

14 Minnow Environmental Inc., "Serpent River Watershed Monitoring Program – Cycle 2," June 2005, 1. Held in Elliot Lake Public Library. Note that the report is commissioned by the businesses that are ultimately responsible for the sites.

15 Rio Algom Limited & Denison Mines Inc., "Community Newsletter: Strong Effective Regulation Helps Improve Elliot Lake Site Environment," 2015, accessed 12 July 2018, https://www.denisonenvironmental.com /assets/docs/des-ral-newsletter-2015.pdf.

16 AO, RG 1–282–4-56 Bin 397141, File: Serpent River 1964–67, A.E. Armstrong, 9 February 1967.

17 AO, RG 1–282, B397141, Container 6, "Meeting at Elliot Lake to Discuss Problems Arising from Radioactive Pollution of the Serpent River Drainage System," 2.

18 Decommissioning Review and Advisory Committee, *Respect and Responsibility: The Stewardship of the Serpent River Watershed, Proposal for a New Structure by the Decommissioning Review and Advisory Committee: Final Report*, March 2000, 6. Held at Elliot Lake Public Library.

19 Ibid.

20 For more information about the cost-sharing arrangements between different levels of government with regards to Elliot Lake in the context of the Cold War, see chapter three.

21 Decommissioning Review and Advisory Committee, *Respect and Responsibility*, 6.

22 Interview with Peter Johnston by Author, 7 July 2009, Serpent River First Nation.

23 "Poisons Pile Up in Serpent River; Double Standards Anger Indians," *Globe and Mail*, 16 December 1976, 11. The issues at Serpent River made the national press, and while the *Globe and Mail* may be seen as more

conservative, it is national in scope, speaking to the level of interest there
was in the 1970s regarding environmental racism.

24 Ibid. These figures are supported by studies done throughout the 1970s
and compiled in chart form in A.C. Roy, W. Keller, "Status Report: Water
Pollution in the Serpent River Basin," 1976, in AO, RG 12–45, B141785,
"Lakes and Rivers: Serpent River, 1976, 752–2."

25 Ibid. See also AO, RG 12–45, B141785, A.C. Roy, W. Keller, "Status Report:
Water Pollution in the Serpent River Basin," 1976, in "Lakes and Rivers:
Serpent River, 1976, 752–2."

26 Gertrude Lewis recalled that the National Indian Brotherhood (now
the Assembly of First Nations) was helpful in securing a lawyer when
asked by the community for help. Peter Johnston recalled that when the
community asked for help, the National Indian Brotherhood sent an
environmentalist to assist in their presentations to the Environmental
Assessment Board in the late 1970s. Interview with Gertrude Lewis by
Author, 22 February 2008 and with Peter Johnston by Author, 7 July 2009,
Serpent River First Nation. For more information about the community's
presentation to the EAB, and who was involved, see chapter six. On the
involvement of the NIB see AO, RG 12–45, B141785, File: Lakes and Rivers:
Serpent River, 1976, 752–2, "George Manuel, President, NIB to Roméo
LeBlanc," 26 August 1976.

27 Interview with Gertrude Lewis by Author, 22 February 2008, Serpent River
First Nation.

28 AO, RG 12–45, B141785, File: Lakes and Rivers: Serpent River, 1976, 752–2,
"Minutes of Meeting to Discuss Radiological Concerns at Serpent River
Native Community," 17 November 1976.

29 For more on the problem of providing clean drinking water on reserve see
AO, RG 84–1, B259698, File: Surveys, 1969: Serpent River, "Memorandum
by L.V. Pitts titled 'Ground Water Survey, Spragge-Serpent River Area,'"
30 October 1969.

30 Interview with Gertrude Lewis by Author, 22 February 2008, Serpent River
First Nation.

31 Ibid.

32 Ibid.

33 J.B. Milner, "The Ontario Water Resources Commission Act, 1956," The
University of Toronto Law Journal 12, no. 1 (1957): 100–2.

34 Ontario, Official Report of Debates: Legislative Assembly of Ontario, 14 June
1965, p. 4136, Hon. Mr. Dymond, MPP (Toronto: Queen's Printer, 1963–5).

35 Deputy Minister's Committee, "Report on Radiological Water Pollution
in the Elliot Lake and Bancroft Areas" (Government of Ontario, 1965),
foreword. For the data that was collected that form the basis of the report,
see AO, RG 84–22, B125018, File: Elliot Lake (Uranium Mines) Analyses 1960.

36 "Thompson's Liberals set up committee on penal reform," *Toronto Daily Star*, 26 November 1964, 53.

37 Ibid.

38 Ontario, *Official Report of Debates: Legislative Assembly of Ontario*, 14 June 1965, p. 4136, Hon. Mr. Dymond, MPP (Toronto: Queen's Printer, 1963–5).

39 Ontario, *Official Report of Debates: Legislative Assembly of Ontario*, 14 June 1965, p. 4136, Hon. Mr. Dymond, MPP and Mr. Renwick, MPP (Toronto: Queen's Printer, 1963–5).

40 Barrie Zwicker, "Hold-Up Report on A-Pollution until after Vote," *Globe and Mail*, 2 November 1965, 1.

41 Ibid.

42 Ibid.

43 Ibid.

44 Deputy Minister's Committee, "Report on Radiological Water Pollution in the Elliot Lake and Bancroft Areas" (Government of Ontario, 1965), iv.

45 Deputy Minister's Committee, "Report on Radiological Water Pollution in the Elliot Lake and Bancroft Areas" (Government of Ontario, 1965), iv.

46 There was some discussion about the water quality for the town in the *Standard*. See Editorial, "Elliot Lake Water Still Safe for Drinking," *Standard*, 18 November 1964, 4: "Although it may be news to other parts of Canada that there are waters in the Elliot Lake area that are contaminated by radioactive waste from the uranium mines, it is hardly new to Elliot Lakers." See also "Elliot Lake Water Still Safe to Drink," *Standard*, 17 July 1963, 1, which described the 300 tonne acid spill at Lacnor mine and "Municipal Beach Is Again Closed Down: Water Remains Safe to Drink," *Standard*, 24 July 1963, 1. "Elliot Lake Weathers Water Scare: Water Supply Safe," *Standard*, 18 November 1964, 1. A *Maclean's* editorial pointed to the disturbing fact that many people did not seem bothered by (or did not believe) the fact that water resources were in danger: "Since When Did the Truth Become More Dangerous than Danger Itself?" *Maclean's*, 14 December 1964, 4. See, for example, "Elliot Lakers 'Fed Up' with Media: Foster," *Standard*, 14 December 1977, 1. In 1983, some settler communities met at the Lions hall in Serpent River to discuss the issue of water contamination. See "Serpent River Citizens Fear Acid Spillage," *Standard*, 18 March 1983, 1.

47 Deputy Minister's Committee, "Report on Radiological Water Pollution in the Elliot Lake and Bancroft Areas" (Government of Ontario, 1965), v.

48 Ibid.

49 A decade later, the government was still hopeful that this would be possible. See AO, B141785, File Lakes and Rivers: Serpent River, 1976, 752–2, "Status Report, 1976."

50 Deputy Minister's Committee, "Report on Radiological Water Pollution in the Elliot Lake and Bancroft Areas" (Government of Ontario, 1965), iv.

51 Ibid., v.

52 Eric Colwill, "Pollution of Waterways in District Concern to Residents of Spanish Area," *Standard*, 15 December 1965, 1.

53 Ibid.

54 Eric Colwill, "Pollution of Waterways in District Concern to Residents of Spanish Area," *Standard*, 15 December 1965, 1. Concerns about sport fishing and commercial fishing persisted for more than a decade. See various correspondence from 1973 in AO, RG 12–88, B211794, File: River Basins, Lake Huron.

55 AO, RG 1–282, B397141, Container 6, "Letter from J.S. Ball to C.F. Schenk," 27 April 1966.

56 "Elliot Lake Weathers Water Scare: Water Supply Safe," *Standard*, 18 November 1964, 1. The title of the article is ironic given the information contained in it. After describing the spawning issues identified by the Department of Lands and Forests, the article then goes on to state that "scientists and medical authorities responsible insist that there is no danger whatsoever at this time in Elliot Lake."

57 Fisheries and Oceans Canada, *Ontario-Great Lakes Area Fact Sheets: Lake Trout*, accessed 12 July 2020, http://www.dfo-mpo.gc.ca/regions/central/pub/factsheets-feuilletsinfos-ogla-rglo/laketrout-touladi-eng.htm.

58 David R. Browne, *Freshwater Fish in Ontario's Boreal: Status, Conservation and Potential Impacts of Development* (N.p.: Wildlife Conservation Society Canada, 2007), 33.

59 Ibid., 29–33.

60 AO, RG 84–22, B125001, Container 9, G.M. Galimbert to D.S. Caverly, "Industrial Pollution in the Serpent River Watershed – Whiskey, Kindle, and Hook Lakes," 26 August 1964.

61 Ibid.

62 Ibid.

63 Ibid.

64 Ibid.

65 Ibid.

66 See, for example, AO, RG 84–1, B259698, File: Surveys, 1969: Serpent River, Memorandum by L.V. Pitts titled "Ground Water Survey, Spragge-Serpent River Area," 30 October 1969.

67 The letter does not name the lakes explicitly, but the 1965 report focused on these two lakes. Deputy Minister's Committee, "Report on Radiological Water Pollution in the Elliot Lake and Bancroft Areas" (Toronto: Government of Ontario, 1965).

68 AO, RG 84–22, B125001, Container 9, "Letter from G.M. Galimbert to Dr. D.J. Dewar," 13 August 1964.
69 Ibid.
70 AO, RG 1–282–4-56 File: Serpent River 1964–67, "Memo to F.A. MacDougall," 22 October 1964.
71 George Manuel and Michael Posluns, *The Fourth World: An Indian Reality* (Don Mills: Collier Macmillan Canada, 1974), 189.
72 AO, RG 1–282–4-56 File: Serpent River 1964–67, R.W. McCauley, "Meeting at Elliot Lake to Discuss Problems Arising From Radioactive Pollution of the Serpent River Drainage System," 1964.
73 Ibid.
74 Ibid.
75 Ibid.
76 Barrie Zwicker, "Facts Secret Two Years – Elliot Lake Contaminated by Radioactive Waste," *Globe and Mail*, 13 November 1964, 1.
77 Ibid.
78 Ibid.
79 "Since When Did the Truth Become More Dangerous than Danger Itself?" *Maclean's*, 14 December 1964, 4.
80 Ibid.
81 See also AO, B211794, "Lake Huron Serpent River – River Basins, Lake Huron, RB-22: Streams, Serpent, vol. IV."
82 The members of SRFN continued to fish commercially in Lake Huron during the 1960s but their traditional fishing grounds, the mouth and "half of the Serpent River" were no longer safe or productive. For a description of traditional territories see LAC, RG 10, vol. 11347, File B/20–2-8, "Serpent River Reserve Fishing Rights," 5 December 1949. For an overview of how fishing changed in see LAC, RG 10, vol. 13102, File 411B/20–2-201.
83 "Since when did the truth become more dangerous than danger itself?" Ibid.
84 Olive P. Dickason with David T. McNab, *Canada's First Nations: A History of Founding Peoples from Earliest Times*, 4th Edition (Don Mills: Oxford University Press, 2009), 388. For an examination of enfranchisement and loss of Indian Status before 1960, see Robin Jarvis Brownlie, "'A better citizen than lots of white men': First Nations Enfranchisement: an Ontario Case Study, 1918–1940," *Canadian Historical Review* 87, no. 1 (March, 2006): 29–52.
85 Interviews with Gertrude Lewis, 22 February 2008, and with Peter Johnston, 7 July 2009, Serpent River First Nation.
86 Lorraine Rekmans, Keith Lewis, and Anabel Dwyer, eds., 33. The editors noted that the group session where these stories were told was held at the Kenabutch Health Centre on 19 March 1999.
87 Ibid., 41–3.

88 Ibid., 42.

89 AO, RG 12–45, B141785, Lakes and Rivers 1976, "Letter from E.L. LeVert to Chief and Council," 30 July 1974. Emphasis added. This letter was found in provincial documents but has not been located in the DIA records available at LAC. It is possible that a copy was not retained at DIA or was misplaced.

90 AO, RG 12–45, B141785, Lakes and Rivers 1976, "Letter from George Manuel to Roméo Leblanc," 25 August 1976.

91 Ibid.

92 For works on Grassy Narrows, see Anastasia M. Shkilnyk, *A Poison Stronger Than Love: The Destruction of an Ojibwa Community* (New Haven: Yale University Press, 1985); George Hutchison and Dick Wallace, *Grassy Narrows* (Toronto: Van Nostrand Reinhold Ltd., 1977); Christopher Vecsey, "Grassy Narrows Reserve: Mercury Pollution, Social Disruption, and Natural Resources: A Question of Autonomy," *American Indian Quarterly* 11, no. 4 (Autumn 1987): 287–314.

93 The Red Power movement of the 1970s had contributed to the development of Indigenous political organizations as they became increasingly concerned with rights and environmental issues. See Donald Purich, *Our Land: Native Rights in Canada* (Toronto: James Lorimer and Company, 1986), especially the chapter entitled, "The Future of Native Rights"; J. Rick Ponting and Roger Gibbons, *Out of Irrelevance: A Socio-Political Introduction to Indian Affairs in Canada* (Toronto: Butterworth, 1980), especially Part III: The Politicization of Indian Affairs –The National Indian Brotherhood (NIB); Peter McFarlane, *Brotherhood to Nationhood: George Manuel and the Making of the Modern Indian Movement* (Toronto: Between the Lines, 1993); George Manuel and Michael Posluns (with a foreword by Vine Deloria, Jr.), *The Fourth World: An Indian Reality* (Don Mills: Collier Macmillan Canada, 1974).

94 AO, RG 12–45, B141785, Lakes and Rivers 1976, "Letter from George Manuel to Roméo Leblanc," 25 August 1976.

95 Other First Nations groups in Ontario actively supported SRFN. See the petitions and letters written to the Minister of the Environment, Keith Norton in 1981 in AO, RG 12–88, B214163 File Lakes and Rivers Serpent River 1981.

96 AO, RG 12–45, B141785, Lakes and Rivers 1976, "Letter from Roméo Leblanc to George Manuel," 18 November 1976.

97 Ibid.

98 Ibid.

99 Ibid.

100 AO, B141785, Lakes and Rivers 1976, "Letter from Dr. Peter J. Connop to Chief Loreen [*sic*] Lewis," 30 July 1974. Emphasis added.

101 AO, B141785, Lakes and Rivers 1976, "Letter from Bruce Rawson to Everett Biggs," 17 December 1976.
102 A.C. Roy and W. Keller, *Status Report: Water Pollution in the Serpent River Basin* (Toronto: Ministry of the Environment, 1976), 1.
103 Ibid., 2.
104 Ibid., 3–4.
105 Introductory letter signed by R.E. Moore, Regional Director, 1976. Ontario Ministry of the Environment, *Status Report: Water Pollution in the Serpent River Basin*, 1976.
106 AO, RG 12–45, B141785, Lakes and Rivers 1976, "Minutes of meeting to discuss radiological concerns at Serpent River Native Community," 1. Recall that the provincial standards for radioactivity were 3 pCi/L and the federal standards were 10 pCi/L. "Poisons Pile Up in Serpent River; Double Standards Anger Indians," *Globe and Mail*, 16 December 1976, 11; Interview with Peter Johnston by Author, 7 July 2009, Serpent River First Nation.
107 It is unknown what the results of those tests were.
108 AO, RG 12–45, B141785, Lakes and Rivers 1976, "Minutes of meeting to discuss radiological concerns at Serpent River Native Community," 2.
109 AO, RG 12–45, B141785, Lakes and Rivers 1976, "Minutes of meeting to discuss radiological concerns at Serpent River Native Community," 2.
110 Ibid., 1.
111 Ibid., 1. Dr. P. Connop was contacted in advance for general commentary, so the Department of Health and Welfare did not send a representative to the meeting.

6. "Ooh yes, we all went up to Elliot to protest": Resilience and Resistance at Serpent River First Nation

1 Interview with Peter Johnston by Author, 7 July 2009, Serpent River First Nation.
2 Olivia Ward, "Serpent River Pollution Site a Sulphurous Hell," *Toronto Star*, 21 July 1985, H1.
3 Editorial Board, "Footdragging at Serpent River," *Toronto Star*, 23 July 1985, A12.
4 The National Indian Brotherhood was formed in 1968 and the Union of Ontario Indians was formed in 1949. For an earlier instance of Indigenous rights assertion, see Robin Jarvis Brownlie, "'Nothing left for me or any other Indian': the Georgian Bay Anishinabek and Inter-War Articulations of Aboriginal Rights," *Ontario History* 96, no. 2 (Autumn 2004): 116–42.
5 Ron Sitt, "Energy Source Uranium Number one – Gillespie," *Sault Star*, 31 October 1978.

6 Ibid.
7 Larry R. Stewart, "Canada's Role in the International Uranium Cartel," *International Organization* 35, no. 4 (Autumn 1981), 658. Stewart's article is also fascinating in how it demonstrates the fact that although Canadians (especially opposition politicians) did not seem to object so much to the cartel as it informed international relations and protection of the uranium industry at home, as they disliked the fact that it was a secret.
8 See Robert Bothwell, Ian Drummond, and John English, *Canada Since 1945: Power, Politics, and Provincialism*, rev. ed. (Toronto: University of Toronto Press, 1993), 338–59.
9 *Standard*, 29 December 1976, 1.
10 As has been discussed, Ontario Hydro had been purchasing Elliot Lake uranium for power purposes since the mid-1960s. There had also been a contract with Japan, signed in 1967. See Dixon, 262. The Pearson government had ended its large scale stockpiling program designed specifically to save jobs in Elliot Lake in 1964 (see chapter three), but its federal stockpiling program had ceased in 1970. The contract renewal with Ontario Hydro in 1976 was thus an important development.
11 "Renegotiation of Contracts Ups Rio Profit" and "Outlook for Uranium Strong," *Standard*, 11 May 1977, 3.
12 "Outlook for Uranium Strong," *Standard*, 11 May 1977, 3.
13 "Efforts Stepped Up," *Standard*, 29 January 1976, 8.
14 *Standard*, 29 December 1976, 1.
15 "Environmental Assessment Board Told 10 Lakes Are Beyond Reclaiming," *Standard*, 27 April 1977.
16 "Environment Minister Sets Date of Preliminary Public Hearing," *Standard*, 28 October 1976, 1. Ontario Environment Minister George Kerr set the 30 November 1976 date.
17 Environmental Assessment Board, *The Expansion of the Uranium Mines in the Elliot Lake area: Interim Report Community Assessment*, March 1979, 5–6.
18 Ibid.
19 Ibid., 19–21, 27.
20 Housing was a main concern for the community when expansion was hotly anticipated. There are numerous *Standard* articles that deal with the concern for available housing, both at the time, and in the future should the mines expand. Throughout this time there was general anticipation for the expansion reflected in the local paper, and it spun the EAB's findings as supporting the general goals of the mining community in terms of available jobs, housing, and being good for business overall. Although there were some complaints about the town in terms of sidewalks, nightlife, traffic, etc. "the report concluded, however, on a positive note. 'The town has a friendly, quiet, small-town atmosphere,' it states, adding

that most people feel shortages will be overcome with time." The *Standard* went on to quote the EAB's findings that in general, "Elliot Lake has been perceived as a good place to raise a family." This can be found in "Report Details Town's Needs, Offers Solutions to Problems," *Standard*, 12 April 1978, 1.

21 Environmental Assessment Board, *The Expansion of the Uranium Mines in the Elliot Lake area: Interim Report Community Assessment*, March 1979, 37–8.

22 Interview with Terry and Betty Jacobs by Author, 8 December 2008, Serpent River First Nation.

23 Ibid.

24 See Thomas Berger, *Northern Frontier/Northern Homeland: The Report of the Mackenzie Valley Pipeline Inquiry*, 2 vols. (Ottawa: Ministry of Supply and Services, 1977) and Martin O'Malley, *The Past and Future Land: An Account of the Berger Inquiry into the Mackenzie Valley Pipeline* (Toronto: Peter Martin Associates, 1976). P.H. Pearse, ed., *The Mackenzie Pipeline: Arctic Gas and Canadian Energy Policy* (Montreal: McGill-Queen's University Press, 1974).

25 For a comprehensive study of Northern resource development, see Liza Piper, *The Industrial Transformation of Subarctic Canada*. Liza Piper and John Sandlos, "A Broken Frontier: Ecological Imperialism in the Canadian North," *Environmental History* 12, no. 4 (October 2007): 759–95; Liza Piper, "Subterranean Bodies: Mining the Large Lakes of North-west Canada, 1921–1960," *Environment and History* 13, no. 2 (May 2007): 155–86.

26 Berger, *Northern Frontier/Northern Homeland: The Report of the Mackenzie Valley Pipeline Inquiry*, 224.

27 Richard Howitt, *Rethinking Resource Management: Justice, Sustainability and Indigenous Peoples* (New York: Routledge, 2001), 42.

28 For more on the 1973 *Calder* decision which acknowledged the existence of Aboriginal title to land, see Daniel Raunet, *Without Surrender, Without Consent: A History of the Nishga Land Claims* (Vancouver: Douglas and McIntyre, 1996); Hamar Foster, Heather Raven, and Jeremy Webber, *Let Right be Done: Aboriginal Title, the Calder Case, and the Future of Indigenous Rights* (Vancouver: University of British Columbia Press, 2007).

29 J.R. Miller, "Aboriginal Rights, Land Claims, and the Struggle to Survive," in *Sweet Promises: A Reader on Indian-White Relations in Canada*, ed. J.R. Miller (Toronto: University of Toronto Press, 1991), 405–20. A more recent work is that of Hans M. Carlson, *Home Is the Hunter: The James Bay Cree and Their Land*, see especially chapter eight, entitled, "Flooding the Garden"; Alan Penn, "Uneasy Coexistence: La Grande and the James Bay Cree," in *On the Land: Confronting the Challenges to Aboriginal Self-Determination in Northern Quebec and Labrador*, ed. Bruce W. Hodgins and Kerry A. Cannon (Toronto: Betelgeuse, 1995): 129–44.

30 See James F. Hornig, ed., *Social and Environmental Impacts of the James Bay Hydroelectric Project*; Richard F. Salisbury, *A Homeland for the Cree: Regional Development in James Bay, 1971–1981*; Paul Rynard, "'Welcome In, but Check Your Rights at the Door': The James Bay and Nisga'a Agreements in Canada," *Canadian Journal of Political Science*, 33, no. 2 (June 2000): 211–43. Caroline Desbiens, "'Water all around, you cannot even drink': the scaling of water in James Bay/Eeyou Istchee," *Area* 39, no. 3 (September 2007): 259–67; Martin Papillon, "Aboriginal Quality of Life Under a Modern Treaty: Lessons from the Experience of the Cree Nation of Eeyou Istchee and the Inuit of Nunavik," *IRPP Choices* 14, no. 9 (August 2008). Jean L. Manore studies an earlier period of hydroelectricity in *Cross-Currents: Hydroelectricity and the Engineering of Northern Ontario*.

31 Hugh Shewell, *"Enough to Keep them Alive,"* 170.

32 Burton Jacobs, "Kicking out the Indian Agent," in *Nation to Nation: Aboriginal Sovereignty and the Future of Canada*, ed. John Bird, Lorraine Land, and Murray MacAdam (Toronto: Irwin Publishing, 2002), 141–7.

33 *A Survey of the Contemporary Indians of Canada: Economic, Political and Educational Needs*, vols. 1 and 2 (Ottawa: Government of Canada, 1967–8). This report is also known as the Hawthorn Report, after its editor, Harry B. Hawthorn. It advocated the term "Citizens Plus."

34 The White Paper, proposed by Pierre Trudeau's government, was an attempt to bring Indigenous administration in line with his "just society" idea. According to Trudeau, the "special" Indian Status afforded to First Nations people was what held them back. See Sally Weaver, *Making Canadian Indian Policy: The Hidden Agenda, 1968–70* (Toronto: University of Toronto Press, 1981).

35 See my previous discussion of the Robinson-Huron Treaty for more information on issues surrounding this Western/Euro-Canadian interpretation of the Treaty.

36 Interview with Peter Johnston by Author, 7 July 2009, Serpent River First Nation. Johnston's view of preventing expansion at Elliot Lake may stem from the fact that he worked for Rio Algom and "had first-hand knowledge of what was happening and what the potential there was for things to go wrong in the future which might still happen." His first-hand view as an employee, which was not an easy position for him to occupy, was one of his personal motivations for ensuring that expansion did not continue and may serve to explain why some of the other community members were concerned that it move on responsibly – after proper compensation for past environmental damage – rather than not at all.

37 Environmental Assessment Board, *The Expansion of the Uranium Mines in the Elliot Lake Area – Interim Report – Community Assessment*, March 1979, 3. There were people concerned with their tourism businesses present as

well. Interview with Gertrude Lewis by Author, 22 February 2008, Serpent River First Nation.

38 Interview with Gertrude Lewis by Author, 22 February 2008, Serpent River First Nation.

39 Lorraine Rekmans, Keith Lewis and Anabel Dwyer, eds., *This Is My Homeland*, 95.

40 Ibid.

41 For more on women and Indian Act governance structures, see Cora Voyageur, *Firekeepers of the Twenty-First Century: First Nations Women Chiefs* (Montreal: McGill-Queen's University Press, 2008).

42 Lorraine Rekmans, Keith Lewis and Anabel Dwyer, eds., *This Is My Homeland*, 94.

43 Interview with Peter Johnston by Author, 7 July 2009, Serpent River First Nation.

44 Both Terry Jacobs and Peter Johnston noted that many of the community's men worked at the plant.

45 See chapters four and five for the effects the industry's pollution had on traditional pursuits.

46 See the introduction and chapter two for a more in-depth explanation of Anishinaabe teachings.

47 Tony Frangomeni, "Fall Public Hearings Set by Provincial Ministry," *Standard*, 30 September 1976, 1.

48 Ibid.

49 This report is discussed in detail in the previous chapter.

50 Richard Sandberg, "'Clean Up Polluted Water' Union Men Demand of Government," *Standard*, 15 July 1976, 1. See also "Slow Up in Expansion Program Needed Here Says Union Leader," *Standard*, 14 September 1977, 1. Seguin spoke to the *Standard* about the board, which was, at the time, in temporary adjournment. The union supported expansion, but it insisted that it be at a rate that took workers, the town, and the environment into consideration.

51 Rachel Carson, *Silent Spring*, 40th anniversary ed. (New York: Houghton Mifflin Company, 2002).

52 Rex Weyler, *Greenpeace: How a Group of Ecologists, Journalists and Visionaries Changed the World* (Vancouver: Raincoast Books, 2004).

53 Ryan O'Connor, *The First Green Wave: Pollution Probe and the Origins of Environmental Activism in Ontario* (Vancouver: University of British Columbia Press, 2014). See also Jennifer Bonnell, "An Intimate Understanding of Place: Charles Sauriol and Toronto's Don River Valley, 1927–89," *Canadian Historical Review* 92, no. 4 (2011): 607–36.

54 "A Catalyst for Change: Earth Day Canada," *Maclean's*, 122, no. 14 (20 April 2009), 49. See also Chad and Pam Gaffield, eds., *Consuming Canada: Readings in Environmental History* (Toronto: Copp Clark Ltd., 1995).

For Canadian environmental policy, see Bruce Doern and Thomas
Conway, *The Greening of Canada: Federal Institutions and Decisions* (Toronto:
University of Toronto Press, 1994). A more recent book is Melody Hessing,
Michael Howlett, and Tracy Summerville, *Canadian Natural Resource
and Environmental Policy: Political Economy and Public Policy* (Vancouver:
University of British Columbia Press, 2005). Kathryn Harrison, *Passing the
Buck: Federalism and Canadian Environmental Policy* (Vancouver: University
of British Columbia Press, 1996).
55 J.W. Black, "Elliot Lake," *Globe and Mail*, 21 November 1964, 6.
56 Archives of Ontario RG 84–22, File: Elliot Lake Uranium Mines Pollution
Correspondence Information, "Letter from Ronald Hancock to D.S.
Caverly, General Manager, OWRC," 16 November 1964. See the entire file
for more examples and the responses (usually one-and-a-half pages in
length) provided by Caverly or other OWRC officials.
57 Interview with Gertrude Lewis by Author, 22 February 2008, Serpent River
First Nation. When Gertrude mentioned the head of the union, she was
most likely referring to Homer Seguin.
58 See, for example, "Environmental Assessment Board Told 10 Local Lakes
Are beyond Reclaiming," *Standard*, 27 April 1977, 1. Dr. Donald Gobor, the
project manager of Denison and Rio Algom's consulting firm, McLaren,
presented the information himself to the board. It should be noted that the
local response to negative media attention to the area was unwelcome. See
"Elliot Lakers 'fed up' with media: Foster," *Standard*, 14 December 1977, 1.
MP Maurice Foster is quoted throughout the article as saying, "People are
fed up with sensationalist journalists coming here to tell Canada that there
are all these problems … they don't realize that people live here, raise their
families here, and they don't go around scared to death … If the town was
like the way the CBC would have you think, then why do people spend
their whole life here?"
59 Interview with Gertrude Lewis by Author, 22 February 2008, Serpent River
First Nation.
60 Ibid.
61 Ibid.
62 Environmental Assessment Board, *The Expansion of the Uranium Mines in
the Elliot Lake Area: Final Report*, May 1979, 251.
63 "Rio Spill not the first as both companies seek prevention measures,"
Standard, 19 April 1978, 1. The article also outlines previous issues Rio
and Denison had had in the 1970s, as well as the modern equipment
that the companies were using to try to increase their responsible waste
management systems. The concerns did not end in the 1970s, nor were
they only held by SRFN as the settler community of Serpent River held
a meeting in March 1983. "Serpent River Citizens Fear Acid Spillage,"
Standard, 18 March 1983, 1.

64 "Big Clean Up Job Ahead after Recent Rio Tailings Spill," *Standard*, 19 April 1978, 1.
65 Environmental Assessment Board, *The Expansion of the Uranium Mines in the Elliot Lake Area: Final Report* (May 1979), 251.
66 Ibid. Emphasis added.
67 Ibid., 252.
68 Ibid., x.
69 In 1990, Rio and Denison announced their first round of lay-offs. Denison closed in 1992 and Rio Stanleigh's last day of operation was in 1996. By 1996, 4,200 miners had lost their jobs out of a population of approximately 13,500 people. See Anne-Marie Mawhiney and Jane Pitblado, "Introduction," in *Boom Town Blues, Elliot Lake: Collapse and Revival in a Single-Industry Community* (Toronto: Dundurn Press, 1999), 12–14.
70 Ibid., 13–14.
71 Ibid.
72 Institute for Environmental Studies, "Rehabilitation of the Cutler Acid Site, on the Serpent River Indian Reserve – A Feasibility Study," Final Report, 1981.
73 Ibid., charts on 175–6.
74 Discussed at length in chapter three.
75 As quoted in Olivia Ward, "Serpent River Pollution Site a Sulphurous Hell," Toronto Star, 21 July 1985. See also Institute for Environmental Studies, "Rehabilitation of the Cutler Acid Site, on the Serpent River Indian Reserve – A Feasibility Study," Final Report, 1981, 97.
76 Ibid.
77 The International Institute of Concern for Public Health describes itself as "a Canadian-based non-profit organization dedicated to helping communities assess and improve their environmental health status." On the IICPH see http://www.iicph.org/, accessed 22 April 2011. I use this data here only to suggest a pattern in the relationship between the acid plant and community health. It was not an exhaustive study, but it is the only one of its kind to provide statistics about the health of residents due in no small part to privacy concerns and the fact that this is a fairly recent situation. See also Elaine Carey, "Honours Piling Up for the Rebel Nun," *Toronto Star*, 25 January 1987, D5.
78 LAC, MG 31 K39 vol. 36, Serpent River Band, "Report of Progress on Environmental Intervention Study Period: Jan 1-March 31, 1982," n.d., 1.
79 LAC, MG 31 K39 vol. 36, "Serpent River Report, 1985," by the International Institute of Concern for Public Health, i.
80 LAC, MG 31 K39 vol. 36, "Joint Health Report: Serpent River, Mississaugi and Spanish River Reserves January, 1984," by the International Institute of Concern for Public Health, 2.
81 Ibid.

82 Ibid., 4.

83 Ibid., 4. Bertell breaks down the numbers for each reserve into subcategories: occupational exposure, age, and fish and game consumption. Because she did not use the same subcategories for each community, I have averaged the numbers given for each community to give an approximate comparison in order to suggest a pattern.

84 Ibid., 4.

85 This may also have to do with the fact that Sagamok and Mississauga First Nations are located on different rivers.

86 LAC, MG 31 K39 vol. 36, "Serpent River Report, 1985," by the International Institute of Concern for Public Health, 17.

87 LAC, MG 31 K39 vol. 36, "Report on the Serpent River Project," 30 November 1985, 5.

88 Ibid., 4.

89 I include the comparison because the two communities would have had similar socio-economic and ethnic backgrounds with the only significant difference being that the Serpent River First Nation had an acid plant and the Mississauga First Nation did not.

90 LAC, MG 31 K39 vol. 36, "Report on the Serpent River Project," 30 November 1985, 4–6. Bertell also found that 57.1 per cent of acid plant workers and 13.6 per cent of other males reported deafness (the latter had 0.6 per cent partial deafness). She suspected that the hearing loss in adult workers was related to excessive noise at the plant, but she also had some concern that the hearing loss in children may have been related to swimming in the bay near the acid site (where refuse from the plant was dumped throughout its operation): "Children swimming in Aird Bay, in the acidic effluence from the contaminated site have reported pains in their ears. Some of the acid plant worker deafness was probably due to noise."

91 LAC, MG 31 K39 vol. 36, "Serpent River Report, 1985," by the International Institute of Concern for Public Health, 16.

92 Ibid., 17.

93 Olivia Ward, "Serpent River Pollution Site a Sulphurous Hell," *Toronto Star*, 21 July 1985, H1, H5.

94 Ibid, H5.

95 Ibid, H5.

96 Interview with Peter Johnston by Author, 7 July 2009, Serpent River First Nation.

97 "Chemical Waste: Band Could Block Highway, *Standard*, 9 February 1986, 1.

98 Ibid.

99 Peter Haggart, "Reserve's Acid: Band Chief More Hopeful, but No Clean-Up Promised," *Standard*, 16 February 1986, 1. The *Toronto Star* reported that a 31 May meeting had been scheduled to include federal

Indian and Northern Affairs Minister David Crombie, federal Environment Minister Tom McMillan, and federal Health Minister Jake Epp. David Israelson, "Indian Band Ready to Block Highway over Cleanup Dispute," *Toronto Star*, 14 February 1986, A14.

100 For more on the Oka and its ties to the growth of Indigenous nationalism, see Gerald (Taiaiake) R. Alfred, *Heeding the Voices of Our Ancestors: Kahnawake Mohawk Politics and the Rise of Native Nationalism* (Don Mills: Oxford University Press, 1995).

101 Nicholas Blomley, "'Shut the Province Down': First Nations Blockades in British Columbia, 1984–1995," *BC Studies* 111 (Autumn 1996): 5–35. Quote from page 6. See also C. Radha Jhappan, "Indian Symbolic Politics: The Double-Edged Sword of Publicity," *Canadian Ethnic Studies* 22 (1990): 19–39.

102 See Anna Willow's work on the use of blockades at Grassy Narrows in response to clear-cutting: "Clear-Cutting and Colonialism: The Ethnopolitical Dynamics of Indigenous Environmental Activism in Northwestern Ontario," *Ethnohistory* 56, no. 1 (2009): 35–67; Anna J. Willow, *Strong Hearts, Native Lands: Anti-Clearcutting Activism at Grassy Narrows First Nation* (Winnipeg: University of Manitoba Press, 2012).

103 "Chemical Waste: Band Could Block Highway," *Standard*, 9 February 1986, 1; Peter Haggart, "Reserve's Acid: Band Chief More Hopeful, but No Clean-Up Promised," *Standard*, 16 February 1986, 1.

104 David Israelson, "Band Sets Deadlines for Clean-Up on Reserve," *Toronto Star*, 28 September 1986, A18.

105 Ibid.

106 AO, RG 12–45, B320348, File: Waste Sites 1986, Cutler Acid Site – Serpent River, "Letter from Chief Earl Commanda to Hon. James Bradley," 22 July 1986. Not everyone was pleased with the Pronto idea, as one Lake Lauzon resident was concerned about potential pollution as a result of this type of action. See correspondence in same file.

107 Ibid.

108 Douglas Armour, "Leaders' Threat: Reserve Will Take Its Own Steps unless Government Moves on Acid," *Standard*, 1 October 1986, 1.

109 Ibid.

110 Ibid.; Rudy Platiel, "Serpent River Indians Seek Action on Contaminated Soil," *Globe and Mail*, 29 September 1986, A14; "Reserve Cleanup Awaits Decision," *Globe and Mail*, 24 October 1986, A9.

111 Anon., "Native Set Protest Fire to Push Ottawa on Waste," *Toronto Star*, 29 June 1988, A7.

112 Jim Patrick, "Serpent River Band Tells a History of Complaint," *Standard*, 29 June 1988, 1.

113 Serpent River Band, "The Cutler Acid Site: Presentation to the Standing Committee on Aboriginal Affairs," 28 January 1987. The author of the

report is unknown, but it was prepared for the leadership's presentation. The report is held in the private papers of Gertrude Lewis. *Miigwetch* to her for her permission to use them for this project.

114 Speaking notes written by Gertrude Lewis, held privately in her papers. *Miigwetch* to Gertrude for lending them to me and providing consent to quote from them.

115 Serpent River Band, "The Cutler Acid Site: Presentation to the Standing Committee on Aboriginal Affairs," 28 January 1987, 3–4.

116 Ibid., 3.

117 Elmer Sopha, MPP, Sudbury to Minister of Indian Affairs, 1969, quoted in Serpent River Band, "The Cutler Acid Site: Presentation to the Standing Committee on Aboriginal Affairs," 28 January 1987, 2.

118 Editorial, *Toronto Star*, 23 July 1985, quoted in Serpent River Band, "The Cutler Acid Site: Presentation to the Standing Committee on Aboriginal Affairs," 28 January 1987, 4. For the original article see Editorial Board, "Footdragging at Serpent River," *Toronto Star*, 23 July 1985, A12.

119 Serpent River Band, "The Cutler Acid Site: Presentation to the Standing Committee on Aboriginal Affairs," 28 January 1987, 6.

120 "Natives Set Protest Fire to Push Ottawa on Waste," *Toronto Star*, 29 June 1988, A7.

121 Ibid.

122 Interview with Peter Johnston by Author, 7 July 2009, Serpent River First Nation.

123 Anon., "$5.7 Million Given to Compensate Band in Toxic Waste Case," *Toronto Star*, 20 July 1988, A7.

124 Judy Robinson, "Government Gives Reserve $6 million for Toxic Cleanup," *The Globe and Mail*, 18 July 1988, A9.

125 Ibid.

126 Jim Patrick, "Noranda won't help with Cutler Clean-Up," *Standard*, 23 November 1988, 1.

127 Jeff Wilkinson, "Chemical Company Compensating Band," *Standard*, 18 December 1988, 1.

128 Ibid.

Conclusion

1 Interview with Peter Johnston by Author, 7 July 2009, Serpent River First Nation.

2 Interview with Gertrude Lewis by Author, 22 February 2008, Serpent River First Nation. Gertrude passed away in September 2012.

3 Interview with Terry and Betty Jacobs by Author, 8 December 2008, Serpent River First Nation.

4 Ibid.
5 Interview with Arnelda Jacobs by Author, 8 July 2009, Serpent River First Nation.
6 Interview with Valerie Commanda by Author, 7 July 2009, Serpent River First Nation.
7 United Nations Declaration on the Rights of Indigenous Peoples, 2007, accessed 24 July 2018, http://www.un.org/esa/socdev/unpfii/documents/DRIPS_en.pdf.
8 Truth and Reconciliation Commission, "Calls to Action," 2015, accessed 24 July 2018, http://trc.ca/assets/pdf/Calls_to_Action_English2.pdf.
9 Pele Mountain Resources, "The City of Elliot Lake Extends Exclusive Sustainable Energy Development Agreement with Pele Mountain," 2 May 2018, accessed 24 July 2018, http://www.pelemountain.com/nr/20180502.php and retrievable at https://web.archive.org/web/20190216061054/http://www.pelemountain.com/nr/20180502.php.
10 For more information about the decommissioning and monitoring aspects of the work being done by Denison Environmental, see Denison Environmental Services, accessed 27 February 2011, http://www.denisonenvironmental.com/.
11 Jessica Brousseau, "Sub-committee members present draft agreement for cottage lot development," *Standard*, 16 April 2015, 12.
12 Ibid.
13 Ibid.
14 Rosalind Russell, "Serpent River First Nation Agrees to Work with Elliot Lake Council," *My Algoma Manitoulin Now*, 20 June 2018, accessed 24 July 2018, https://www.myalgomamanitoulinnow.com/18002/serpent-river-first-nation-agrees-to-work-with-elliot-lake-council/.
15 David Briggs, "Elliot Lake Raises Serpent River First Nation Flag," *Standard*, 27 June 2018, accessed 24 July 2018, http://www.elliotlakestandard.ca/2018/06/27/elliot-lake-raises-serpent-river-first-nation-flag.
16 David Briggs, "Elliot Lake Enters Phase Two of NWMO Search," *Standard*, 26 February 2015, 16.
17 Gloria Galloway, "Ontario First Nations Demand a Say over Nuclear Waste Storage," *Globe and Mail*, 21 May 2015, accessed 15 June 2015, http://www.theglobeandmail.com/news/politics/ontario-first-nations-demand-a-say-over-nuclear-waste-storage/article24540670/.
18 Letter quoted in ibid.
19 NWMO, "Blind River, Elliot Lake and Area," December 2017, accessed 24 July 2018, https://www.nwmo.ca/en/Site-selection/Study-Areas/Areas-No-Longer-Being-Studied/Blind-River-Elliot-Lake-and-Area.

Bibliography

Oral History Interviews

Mrs. Valerie Commanda, 7 July 2009
Mrs. Arnelda Jacobs, 8 July 2009
Mrs. Betty Jacobs, 8 December 2008
Mr. Terry Jacobs, 8 December 2008
Mr. Peter Johnston, 7 July 2009
Mr. Frank Lewis, 16 May 2014
Mrs. Gertrude Lewis, 22 February 2008

Documentary Primary Sources

Federal Archives

Aboriginal Affairs and Northern Affairs Development Canada (AANDC) – Indian Lands Registry
Library and Archives Canada (LAC) – Official Government Records
   Annual Reports for the Department of Indian Affairs
   Record Group 2 (Records of the Privy Council)
   Record Group 10 (Department of Indian Affairs)
   Record Group 20 (Department of Industry, Trade and Commerce)
   Record Group 22 (Department of Indian and Northern Affairs)
Library and Archives Canada – Personal Papers
   Manuscript Group 31 K39 (Dr. Rosalie Bertell Fonds)
   Manuscript Group 26–N4 (Lester B. Pearson Papers)

Regional and Local Archives

Archives of Ontario
   RG 1-282 – Ministry of Natural Resources
   RG 12-45 – Lakes and Rivers

RG 19 – Records of the Ontario Municipal Board
RG 84-22 – Industrial Waste/Municipal Files
Laurentian University Library Archives
    Catharine Dixon Fonds
    USWA Local 5417 Fonds
Archives of the Serpent River First Nation
    Interviews Transcripts by Anna Stanley
    Interview Transcripts by Perry Shawana
Archives of the City of Elliot Lake
    Denison Papers

Privately Held Papers

Personal Papers of Gertrude Lewis, Serpent River First Nation, Cutler, Ontario.
Personal Papers of Valerie Commanda, Serpent River First Nation, Cutler, Ontario

Primary Sources

Newspapers and Periodicals

Globe and Mail
Global News
Leader-Spectator
Maclean's
Marketwatch.com
My Algoma Manitoulin Now
Sault Daily Star (Sault Ste. Marie, Ontario)
Sault Star (Sault St. Marie, Ontario)
Spectator (Bruce Mines, Ontario)
Standard (Elliot Lake, Ontario)
Toronto Star
Windspeaker

Government Documents

Berger, Thomas. *Northern Frontier/Northern Homeland: The Report of the Mackenzie Valley Pipeline Inquiry.* 2 vols. Ottawa: Ministry of Supply and Services, 1977.
Cairns, H.A.C., S.M. Jamieson, K. Lysyk, M.A. Tremblay, F.G. Vallee, and J. Ryan. *A Survey of the Contemporary Indians of Canada: Economic, Political and Educational Needs and Policies.* 2 vols. Ottawa: Government of Canada, 1967–8.

Canada Indian Affairs, *Report of the Special Commissioners Appointed on the 8th of September, 1856, to Investigate Indian Affairs in Canada.* Sessional Papers, Appendix 21. Toronto: Stewart Derbishire and George Desbarats, 1858.

Centers for Disease Control and Prevention. "NIOSH [National Institute for Occupational Safety and Health] Pocket Guide to Chemical Hazards – Sulfuric Acid." Accessed 26 February 2011. http://www.cdc.gov/niosh /npg/npgd0577.html.

Crown-Indigenous Relations and Northern Affairs Canada. *Copy of the Robinson Treaty Made in the Year 1850 with the Ojibewa Indians of Lake Huron Conveying Certain Lands to the Crown.* Accessed 20 July 2021. https://www .rcaanc-cirnac.gc.ca/eng/1100100028984/1581293724401.

Government of Canada. *Canada Department of Citizenship and Immigration Report of Indian Affairs Branch 1956–57.* Ottawa: Queen's Printer, 1957.

– *Canada Department of Citizenship and Immigration Report of Indian Affairs Branch for the Fiscal Year Ended March 31, 1959.* Ottawa: Queen's Printer, 1960.

– *Report of the Royal Commission on Aboriginal Peoples.* 5 vols. Ottawa: Queen's Printer, 1991.

Government of Canada, Fisheries and Oceans Canada. *Ontario-Great Lakes Area Fact Sheets: Lake Trout.* Accessed 12 July 2010. http://www.dfo-mpo .gc.ca/regions/central/pub/factsheets-feuilletsinfos-ogla-rglo/laketrout -touladi-eng.htm.

Government of Canada, Indian Affairs Branch. *Indian in Transition: The Meeting of the Ways Learning for Earning.* Ottawa: Government of Canada, 1961.

Government of Ontario. *Official Report of Debates: Legislative Assembly of Ontario.* Toronto: Queen's Printer, 1963–5.

Government of Ontario, Deputy Minister's Committee. *Report on Radiological Water Pollution in the Elliot Lake and Bancroft Areas.* Toronto: Government of Ontario, 1965.

Government of Ontario, Environmental Assessment Board. *The Expansion of the Uranium Mines in the Elliot Lake Area: Final Report.* Toronto: Queen's Printer, 1979.

– *The Expansion of the Uranium Mines in the Elliot Lake Area: Interim Report Community Assessment.* Toronto: Queen's Printer, 1979.

Library of Parliament. "Stanley James Korchinski, M.P." Accessed 17 July 2020. https://lop.parl.ca/sites/ParlInfo/default/en_CA/People/Profile ?personId=13510.

National Inquiry into Missing and Murdered Indigenous Women and Girls. *Reclaiming Power and Place: The Final Report of the National Inquiry into Missing and Murdered Indigenous Women and Girls.* 2019. Accessed 17 July 2020. https://www.mmiwg-ffada.ca/wp-content/uploads/2019/06/Final _Report_Vol_1a-1.pdf.

– *A Legal Analysis of Genocide*. Accessed 17 July 2020. https://www.mmiwg
-ffada.ca/wp-content/uploads/2019/06/Supplementary-Report
_Genocide.pdf.

Spence, H.S., and F.N. Senftle. *Prospectors' Guide for Uranium and Thorium
Minerals in Canada*. Ottawa: Bureau of Mines, Department of Mines and
Resources, 1949.

Surtees, Robert J. *The Robinson Treaties (1850)*. Ottawa: Treaties and Historical
Research Centre: Indian and Northern Affairs Canada, 1986. Crown-
Indigenous Relations and Northern Affairs Canada. Accessed 17 July 2020.
https://www.rcaanc-cirnac.gc.ca/eng/1100100028974/1564412549270.

– *Manitoulin Island Treaties*. Ottawa: Treaties and Historical Research Centre,
Indian and Northern Affairs Canada, 1986. Crown-Indigenous Relations
and Northern Affairs Canada. Accessed 20 July 2020. https://www.rcaanc
-cirnac.gc.ca/eng/1100100028959/1564583230395.

Published Primary Sources

Decommissioning Review and Advisory Committee. *Respect and
Responsibility: The Stewardship of the Serpent River Watershed, Proposal for a
New Structure by the Decommissioning Review and Advisory Committee: Final
Report*. N.p.: 2000.

Leonard, John William. *The Industries of Detroit*. Detroit: J.M. Elstner and
Co., 1887.

Roberts, Leslie. *Noranda*. Toronto: Clarke Irwin, 1956.

Thwaites, Reuben Gold, ed. *Jesuit Relations and Allied Documents*. vol. 33.
Cleveland: The Burrows Brothers Company, 1898.

Websites

Denison Environmental Services. "Home." Accessed 27 February 2011. http://
www.denisonenvironmental.com/.

Julia Jarvis. "Biography of William Benjamin Robinson." *Dictionary of
Canadian Biography Online*. Toronto and Quebec: University of Toronto and
Université Laval, 2000. Accessed 3 December 2012. http://www.biographi
.ca/009004-119.01-e.php?id_nbr=5234.

Pele Mountain. Accessed 20 June 2018. http://www.pelemountain.com.

Nuclear Waste Management Organization. "Blind River, Elliot Lake and
Area." December 2017. Accessed 24 July 2018. https://www.nwmo.ca
/en/Site-selection/Study-Areas/Areas-No-Longer-Being-Studied
/Blind-River-Elliot-Lake-and-Area.

Rio Algom Ltd. & Denison Mines Inc. "Community Newsletter: Strong
Effective Regulation Helps Improve Elliot Lake Site Environment." 2015.

Accessed 12 July 2018. https://www.denisonenvironmental.com/assets
/docs/des-ral-newsletter-2015.pdf (document no longer available).
Robinson-Huron Treaty 1850. Accessed 23 May 2018. http://rht1850.ca/.
Truth and Reconciliation Commission of Canada. Accessed 17 July 2020.
http://www.trc.ca/.
United Nations Declaration on the Rights of Indigenous Peoples, 2007.
Accessed 24 July 2018. http://www.un.org/esa/socdev/unpfii/documents
/DRIPS_en.pdf.

Secondary Sources

Abel, Kerry. *Changing Places: History, Community, and Identity in Northeastern
Ontario*. Montreal: McGill-Queen's University Press, 2006.
– *Drum Songs: Glimpses of Dene History*. Montreal: McGill-Queen's University
Press, 2005.
Abel, Kerry, and Jean Friesen, eds. *Aboriginal Resource Use in Canada: Historical
and Legal Aspects*. Winnipeg: University of Manitoba Press, 1991.
Absolon (Minogiizhigokwe), Kathleen E. *Kaandossiwin: How We Come to
Know*. Black Point: Fernwood Press, 2011.
Absolon, Kathy, and Cam Willett, "Putting Ourselves Forward: Location
in Aboriginal Research." In *Research as Resistance: Critical, Indigenous, and
Anti-Oppressive Approaches*, edited by Leslie Brown and Susan Strega.
97–125. Toronto: Canadian Scholars' Press/Women's Press, 2005.
Acland, Charles R., and William J. Buxton, eds. *Harold Innis in the New
Century*. Montreal: McGill-Queen's University Press, 1999.
Adams, Mary Louise. "Youth, Corruptibility, and English-Canadian Postwar
Campaigns against Indecency, 1948–1955." *Journal of the History of Sexuality*
6, no. 1 (July 1995): 89–117.
– *The Trouble with Normal: Postwar Youth and the Making of Heterosexuality*.
Toronto: University of Toronto Press, 1997.
Adamson, Nancy. "Feminists, Libbers, Lefties, and Radicals: The Emergence
of the Women's Liberation Movement." In *A Diversity of Women: Ontario,
1945–1980*, edited by Joy Parr, 252–80. Toronto: University of Toronto
Press, 1995.
Agyeman, Julian, ed. *Speaking for Ourselves: Environmental Justice in Canada*.
Vancouver: University of British Columbia Press, 2009.
Albert, Marion. *Trade History, North Shore of Lake Huron: A Review of Events
That Shaped the Economy of the North Shore, 1600–1996*. Blind River: Town of
Blind River, 1996.
Alfred, Gerald (Taiaiake) R. *Heeding the Voices of Our Ancestors: Kahnawake
Mohawk Politics and the Rise of Native Nationalism*. Don Mills: Oxford
University Press, 1995.

Ali, Saleem. *Mining, the Environment, and Indigenous Development Conflicts.* Tucson: University of Arizona Press, 2003.

Amundson, Michael A. *Yellowcake Towns: Uranium Mining Communities in the American West.* Boulder: University Press of Colorado, 2002.

Anastakis, Dimitry, ed. *The Sixties: Passion, Politics, and Style.* Montreal: McGill-Queen's University Press, 2008.

Anastakis, Dimitry, Mary-Ellen Kelm, and Suzanne Morton. "New Approaches to Indigenous History." *Canadian Historical Review* 98, no. 1 (2017): 60–3.

Anderson, David G. and Mark Nuttall, eds. *Cultivating Arctic Landscapes: Knowing and Managing Animals in the Circumpolar North.* New York: Berghahn Books, 2004.

Anderson, Kim. *Life Stages and Native Women: Memory, Teachings, and Story Medicine.* Winnipeg: University of Manitoba Press, 2011.

Angus, James T. "How the Dokis Indians Protected Their Timber." *Ontario History* 81 (1989): 181–99.

Archibald, Jo-ann. *Indigenous Storywork: Educating the Heart, Mind, Body, and Spirit.* Vancouver: University of British Columbia Press, 2008.

Asch, Michael, ed. *Aboriginal and Treaty Rights in Canada: Essays on Law, Equity, and Respect for Difference.* Vancouver: University of British Columbia Press, 1997.

Baillargeon, Denyse. *Babies for the Nation: The Medicalization of Motherhood in Quebec, 1910–1970.* Waterloo: Wilfrid Laurier University Press, 2009.

Baldwin, A., L. Cameron, and A. Kobayashi, eds. *Rethinking the Great White North: Race, Nature, and the Historical Geographies of Whiteness in Canada.* Vancouver: University of British Columbia Press, 2011.

Barker, Adam J. "The Contemporary Reality of Canadian Imperialism: Settler Colonialism and the Hybrid Colonial State." *American Indian Quarterly* 33, no. 3 (2009): 325–51.

Barnes, Michael. *Great Northern Ontario Mines.* Burnstown: General Store Publishing House, 1998.

– *Kirkland Lake: On the Mile of Gold.* Kirkland Lake: Economic Development and Tourism Department, 1994.

Bellfy, Phil. *Three Fires Unity: The Anishnaabeg of the Lake Huron Borderlands.* Lincoln: Nebraska University Press, 2011.

Benton-Banai, Edward. *The Mishomis Book: The Voice of the Ojibway.* Minneapolis: University of Minnesota Press and Indian Country Communications, Inc., 2010.

Berkhofer, Robert F. *The White Man's Indian: Images of the American Indian from Columbus to the Present.* New York: Vintage, 1979.

Berland, Jody. "Space at the Margins: Critical Theory and Colonial Space after Innis." In *Harold Innis in the New Century,* edited by Charles R. Acland and William J. Buxton, 281–309. Montreal: McGill-Queen's University Press, 1999.

Bielawski, Ellen. *Rogue Diamonds: The Rush for Northern Riches on Dene Land.* Toronto: Douglas and McIntyre, 2003.

Binnema, Theodore, and Kevin Hutchings. "The Emigrant and the Noble Savage: Sir Francis Bond Head's Romantic Approach to Aboriginal Policy in Upper Canada, 1836–1838." *Journal of Canadian Studies* 39, no. 1 (2005): 115–38.

Blomley, Nicholas. "'Shut the Province Down': First Nations Blockades in British Columbia, 1984–1995." *BC Studies* no. 111 (Autumn 1996): 5–35.

Bocking, Stephen. "Indigenous Knowledge and the History of Science, Race, and Colonial Authority in Northern Canada." In *Rethinking the Great White North: Race, Nature, and the Historical Geographies of Whiteness in Canada,* edited by A. Baldwin, L. Cameron, and A. Kobayashi, 39–61. Vancouver: University of British Columbia Press, 2011.

Bohaker, Heidi, and Franca Iacovetta. "Making Aboriginal People 'Immigrants Too': A Comparison of Citizenship Programs for Newcomers and Indigenous Peoples in Postwar Canada, 1940s–1960s." *Canadian Historical Review* 90, no. 3 (September 2009): 427–61.

Bonnell, Jennifer. "An Intimate Understanding of Place: Charles Sauriol and Toronto's Don River Valley, 1927–89." *Canadian Historical Review* 92, no. 4 (2011): 607–36.

– *Reclaiming the Don: An Environmental History of Toronto's Don River Valley.* Toronto: University of Toronto Press, 2014.

Borrows, John. "Challenging Historical Frameworks: Aboriginal Rights, The Trickster, and Originalism." *Canadian Historical Review* 98, no. 1 (2017): 114–35.

– "Living Between the Water and the Rocks: First Nations, Environmental Planning and Democracy." *University of Toronto Law Journal* 47 (1997): 417–66.

– "Wampum at Niagara: The Royal Proclamation, Canadian Legal History, and Self-Government." In *Aboriginal and Treaty Rights in Canada: Essays on Law, Equity, and Respect for Difference,* edited by Michael Asch, 155–72. Vancouver: University of British Columbia Press, 1997.

– *Recovering Canada: The Resurgence of Indigenous Law.* University of Toronto Press, 2002.

Bothwell, Robert. *Alliance and Illusion: Canada and the World, 1945–1984.* Vancouver: University of British Columbia Press, 2007.

– *Eldorado: Canada's National Uranium Company.* Toronto: University of Toronto Press, 1984.

– *The Big Chill: Canada and the Cold War.* Concord: Irwin, 1998.

Bothwell, Robert, Ian Drummond, and John English. *Canada since 1945: Power, Politics, and Provincialism.* Rev. ed. Toronto: University of Toronto Press, 1993.

Bradbury, John H. "Towards an Alternative Theory of Resource-Based Town Development in Canada." *Economic Geography* 55, no. 2 (1979): 147–66.

Bray, Matt, and Ashley Thomson, eds. *At the End of the Shift: Mines and Single-Industry Towns in Northern Ontario*. Sudbury: Dundurn Press/Laurentian University, 1992.

Brookfield, Tarah. *Cold War Comforts: Canadian Women, Child Safety, and Global Insecurity*. Waterloo: Wilfrid Laurier University Press, 2012.

Brown, Jennifer S.H. *Strangers in Blood: Fur Trade Indian Families in Indian Country*. Vancouver: University of British Columbia Press, 1980.

Brown, Leslie, and Susan Strega, eds. *Research as Resistance: Critical, Indigenous, and Anti-Oppressive Approaches*. Toronto: Canadian Scholars' Press/Women's Press, 2005.

Brown, Rosemary. "The Exploitation of the Oil and Gas Frontier: Its Impact on Lubicon Lake Cree Women." In *Women of the First Nations: Power, Wisdom, and Strength*, edited by Christine Miller and Patricia Chuchryk, 151–65. Winnipeg: University of Manitoba Press, 1997.

Browne, David R. *Freshwater Fish in Ontario's Boreal: Status, Conservation and Potential Impacts of Development*. N.p.: Wildlife Conservation Society Canada, 2007.

Brownlie, Robin Jarvis. "'A better citizen than lots of white men': First Nations Enfranchisement: an Ontario Case Study, 1918–1940." *Canadian Historical Review* 87, no. 1 (March 2006): 29–52.

– "'Living the same as the white people': Mohawk and Anishinabe Women's Labour in Southern Ontario in the 1920s and 30s." *Labour/Le Travail* 61 (Spring 2008): 41–68.

– "'Nothing left for me or any other Indian': The Georgian Bay Anishinabek and Inter-War Articulations of Aboriginal Rights." *Ontario History* 96, no. 2 (Autumn 2004): 116–42.

– *A Fatherly Eye: Indian Agents, Government Power, and Aboriginal Resistance in Ontario, 1918–1939*. Don Mills: Oxford University Press, 2003.

Brownlie, Robin Jarvis, and Mary-Ellen Kelm. "Desperately Seeking Absolution: Native Agency as Colonialist Alibi?" *Canadian Historical Review* 75, no. 4 (1994): 543–56.

Buckley, Helen. *From Wooden Ploughs to Welfare: Why Indian Policy Failed in the Prairie Provinces*. Montreal: McGill-Queen's University Press, 1992.

Buckner, Philip, and R.D. Francis, eds. *Canada and the British World: Culture, Migration, and Identity*. Vancouver: University of British Columbia Press, 2006.

Campbell, Claire. "'Behold Me a Sojourner in the Wilderness': Early Encounters with the Georgian Bay." *Michigan Historical Review* 28, no. 1 (Spring 2002): 32–62.

Campbell, Lara, Dominique Clement, and Gregory S. Kealey, eds. *Debating Dissent: Canada and the Sixties*. Toronto: University of Toronto Press, 2012.

Carlson, Hans. *Home Is the Hunter: The James Bay Cree and Their Land*. Vancouver: University of British Columbia Press, 2008.

– "A Watershed of Words: Litigating and Negotiating Nature in Eastern James Bay, 1971–1975." *Canadian Historical Review* 85, no. 1 (2004): 63–84.

Carlson, Keith Thor, ed. *You Are Asked to Witness: The Sto:lo in Canada's Pacific Coast History.* Chilliwack: Sto:lo Heritage Trust, 1997.

Carlson, Keith Thor. *The Power of Place, The Problem of Time: Aboriginal Identity and Historical Consciousness in the Cauldron of Colonialism.* Toronto: University of Toronto Press, 2010.

Carlson, Keith Thor, and Jonathan Clapperton. "Introduction. Special Places and Protected Spaces: Historical and Global Perspectives on Non-National Parks in Canada and Abroad." *Environment and History* 18 (2012): 475–96.

Carlson, Keith Thor, Melinda Marie Jette, and Kenichi Matsui. "An Annotated Bibliography of Major Writings in Aboriginal History, 1990–99." *Canadian Historical Review* 82, no. 1 (2001): 122–71.

Carson, Rachel. *Silent Spring – 40th Anniversary Edition.* New York: Houghton Mifflin Company, 2002.

Carter, Sarah. *Lost Harvests: Prairie Indian Reserve Farmers and Government Policy.* Montreal: McGill-Queen's University Press, 1990.

Charles, R. Menzies, ed. *Traditional Ecological Knowledge and Natural Resource Management.* Lincoln: University of Nebraska Press, 2006.

Child, Brenda J. *Holding Our World Together: Ojibwe Women and the Survival of Community.* Toronto: Viking, 2012.

Christie, Nancy, and Michael Gauvreau, eds. *Cultures of Citizenship in Post-war Canada, 1940–1955.* Montreal: McGill-Queen's University Press, 2003.

Chute, Janet E. "Pursuing the Great Spirit's Plan: Nineteenth-Century Ojibwa Attitudes Towards the Future of Logging and Mining on Unsurrendered Indian Lands North of Lakes Huron and Superior." In *Social Relations in Resource Hinterlands: Papers from the 27th Annual Meeting of the Western Association of Sociology and Anthropology,* edited by Thomas W. Dunk, 173–203. Thunder Bay: Lakehead University Centre for Northern and Regional Studies, 1991.

– *The Legacy of Shingwaukonse: A Century of Native Leadership.* Toronto: University of Toronto Press, 1998.

Clarke, Frank K. "'Keep Communism Out of Our Schools': Cold War Anti-Communism at the Toronto Board of Education, 1948–1951." *Labour/ Le Travail* 49 (Spring 2002): 93–120.

Coates, Ken. "Writing First Nations History into Canadian History: A Review of Recent Scholarly Works." *Canadian Historical Review* 81, no. 1 (2000): 99–114.

Colorado, Pam. "Bridging Native and Western Science." *Convergence* 21, no. 2 (1988): 49–68.

Cook, Katsi. "Powerful Like a River: Reweaving the Web of Our Lives in Defense of Environmental and Reproductive Justice." In *Original*

Instructions: Indigenous Teachings for a Sustainable Future, edited by Melissa K. Nelson, 154–67. Rochester: Bear and Company, 2008.

Cook, Ramsay, ed. *The Voyages of Jacques Cartier*. Toronto: University of Toronto Press, 1993.

Copway, George. *The Traditional History and Characteristic Sketches of the Ojibway Nation*. Toronto: Coles, 1972.

Cruikshank, Julie. "Uses and Abuses of 'Traditional Knowledge': Perspectives from the Yukon Territory." In *Cultivating Arctic Landscapes: Knowing and Managing Animals in the Circumpolar North*, edited by David G. Anderson and Mark Nuttall, 17–32. New York: Berghahn Books, 2004.

– *Do Glaciers Listen? Local Knowledge, Colonial Encounters, and Social Imagination*. Vancouver: University of British Columbia Press, 2005.

Daschuk, James. *Clearing the Plains: Disease, Politics of Starvation, and the Loss of Aboriginal Life*. Regina: University of Regina Press, 2012.

Dawson, Bruce. "The Roots of Agriculture: A Historiographical Review of First Nations Agriculture and Government Indian Policy." *Prairie Forum* 28, no. 1 (Spring 2003): 99–115.

Delâge, Denys. *Bitter Feast: Amerindians and Europeans in Northeastern North America, 1600–64*. Vancouver: University of British Columbia Press, 1993.

Desbiens, Caroline. *Power from the North: Territory, Identity, and Culture of Hydroelectricity in Quebec*. Vancouver: University of British Columbia Press, 2013.

– "'Water all around, you cannot even drink': The scaling of water in James Bay/Eeyou Istchee." *Area* 39, no. 3 (September 2007): 259–67.

Dickason, Olive Patricia. *Canada's First Nations: A History of Founding Peoples from Earliest Times*, 4th ed. With David T. McNab. Don Mills: Oxford University Press, 2009.

Dixon, Catharine. *As It Happened: The Founding of Elliot Lake Secondary School*. Elliot Lake: Gillidix Publishing Inc., 2001.

– *The Power and the Promise: The Elliot Lake Story*. Elliot Lake: Gillidix Publishing Inc., 1996.

Doern, Bruce, and Thomas Conway. *The Greening of Canada: Federal Institutions and Decisions*. Toronto: University of Toronto Press, 1994.

Dokis, Carly A. *Where the Rivers Meet: Pipelines, Participatory Resource Management, and Aboriginal-State Relations in the Northwest Territories*. Vancouver: University of British Columbia Press, 2015.

Donaghy, Greg, ed. *Canada and the Early Cold War, 1943–1957*. Ottawa: Department of Foreign Affairs and International Trade, 1988.

Downey, Terrence James. *The Political Economy of Uranium: Elliot Lake, 1948–1970*. Master's thesis, The University of Western Ontario, 1972.

Dunaway, Finis. "Gas Masks, Pogo, and the Ecological Indian: Earth Day and the Visual Politics of American Environmentalism." *American Quarterly* 60, no. 1 (2008): 67–99.

Dunk, Thomas W. *It's a Working Man's Town: Male Working Class Culture in Northwestern Ontario*. Montreal: McGill-Queen's University Press, 1991.

–, ed. *Social Relations in Resource Hinterlands: Papers from the 27th Annual Meeting of the Western Association of Sociology and Anthropology*. Thunder Bay: Lakehead University Centre for Northern and Regional Studies, 1991.

Eayrs, James. *In Defence of Canada Volume III: Peacemaking and Deterrence*. Toronto: University of Toronto Press, 1972.

Eggleston, Wilfrid. *Canada's Nuclear Story*. Toronto: Clarke, Irwin and Company, 1965.

Eid, Leroy. "The Ojibwa-Iroquois War: The War the Five Nations did not Win." *Ethnohistory* 36, no. 4 (Fall 1979): 297–324.

Elliot Lake Secondary School. *Dawn of a New Setting, 1980–1997*. Elliot Lake: Elliot Lake Secondary School, 1997.

– *Jewel in the Wilderness: A History of Elliot Lake 1957–1980*. Elliot Lake: Elliot Lake Secondary School, 1980.

English, John. *The Life of Lester Pearson: The Worldly Years, 1949–1972*. Toronto: A.A. Knopf Canada, 1992.

Ens, Gerhard. *Homeland to Hinterland: The Changing Worlds of the Red River Metis in the Nineteenth Century*. Toronto: University of Toronto Press, 1996.

Fahrni, Magda, and Robert Rutherdale, eds. *Creating Postwar Canada: Community, Diversity, and Dissent, 1945–75*. Vancouver: University of British Columbia Press, 2008.

Feldberg, Georgina, ed. *Women, Health and Nation: Canada and the United States since 1945*. Montreal: McGill-Queen's University Press, 2003.

Fisher, Robin. *Contact and Conflict: Indian-European Relations in British Columbia, 1774–1890*. Vancouver: University of British Columbia Press, 1977.

Fixico, Donald L. "The Alliance of the Three Fires in Trade and War, 1630–1812." *Michigan Historical Review* 20, no. 2 (1994): 1–23.

Foster, Hamar, Heather Raven, and Jeremy Webber. *Let Right be Done: Aboriginal Title, the Calder Case, and the Future of Indigenous Rights*. Vancouver: University of British Columbia Press, 2007.

Foster, Peter. *Rags to Riches: The Story of Bow Valley Industries Ltd*. Calgary: Bow Valley Industries, 1985.

Freeman, M.R. "The Nature and Utility of Traditional Ecological Knowledge." *Northern Perspectives* 20, no. 1 (1992): 9–12.

Furniss, Elizabeth. *The Burden of History: Colonialism and the Frontier Myth in a Rural Canadian Community*. Vancouver: University of British Columbia Press, 1999.

Gaffield, Chad, and Pam Gaffield, eds. *Consuming Canada: Readings in Environmental History*. Toronto: Copp Clark Ltd., 1995.

Gamble, Janice, and Elder Tea, eds. *Connected to the Land: Stories from the Serpent's Band*. Serpent River First Nation: Serpent River First Nation Education Department, 2013.

Getty, Ian A.L., and Antoine S. Lussier, eds. *As Long as the Sun Shines and the Water Flows: A Reader in Canadian Native Studies*. Vancouver: University of British Columbia Press, 1995.

Gibson, Ginger, and Deanna Kemp. "Corporate Engagement with Indigenous Women in the Minerals Industry: Making Space for Theory." In *Earth Matters: Indigenous Peoples, the Extractive Industries and Corporate Social Responsibility*, edited by Ciaran O'Faircheallaigh and Saleem Ali, 104–22. Sheffield: Greenleaf Publishing Ltd., 2008.

Gibson, Ginger, and Jason Klinck. "Canada's Resilient North: The Impact of Mining on Aboriginal Communities." *Pimatisiwin* 3, no. 1 (2005): 114–40.

Gleason, Mona. "Disciplining Children, Disciplining Parents: The Nature and Meaning of Advice to Canadian Parents, 1945–1955." *Histoire sociale/Social History* 29, no. 57 (1996): 187–209.

– *Normalizing the Ideal: Psychology, Schooling, and the Family in Postwar Canada*. Toronto: University of Toronto Press, 1999.

Glenn, Evelyn Nakano. "Settler Colonialism as Structure: A Framework for Comparative Studies of US Race and Gender Formation." *Sociology of Race and Ethnicity* 1, no. 1 (2015): 52–72.

Gow, Sharon. "Respect and Responsibility: Community-Based Options for Perpetual Care in the Serpent River Watershed." In *Boom Town Blues, Elliot Lake: Collapse and Revival in a Single-Industry Community*, edited by Anne-Marie Mawhiney and Jane Pitblado, 318–30. Toronto: Dundurn Press, 1999.

Gulig, Anthony G. "'We Beg The Government:' Native People and Game Regulation in Northern Saskatchewan, 1900–1940." *Prairie Forum* 28, no. 1 (Spring 2003): 81–98.

Gutsche, Andrea, Barbara Chisholm, and Russell Floren. *The North Channel and St. Mary's River: A Guide to the History*. Toronto: Lynx Images, 2008.

Harkin, Michael E., and David Rich Lewis, eds. *Native Americans and the Environment: Perspectives on the Ecological Indian*. Lincoln: University of Nebraska Press, 2007.

Harris, Cole. *The Resettlement of British Columbia*. Vancouver: University of British Columbia Press, 1997.

Harris, Richard. *Creeping Conformity: How Canada Became Suburban, 1900–1960*. Toronto: University of Toronto Press, 2004.

Harrison, Kathryn. *Passing the Buck: Federalism and Canadian Environmental Policy*. Vancouver: University of British Columbia Press, 1996.

Havard, Gilles. *The Great Peace of Montreal of 1701: French-Native Diplomacy in the Seventeenth Century*. Translated by Phyllis Aronoff and Howard Scott. Montreal: McGill-Queen's University Press, 2001.

Heard, Shawn. "The City of Elliot Lake to 1991: Before the Roof Fell In." In *Boom Town Blues, Elliot Lake: Collapse and Revival in a Single-Industry*

Community, edited by Anne-Marie Mawhiney and Jane Pitblado, 21–35. Toronto: Dundurn Press, 1999.

Henderson, Stuart. *Making the Scene: Yorkville and Hip Toronto in the 1960s.* Toronto: University of Toronto Press, 2011.

Hessing, Melody, Michael Howlett, and Tracy Summerville. *Canadian Natural Resource and Environmental Policy: Political Economy and Public Policy.* Vancouver: University of British Columbia Press, 2005.

Hill, Susan M. *The Clay We Are Made Of.* Winnipeg: University of Manitoba Press, 2017.

Hjartarson, Josh, Liam McGuinty, and Scott Boutilier. *Beneath the Surface: Uncovering the Economic Potential of Ontario's Ring of Fire.* Toronto: Ontario Chamber of Commerce, 2014.

Hodgins, Bruce W., Ute Lischke, and David T. McNab, eds. *Blockades and Resistance: Studies in Actions of Peace and the Temagami Blockades of 1988–89.* Waterloo: Wilfrid Laurier University Press, 2003.

Hornig, James F., ed. *Social and Environmental Impacts of the James Bay Hydroelectric Project.* Montreal: McGill-Queen's University Press, 1999.

Howard-Bobiwash, Heather. "Women's Class Strategies as Activism in Native Community Building in Toronto, 1950–1975." *American Indian Quarterly* 27, nos. 3–4 (2003): 566–82.

Howitt, Richard. *Rethinking Resource Management: Justice, Sustainability and Indigenous Peoples.* New York: Routledge, 2001.

Hutchison, George, and Dick Wallace. *Grassy Narrows.* Toronto: Van Nostrand Reinhold Ltd., 1977.

Iacovetta, Franca. *Gatekeepers: Reshaping Immigrant Lives in Cold War Canada.* Toronto: Between the Lines, 2006.

Iacovetta, Franca, Valerie J. Korinek, and Marlene Epp, eds. *Edible Histories, Cultural Politics: Towards a Canadian Food History.* Toronto: University of Toronto Press, 2012.

Innis, Harold Adam. *Settlement and the Mining Frontier.* Toronto: Macmillan, 1936.

– *The Fur Trade in Canada: An Introduction to Canadian Economic History.* Rev. ed. Toronto: University of Toronto Press, 1999.

Jacobs, Burton. "Kicking out the Indian Agent." In *Nation to Nation: Aboriginal Sovereignty and the Future of Canada*, edited by John Bird, Lorraine Land, and Murray MacAdam, 141–47. Toronto: Irwin Publishing, 2002.

Janovicek, Nancy. "'Assisting our own': Urban Migration, Self-Governance, and Native Women's Organizing in Thunder Bay, Ontario, 1972–1989." *American Indian Quarterly* 27, no. 3–4 (2003): 548–65.

Jasen, Patricia. "Race, Culture, and the Colonization of Childbirth in Northern Canada." *Social History of Medicine* 10, no. 3 (1997): 383–400.

Jhappan, C. Radha. "Indian Symbolic Politics: The Double-Edged Sword of Publicity." *Canadian Ethnic Studies* 22 (1990): 19–39.

Johnston, Basil. *Ojibway Ceremonies*. Toronto: McClelland and Stewart, 2008.
– *Ojibway Heritage*. Toronto: McClelland and Stewart, 2008.
Jones, Peter. *History of the Ojebway Indians*. London: A.W. Bennett, 1861.
Karl, Hele, ed. *The Nature of Empires and Empires of Nature*. Waterloo: Wilfrid Laurier University Press, 2013.
Keeling, Arn, and John Sandlos. "Environmental Justice Goes Underground? Historical Notes from Canada's Northern Mining Frontier." *Environmental Justice* 2, no. 3 (2009): 117–25.
– "The Complex Legacy of Mining in Northern Canada." In *Mining and Communities in Northern Canada: History, Politics, and Memory*, 5–12. Calgary: University of Calgary Press, 2015.
–, eds. *Mining and Communities in Northern Canada: History, Politics, and Memory*. Calgary: University of Calgary Press, 2015.
– "Claiming the New North: Development and Colonialism at the Pine Point Mine, Northwest Territories, Canada." *Environment and History* 18, no. 1 (2012): 5–34.
Keeling, Arn. "'Born in an Atomic Test Tube': Landscapes of cyclonic development at Uranium City, Saskatchewan." *The Canadian Geographer* 54, no. 2 (Summer 2010): 228–52.
Keeling, Arn, and Patricia Boulter. "From Igloo to Mine Shaft: Inuit Labour and Memory at the Rankin Inlet Nickel Mine." In *Mining and Communities in Northern Canada: History, Politics, and Memory*, edited by Arn Keeling and John Sandlos, 35–58. Calgary: University of Calgary Press, 2015.
Kelley, Ninette, and Michael Trebilcock. *The Making of the Mosaic: A History of Canadian Immigration Policy*. Toronto: University of Toronto Press, 1998.
Kelm, Mary-Ellen. "Diagnosing the Discursive Indian: Medicine, Gender, and the 'Dying Race.'" *Ethnohistory* 52, no. 2 (Spring 2005): 371–406.
– *Colonizing Bodies: Aboriginal Health and Healing in British Columbia, 1900–50*. Vancouver: University of British Columbia Press, 1998.
Kendrick, John. *The People of the Snow: The Story of Kitimat*. Chapel Hill: University of North Carolina Press, 1987.
Kinsman, Gary, Dieter K. Buse, and Mercedes Steedman, eds. *Whose National Security? Canadian State Surveillance and the Creation of Enemies*. Toronto: Between the Lines, 2000.
Kinsman, Gary, and Patrizia Gentile. *The Canadian War on Queers: National Security in Sexual Regulation*. Vancouver: University of British Columbia Press, 2009.
Knight, Rolf. *Indians at Work: An Informal History of Native Labour in British Columbia, 1848–1930*. Vancouver: New Star Books, 1996.
Korinek, Valerie. *Roughing It in the Suburbs: Reading Chatelaine Magazine in the Fifties and Sixties*. Toronto: University of Toronto Press, 2000.

Kovach, Margaret. *Indigenous Methodologies: Characteristics, Conversations, and Contexts*. Toronto: University of Toronto Press, 2009.

Krech III, Shepard. *The Ecological Indian: Myth and History*. New York: W.W. Norton, 1999.

Krupnik, Igor, and Dyanna Jolly, eds. *The Earth Is Faster Now: Indigenous Observations of Arctic Environmental Change*. 2nd ed. Fairbanks: Arctic Research Consortium of the United States, 2010.

Kuhlberg, Mark. "'Nothing It Seems Can Be Done about It': Charlie Cox, Indian Affairs Timber Policy, and the Long Lac Reserve, 1924–40." *Canadian Historical Review* 84, no. 1 (2003): 33–64.

Lackenbauer, P. Whitney, and Matthew Farish, "The Cold War on Canadian Soil: Militarizing a Northern Environment." *Environmental History* 12, no. 4 (2007): 920–50.

LaDuke, Winona. *All Our Relations: Native Struggles for Land and Life*. Cambridge: South End Press, 1999.

Lawrence, Bonita. *"Real" Indians and Others: Mixed-Blood Urban Native Peoples and Indigenous Nationhood*. Vancouver: University of British Columbia Press, 2004.

Leddy, Lianne C. "'Are you only interviewing women for this?': Indigenous Feminism and Oral History." In *Beyond Women's Words: Feminisms and the Practices of Oral History in the Twenty-First Century*, edited by Katrina Srigley, Stacey Zembrzycki, and Franca Iacovetta, 95–108. New York: Routledge, 2018.

– "*Dibaajimowinan* as Method: Environmental History, Indigenous Scholarship, and Balancing Sources." In *Methodological Challenges in Nature-Culture and Environmental History Research*, edited by Jocelyn Thorpe, Stephanie Rutherford, and Anders L. Sandberg, 93–104. New York: Routledge, 2017.

– "Intersections of Indigenous and Environmental History in Canada." *Canadian Historical Review* 98, no. 1 (2017): 83–95.

– "Interviewing Nookomis and Other Reflections: The Promise of Community Collaboration." *Oral History Forum/d'histoire orale* 30 (Special Issue–2010): 1–18.

– "Poisoning the Serpent: Uranium Exploitation and the Serpent River First Nation, 1953–1988." In *The Nature of Empires and Empires of Nature*, edited by Karl Hele, 125–47. Waterloo: Wilfrid Laurier University Press, 2013.

Leduc, Timothy B. *Climate Culture Change: Inuit and Western Dialogues with a Warming North*. Ottawa: University of Ottawa Press, 2010.

Leslie, John F. "Assimilation, Integration, or Termination: The Development of Canadian Indian Policy, 1943–1963." PhD diss., Carleton University, 1999. https://curve.carleton.ca/003068e9-223d-4461-85a5-8dc285681838

Leslie, John F., and Ron Maguire. *The Historical Development of the Indian Act.* Ottawa: Indian and Northern Affairs, 1978.

Levitt, Joseph. *Pearson and Canada's Role in Nuclear Disarmament and Arms Control Negotiations.* Montreal: McGill-Queen's University Press, 1993.

Lischke, Ute, and David T. McNab, eds. *Walking a Tightrope: Aboriginal People and their Representations.* Waterloo: University of Waterloo Press, 2005.

Luby, Brittany. "From Milk-Medicine to Public Re-Education Programs: An Examination of Anishinabek Mothers' Responses to Hydroelectric Flooding in the Treaty #3 District, 1900–1975." *Canadian Bulletin of Medical History* 32, no. 2 (2015): 363–89.

Lucas, Rex A. *Minetown, Milltown, Railtown: Life in Canadian Communities of Single Industry.* Toronto: University of Toronto Press, 1971.

Lutz, John. "After the Fur Trade: The Aboriginal Labouring Class of British Columbia, 1849–90." In *Canadian Working-Class History: Selected Readings,* 3rd ed., edited by Laurel Sefton MacDowell and Ian Radforth, 125–48. Toronto: Canadian Scholars' Press, 2006.

Lutz, John. *Makúk: A New History of Aboriginal-White Relations.* Vancouver, University of British Columbia Press, 2009.

Lutz, John, and Keith Thor Carlson. "Sto:lo People and the Development of the B.C. Wage Economy." In *You Are Asked to Witness,* edited by Keith Thor Carlson, 109–24. Chilliwack: Sto:lo Heritage Trust, 1997.

Lux, Maureen K. *Medicine That Walks: Disease, Medicine and Canadian Plains Native People.* Toronto: University of Toronto Press, 2001.

– *Separate Beds: A History of Indian Hospitals in Canada, 1920s–1980s.* Toronto: University of Toronto Press, 2016.

Lyon, Jim. *Dome Petroleum: The Inside Story of Its Rise and Fall.* New York: Beaufort Books, 1983.

Macdougall, Brenda. "Space and Place within Aboriginal Epistemological Traditions: Recent Trends in Historical Scholarship." *Canadian Historical Review* 98, no. 1 (2017): 64–82.

MacDowell, Laurel Sefton. "The Elliot Lake Uranium Miners' Battle to Gain Occupational Health and Safety Improvements, 1950–80." *Labour/Le Travail* 69 (Spring 2012): 91–117.

MacDowell, Laurel Sefton, and Ian Radforth, eds. *Canadian Working-Class History: Selected Readings.* 3rd ed. Toronto: Canadian Scholars' Press, 2006.

MacLeod, Alistair. *No Great Mischief.* Toronto: McClelland and Stewart, 1999.

MacLeod, D. Peter. "The Anishinabeg Point of View: The History of the Great Lakes Region to 1800 in Nineteenth-Century Mississauga, Odawa, and Ojibwa Historiography." *Canadian Historical Review* 73, no. 2 (1992): 194–210.

Manore, Jean L. *Cross-Currents: Hydro-electricity and the Engineering of Northern Ontario.* Waterloo: Wilfrid Laurier University Press, 1999.

– "Indian Reserves v. Indian Lands: Reserves, Crown Lands, and Natural Resource Use in Northeastern Ontario." In *Ontario Since Confederation: A Reader*, edited by Edgar-André Montigny and Lori Chambers, 195–213. Toronto: University of Toronto Press, 2000.

Manuel, George, and Michael Posluns. *The Fourth World: An Indian Reality*. Don Mills: Collier Macmillan Canada, 1974.

Marshall, Dominique. *The Social Origins of the Welfare State: Québec Families, Compulsory Education, and Family Allowances, 1940–1955*. Waterloo: Wilfrid Laurier University Press, 2006.

Mawhiney, Anne-Marie, and Jane Pitblado, eds. *Boom Town Blues, Elliot Lake: Collapse and Revival in a Single-Industry Community*. Toronto: Dundurn Press, 1999.

McAllister, Mary Louise. "Shifting Foundations in a Mature Staples Industry: A Political Economic History of Canadian Mineral Policy." *Canadian Political Science Review* 1 (June 2007): 73–90.

McCallum, Mary Jane Logan. "Starvation, Experimentation, Segregation, and Trauma: Words for Reading Indigenous Health History." *Canadian Historical Review* 98, no. 1 (2017): 96–113.

– *Indigenous Women, Work, and History, 1940–1980*. Winnipeg: University of Manitoba Press, 2014.

McFarlane, Peter. *Brotherhood to Nationhood: George Manuel and the Making of the Modern Indian Movement*. Toronto: Between the Lines, 1993.

McGregor, Deborah. "Coming Full Circle: Indigenous Knowledge, Environment, and Our Future." *American Indian Quarterly* 28, no. 3 and 4 (2004): 386.

– "Indigenous Women, Water Justice and Zaagidowin." *Canadian Woman Studies* 30, nos. 2–3 (Summer/Fall 2013): 71–8.

– "Honouring Our Relations: An Anishnaabe Perspective on Environmental Justice." In *Speaking for Ourselves: Environmental Justice in Canada*, edited by Julian Agyeman, 27–41. Vancouver: University of British Columbia Press, 2009.

– "Linking Traditional Knowledge and Environmental Practice in Ontario." *Journal of Canadian Studies* 43, no. 3 (Fall 2009): 69–100.

McIntyre, B.G. *Uranium City: The Last Boom Town*. N.p.: Driftwood Publications, 1993.

McKenzie-Brown, Peter. *The Richness of Discovery: Amoco's First 50 Years in Canada, 1948–1998*. Calgary: Amoco Canada Petroleum Co., 1998.

McPherson, Kathryn. "Nursing and Colonization: The Work of Indian Health Services Nurses in Manitoba, 1945–1970." In *Women, Health and Nation: Canada and the United States since 1945*, edited by Georgina Feldberg, 223–46. Montreal: McGill-Queen's University Press, 2003.

Menzies, Charles R., and Caroline Butler. "Introduction: Understanding Ecological Knowledge." In *Traditional Ecological Knowledge and Natural*

Resource Management, edited by Charles R. Menzies. Lincoln: University of Nebraska Press, 2006.

– "The Indigenous Foundation of the Resource Economy of BC's North Coast." *Labour/Le Travail* 61 (Spring 2008): 131–49.

Miller, Christine, and Patricia Chuchryk, eds. *Women of the First Nations: Power, Wisdom, and Strength*. Winnipeg: University of Manitoba Press, 1997.

Miller, J.R. "Aboriginal Rights, Land Claims, and the Struggle to Survive." In *Sweet Promises: A Reader on Indian-White Relations in Canada*, edited by J.R. Miller, 405–20. Toronto: University of Toronto Press, 1991.

– "Owen Glendower, Hotspur and Canadian Indian Policy." In *Sweet Promises: A Reader on Indian-White Relations in Canada*, edited by J.R. Miller, 323–52. Toronto: University of Toronto Press, 1991.

– *Shingwauk's Vision*. Toronto: University of Toronto Press, 1996.

– *Skyscrapers Hide the Heavens: A History of Indian-White Relations in Canada*. Toronto: University of Toronto Press, 1989.

Milloy, John S. *A National Crime: The Canadian Government and the Residential School System*. Winnipeg: University of Manitoba Press, 1999.

– "The Early Indian Acts: Developmental Strategy and Constitutional Change." In *Sweet Promises: A Reader on Indian-White Relations*, edited by J.R. Miller, 145–54. Toronto: University of Toronto Press, 1991.

– *The Plains Cree: Trade, Diplomacy, and War, 1780–1870*. Winnipeg: University of Manitoba Press, 1990.

Milner, J.B. "The Ontario Water Resources Commission Act, 1956." *The University of Toronto Law Journal* 12, no. 1 (1957): 100–2.

Mochoruk, James. "Oral History in a Company Town: Flin Flon, 1926–1946." *Canadian Oral History Association* 7 (1984): 5–12.

Montigny, Edgar-André, and Lori Chambers, eds. *Ontario since Confederation: A Reader*. Toronto: University of Toronto Press, 2000.

Morantz, Toby. *The White Man's Gonna Getcha: The Colonial Challenge to the Crees in Quebec*. Montreal: McGill-Queen's University Press, 2002.

Morton, W.L. *The Kingdom of Canada*. Toronto: McClelland and Stewart, 1963.

Mosby, Ian. "Administering Colonial Science: Nutrition Research and Human Biomedical Experimentation in Aboriginal Communities and Residential Schools, 1942–1952." *Histoire sociale/Social History* 91 (2013): 145–92.

Nadasdy, Paul. *Hunters and Bureaucrats: Power, Knowledge, and Aboriginal-State Relations in the Southwest Yukon*. Vancouver: University of British Columbia Press, 2004.

– "Transcending the Debate over the Ecologically Noble Indian: Indigenous Peoples and Environmentalism." *Ethnohistory* 52, no. 2 (2005): 291–331.

Nelson, Melissa K., ed. *Original Instructions: Indigenous Teachings for a Sustainable Future*. Rochester: Bear and Company, 2008.

Newell, Diane. *Tangled Webs of History: Indians and the Law in Canada's Pacific Coast Fisheries*. Toronto: University of Toronto Press, 1989.

Neylan, Susan. *The Heavens are Changing: Nineteenth-Century Protestant Missions and Tsimshian Christianity*. Montreal: McGill-Queen's University Press, 2003.

Ningewance, Patricia M. *Talking Gookum's Language: Learning Ojibwe*. Winnipeg: Mazinaate Press, 2007.

O'Connor, Ryan. *The First Green Wave: Pollution Probe and the Origins of Environmental Activism in Ontario*. Vancouver: University of British Columbia Press, 2015.

O'Faircheallaigh, Ciaran. *Environmental Agreements in Canada: Aboriginal Participation, EIA Follow-Up and Environmental Management of Major Projects*. Calgary: Canadian Institute of Resources Law, 2006.

O'Faircheallaigh, Ciaran, and Saleem Ali. *Earth Matters: Indigenous Peoples, the Extractive Industries and Corporate Social Responsibility*. Sheffield: Greenleaf Publishing Ltd., 2008.

O'Malley, Martin. *The Past and Future Land: An Account of the Berger Inquiry into the Mackenzie Valley Pipeline*. Toronto: Peter Martin Associates, 1976.

Owram, Doug. *Born at the Right Time: A History of the Baby Boom Generation*. Toronto: University of Toronto Press, 1996.

Palmer, Bryan. *Canada's 1960s: The Ironies of Identity in a Rebellious Era*. Toronto: University of Toronto Press, 2009.

Papillon, Martin. "Aboriginal Quality of Life Under a Modern Treaty: Lessons from the Experience of the Cree Nation of Eeyou Istchee and the Inuit of Nunavik." *IRPP Choices* 14, no. 9 (August 2008).

Parr, Joy, ed. *A Diversity of Women: Ontario, 1945–1980*. Toronto: University of Toronto Press, 1995.

Pearse, P.H., ed. *The Mackenzie Pipeline: Arctic Gas and Canadian Energy Policy*. Montreal: McGill-Queen's University Press, 1974.

Penn, Alan. "Uneasy Coexistence: La Grande and the James Bay Cree." In *On the Land: Confronting the Challenges to Aboriginal Self-Determination in Northern Quebec and Labrador*, edited by Bruce W. Hodgins and Kerry A. Cannon, 129–44. Toronto: Betelgeuse, 1995.

Pennier, Henry. *"Call Me Hank": A Sto:lo Man's Reflections on Logging, Living, and Growing Old*, edited by Keith Thor Carlson and Kristina Fagan. Toronto: University of Toronto Press, 2006.

Piper, Liza. *The Industrial Transformation of Subarctic Canada*. Vancouver: University of British Columbia Press, 2008.

– "Subterranean Bodies: Mining the Large Lakes of North-west Canada, 1921–1960." *Environment and History* 13, no. 2 (May 2007): 155–86.

Piper, Liza, and John Sandlos. "A Broken Frontier: Ecological Imperialism in the Canadian North." *Environmental History* 12, no. 4 (October 2007): 759–95.

Podruchny, Carolyn, and Laura Peers, eds. *Gathering Places: Aboriginal and Fur Trade Histories*. Vancouver: University of British Columbia Press, 2010.

Ponting, J. Rick, and Roger Gibbons. *Out of Irrelevance: A Socio-political Introduction to Indian Affairs in Canada*. Toronto: Butterworth, 1980.

Purich, Donald. *Our Land: Native Rights in Canada*. Toronto: James Lorimer and Company, 1986.

Raibmon, Paige. *Authentic Indians: Episodes of Encounter from the Late-Nineteenth-Century Northwest Coast*. Durham: Duke University Press, 2005.

– "Theaters of Contact: The Kwakwaka'wakw Meet Colonialism in British Columbia and at the Chicago World's Fair." *Canadian Historical Review* 81, no. 2 (June 2000): 157–90.

Raunet, Daniel. *Without Surrender, Without Consent: A History of the Nishga Land Claims*. Vancouver: Douglas and McIntyre, 1996.

Ray, Arthur J. *Indians in the Fur Trade: Their Roles as Trappers, Hunters, and Middlemen in the Lands Southwest of Hudson Bay, 1660–1870*. Toronto: University of Toronto Press, 1974.

Ray, Arthur J., Jim Miller, and Frank Tough. *Bounty and Benevolence: A History of Saskatchewan Treaties*. Montreal: McGill-Queen's University Press, 2000.

Razack, Sherene. *Dying from Improvement: Inquests and Inquiries into Indigenous Deaths in Custody*. Toronto: University of Toronto Press, 2015.

Regan, Paulette. *Unsettling the Settler Within: Indian Residential Schools, Truth Telling, and Reconciliation in Canada*. Vancouver: University of British Columbia Press, 2010.

Rekmans, Lorraine, Keith Lewis, and Anabel Dwyer, eds. *This Is My Homeland: Stories of the Effects of Nuclear Industries by People of the Serpent River First Nation and the North Shore of Lake Huron*. Cutler: Serpent River First Nation, 2003.

Rice, James D. "Beyond 'the Ecological Indian' and 'Virgin Soil Epidemics': New Perspectives on Native Americans and the Environment." *History Compass* 12, no. 9 (2014): 745–57.

Rich, E.E. *The Fur Trade and the Northwest to 1857*. Toronto: McClelland and Stewart, 1967.

Richter, Andrew. *Avoiding Armageddon: Canadian Military Strategy and Nuclear Weapons, 1950–1963*. Vancouver: University of British Columbia Press, 2002.

Ritzenthaler, Robert E. "Southwestern Chippewa." In *Handbook of North American Indians*, vol. 15, edited by Bruce G. Trigger, General Editor William C. Sturtevant, 743–59. Washington: Smithsonian Institution, 1978.

Robson, Robert. "Building Resource Towns: Government Intervention in Ontario in the 1950s." In *At the End of the Shift: Mines and Single-Industry Towns in Northern Ontario*, edited by Matt Bray and Ashley Thomson, 97–119. Sudbury: Dundurn Press/Laurentian University, 1992.

– "Manitoba's Resource Towns: The Twentieth Century Frontier." *Manitoba History* 16 (September 1988): 2–16.
– "Strike in the Single Enterprise Community: Flin Flon, Manitoba–1934." *Labour* 12 (Autumn 1983): 63–86.
– "Wilderness Suburbs: Boom and Gloom on the Prairies, 1945–1986." *Prairie Forum* 13, no. 2 (September 1988): 191–219.
– "The Politics of Resource Town Development: Ontario's Resource Communities, 1883–1970." PhD diss., University of Guelph, 1986.
Rogers, E.S. "Southeastern Ojibwa." In *Handbook of North American Indians*, vol. 15, edited by Bruce G. Trigger, General Editor William C. Sturtevant, 760–71. Washington: Smithsonian Institution, 1978.
Rynard, Paul. "'Welcome In, but Check Your Rights at the Door': The James Bay and Nisga'a Agreements in Canada." *Canadian Journal of Political Science* 33, no. 2 (June 2000): 211–43.
Salisbury, Richard F. *A Homeland for the Cree: Regional Development in James Bay, 1971–1981*. Montreal: McGill-Queen's University Press, 1986.
Sandlos, John. *Hunters at the Margin: Native People and Wildlife Conservation in the Northwest Territories*. Vancouver: University of British Columbia Press, 2007.
Sandlos, John, and Arn Keeling. "Zombie Mines and the (Over)burden of History." *Solutions Journal* 4, no. 3 (2013): 80–3.
Sangster, Joan. "Radical Ruptures: Feminism, Labor, and the Left in the Long Sixties in Canada." *American Review of Canadian Studies* 40, no. 1 (March 2010): 1–21.
Schmalz, Peter S. *The Ojibwa of Southern Ontario*. Toronto: University of Toronto Press, 1991.
Shanahan, David. "The Manitoulin Treaties, 1836 and 1862: The Indian Department and Indian Destiny." *Ontario History* 86, no. 1 (1994): 13–32.
Shewell, Hugh. *"Enough to Keep Them Alive": Indian Welfare in Canada, 1873–1965*. Toronto: University of Toronto Press, 2004.
Shkilnyk, Anastasia M. *A Poison Stronger Than Love: The Destruction of an Ojibwa Community*. New Haven: Yale University Press, 1985.
Silverstein, Cory, and Zeek Cywink. "From Fireside to TV Screen: Self-Determination and Anishnaabe Storytelling Traditions." *Canadian Journal of Native Studies* 20, no. 1 (2000): 35–66.
Simpson, Leanne. *Dancing on Our Turtle's Back: Stories of Nishnaabeg Re-Creation, Resurgence and a New Emergence*. Winnipeg: Arbeiter Ring Publishing, 2011.
– "Looking After the *Gdoo-naaganinaa*: Precolonial Nishnaabeg Diplomatic Relationships." *Wicazo Sa Review* 23, no. 2 (Fall 2008): 29–42.
Smith, Linda Tuhiwai. *Decolonizing Methodologies: Research and Indigenous Peoples*. London: Zed Books, 1999.

Smith, Theresa S. *The Island of the Anishnaabeg: Thunderers and Water Monsters in the Traditional Ojibwe Life-World.* Idaho: University of Idaho Press, 1995.

Smithers, Gregory D. "Beyond the 'Ecological Indian': Environmental Politics and Traditional Ecological Knowledge in Modern North America." *Environmental History* 20 (2015): 83–111.

Stanley, Anna. "Citizenship and the Production of Landscape and Knowledge in Contemporary Canadian Nuclear Fuel Waste Management." *The Canadian Geographer* 52 (2008): 64–82.

– "Labours of Land: Domesticity, Wilderness and Dispossession in the Development of Canadian Uranium Markets." *Gender, Place & Culture* 20, no. 2 (2013): 195–217.

– "Marginalization and Challenge: The Production of Knowledge and Landscape in Canadian Nuclear Waste Management Making." PhD diss., University of Guelph, 2006.

Stasiulis, Daiva, and Nira Yuval-Davis, eds. *Unsettling Settler Societies: Articulations of Gender, Race, Ethnicity and Class.* London: SAGE Publications Ltd, 1995.

Stewart, Larry R. "Canada's Role in the International Uranium Cartel." *International Organization* 35, no. 4 (Autumn 1981): 657–89.

Strong-Boag, Veronica. "Canada's Wage-Earning Wives and the Construction of the Middle Class, 1945–60." *Journal of Canadian Studies* 29, no. 3 (1994): 5–25.

– "Home Dreams: Women and the Suburban Experiment in Canada, 1945–60." *Canadian Historical Review* 72, no. 4 (December 1991): 471–504.

Tanner, Helen Hornbeck, ed. *Atlas of Great Lakes Indian History.* Norman: University of Oklahoma Press, 1987.

Telford, Rhonda. "Aboriginal Resistance in the Mid-Nineteenth Century: The Anishinabe, Their Allies, and the Closing of the Mining Operations at Mica Bay and Michipicoten Island." In *Blockades and Resistance: Studies in Actions of Peace and the Temagami Blockades of 1988–89,* edited by Bruce W. Hodgins, Ute Lischke, and David T. McNab, 71–84. Waterloo: Wilfrid Laurier University Press, 2003.

Thorpe, Jocelyn. *Temagami's Tangled Wild: Race, Gender, and the Making of Canadian Nature.* Vancouver: University of British Columbia Press, 2012.

Titley, E. Brian. *A Narrow Vision: Duncan Campbell Scott and the Administration of Indian Affairs in Canada.* Vancouver: University of British Columbia Press, 1986.

– *The Indian Commissioners: Agents of the State and Indian Policy in Canada's Prairie West, 1873–1932.* Edmonton: University of Alberta Press, 2009.

Tobias, John L. "Canada's Subjugation of the Plains Cree, 1879–1885." *Canadian Historical Review* 64 (1983): 519–48.

– "Protection, Civilization, Assimilation: An Outline History of Canada's Indian Policy." In *As Long as the Sun Shines and the Water Flows: A Reader in*

Canadian Native Studies, edited by Ian A.L. Getty and Antoine S. Lussier, 39–55. Vancouver: University of British Columbia Press, 1995.

Tough, Frank. *"As their Natural Resources Fail": Native Peoples and the Economic History of Northern Manitoba, 1870–1930.* Vancouver: University of British Columbia Press, 1996.

Trigger, Bruce G. "Jesuits and the Fur Trade." In *Sweet Promises: A Reader on Indian-White Relations in Canada*, edited J.R. Miller, 3–18. Toronto: University of Toronto Press, 1991.

– *The Children of Aataentsic: A History of the Huron People to 1660.* Montreal: McGill-Queen's University Press, 1976.

Tsetta, Shirley, Ginger Gibson, Linda McDevitt, and Sarah Plotner. "Telling a Story of Change the Dene Way: Indicators for Monitoring in Diamond Impacted Communities." *Pimatisiwin* 3, no. 1 (2005): 59–69.

Turner, Nancy, and Helen Clifton. "'It's So Different Today': Climate Change and Indigenous Lifeways in British Columbia, Canada." *Global Environmental Change* 19 (2009): 180–90.

"Uranium Exploration in the U.S." *Bulletin of the Atomic Scientists* VI, 6 (June 1950): 177.

Van Kirk, Sylvia. *Many Tender Ties: Women in Fur-Trade Society 1660–1870.* Winnipeg: Watson and Dwyer, 1980.

Vecsey, Christopher. "Grassy Narrows Reserve: Mercury Pollution, Social Disruption, and Natural Resources: A Question of Autonomy." *American Indian Quarterly* 11, no. 4 (Autumn 1987): 287–314.

Voorhis, Ernest. *Historic Forts and Trading Posts of the French Regime and of the English Fur Trading Company.* Ottawa: Department of the Interior, 1930.

Voyageur, Cora. *Firekeepers of the Twenty-First Century: First Nations Women Chiefs.* Montreal: McGill-Queen's University Press, 2008.

Wallace, C.M., and Ashley Thomson, eds. *Sudbury: Rail Town to Regional Capital.* Toronto: Dundurn Press, 1993.

Walters, Krista. "'A National Priority': Nutrition Canada's Survey and the Disciplining of Aboriginal Bodies, 1964–1975." In *Edible Histories, Cultural Politics: Towards a Canadian Food History*, edited by Franca Iacovetta, Valerie J. Korinek, and Marlene Epp, 433–52. Toronto: University of Toronto Press, 2012.

Weaver, Sally. *Making Canadian Indian Policy: The Hidden Agenda, 1968–70.* Toronto: University of Toronto Press, 1981.

Weyler, Rex. *Greenpeace: How a Group of Ecologists, Journalists and Visionaries Changed the World.* Vancouver: Raincoast Books, 2004.

Wheeler, Winona. "Reflections on the Social Relations of Indigenous Oral Histories." In *Walking a Tightrope: Aboriginal People and their Representations*, edited by Ute Lischke and David T. McNab, 189–213. Waterloo: University of Waterloo Press, 2005.

Whitaker, Reg, and Steve Hewitt. *Canada and the Cold War*. Toronto: James Lorimer, 2003.

Whitaker, Reg, and Gary Marcuse. *Cold War Canada: The Making of a National Insecurity State, 1945–1957*. Toronto: University of Toronto Press, 1994.

White, Richard. *The Middle Ground: Indians, Empires, and Republics in the Great Lakes Region, 1650–1815*. Cambridge: Cambridge University Press, 1991.

White, Richard, and William Cronon. "Ecological Change and Indian-White Relations." In *Handbook of North American Indians*, vol. 4, edited by Wilcomb E. Washburn, General Editor William C. Sturtevant, 417–29. Washington: Smithsonian Institution, 1988.

Widdowson, Frances, and Albert Howard. *Disrobing the Aboriginal Industry: The Deception Behind Indigenous Cultural Preservation*. Montreal: McGill-Queen's University Press, 2008.

Wiebe, Sarah Marie. *Everyday Exposure: Indigenous Mobilization and Environmental Justice in Canada's Chemical Valley*. Vancouver: University of British Columbia Press, 2016.

Wightman, Nancy M., and W. Robert Wightman. "The Mica Bay Affair: Conflict on the Upper Lakes Mining Frontier, 1840–1850." *Ontario History* 83 (1991): 193–208.

Willow, Anna J. "Clear-Cutting and Colonialism: The Ethnopolitical Dynamics of Indigenous Environmental Activism in Northwestern Ontario." *Ethnohistory* 56, no. 1 (2009): 35–67.

– *Strong Hearts, Native Lands: Anti-Clearcutting Activism at Grassy Narrows First Nation*. Winnipeg: University of Manitoba Press, 2012.

Wilson, Sean. *Research Is Ceremony: Indigenous Research Methods*. Black Point: Fernwood, 2008.

Witgen, Michael. *An Infinity of Nations: How the Native New World Shaped Early North America*. Philadelphia: University of Pennsylvania Press, 2012.

Witgen, Michael. "The Rituals of Possession: Native Identity and the Invention of Empire in Seventeenth-Century Western North America." *Ethnohistory* 54, no. 4 (Fall 2007): 639.

Films

Isacsson, Magnus, dir. *Uranium*. Montreal: National Film Board of Canada, 1990.

Rio Algom. *Carved from the Rock: The Story of Elliot Lake*. Toronto: National Dream Production, 2005.

Index

Printed and bound by CPI Group (UK) Ltd, Croydon, CR0 4YY

14/04/2025

14656924-0001